THE CAR BUILDER'S HANDBOOK

TIPS AND TECHNIQUES FOR BUILDERS OF KIT CARS AND STREET RODS

DOUG McCLEARY

HPBooks

HPBooks
are published by
The Berkley Publishing Group
A division of Penguin Putnam Inc.
375 Hudson Street
New York, New York 10014

First edition: December 1997

© 1997 Doug McCleary
10 9 8 7 6 5

Library of Congress Cataloging-in-Publication Data

McCleary, Doug.
    The car builder's handbook: tips and techniques for builders of
kit cars and street rods/Doug McCleary.—1st ed.
        p.   cm.
    ISBN 1-55788-278-9
    1. Automobiles, Home-built—Design and construction—Handbooks,
manuals, etc.   I. Title
TL240.M367   1997   97-29003
629.222—dc21   CIP

Book Design & Production by Bird Studios
Interior photos by the author unless otherwise noted
Cover photo by Michael Lutfy

ACKNOWLEDGMENTS

I WOULD LIKE TO THANK THE FOLLOWING PEOPLE FOR THEIR SUGGESTIONS AND ENCOURAGEMENT:

Peter Portante, ERA Cars; Bob Jaremsek, Rowley Corvette; Earl Davis, K&N Engineering; Dick Anderson, Gary Wade, Dick Anderson; Carrera Shocks; John Glenn, Thermo Tec; Jim Kuenz, E-A-R Composites; Steve Cornelius, Wilwood Engineering; Ralph Lisena, Engineered Components Inc.; Rick Moore, Jim Kull, Stabalus Gas Springs; James Eldrige, Specialty Power Windows; Jeff Tinnion, Energy Suspension; Klouse Bornhaeuser, Mark MacDaniel, VDO/Yazaki; Ken Arendt, Stewart Warner Instruments; Mark Hammel, Accel; Tony Garisto, Sanderson Headers; Mark Ryan, Doug Thorly Headers; Chad Meredith, MAC Products; Steve Anderson, Paul Carver, Flow Master; Ron Francis, Ron Francis Wire Works; Kevin Simpson, Painless Wire Works; Mark Hooper, Rhode Island Wiring Services; Jim Stafford, Centech Wiring; Mickey Laurea, Total Performance; Marty Kot, Ford Motorsport; Mike Zoner, Callaway Cars; Mark McFail, Chevrolet Motorsport Tech; Bill Howell, Howell Engine Development Industries; Guy Hait, Woody Warren, Holley Carburetors; Kevin Zaske, Digital Fuel Injection; Don School, S&W Race Cars; Chris, Perfection Automotive Products; Dean Harvey, Competition Cams; Jim Losee, Edelbrock; Martin Peters, B.F. Goodrich; Scott Cambell, Fiber Glast Developments Corp.; Peter & Chris Quidley, Quidley Fine Art; Peter Kaskiewicz, P.P.G.; Brian Langley, Prism Powder Coat; Mary Wescott, Wescott's Auto Restyling; David Stutts, Vintage Air; Mike Roux, Canaska Motorsports; Joe Musteric, Kelly Springfield Tire; Rick Spokis, Crankshaft Connection; Vince Veary, Tom Benoit, Tweeter Etc; Rob Ryan; Bill Moore; McMullen Argus; Alan L. Colvin, The Car Channel; Mark and David Smith, Factory Five Racing; and Mostly Mary and our children. ∎

CONTENTS

INTRODUCTION V

CHAPTER 1
GETTING STARTED 1

CHAPTER 2
CHASSIS TIPS 15

CHAPTER 3
SUSPENSION TIPS 25

CHAPTER 4
BRAKE TIPS 36

CHAPTER 5
ENGINE TIPS 47

CHAPTER 6
DRIVETRAIN TIPS 71

CHAPTER 7
BODY TIPS 79

CHAPTER 8
ROLL BARS 109

CHAPTER 9
DRIVER CONTROLS & AIDS 114

CHAPTER 10
ELECTRICAL 120

CHAPTER 11
INTERIOR TIPS 140

CHAPTER 12
FINE-TUNING 148

TABLES 153

INDEX 166

INTRODUCTION

Over the last 20 years, I have built many kit cars to order. During each one, I made mistakes and ultimately learned from them. Many times I was forced to work with substandard parts and designs from manufacturers that were underfunded. As a beginner, I had to teach myself many basic skills and solve problems by trial and error, because I was unable to find general, useful information that addressed the needs of someone building a car from scratch or from a kit. Certainly there were many books available on broad subjects, like paint and body, electrical, engine rebuilding, etc., and I still recommend that you read them. However, there was nothing I could find that was written from the perspective of a novice car builder. This book is intended to be such a guide.

As such, it is not a replacement for a factory shop manual, if one exists for your car. If you have a donor car, you will need one for that too, as well as the assembly manual for your kit, and any other specialty manual such as a book on automotive electrical or fiberglass (both available from HPBooks, see list on page 170). And, try as I might have, I'm certain that I didn't cover every problem that you will encounter. Such a book

would be just about impossible to write. Think of *The Car Builder's Handbook* as just another tool necessary for the assembly of any fiberglass-bodied car.

Throughout this book, I've tried to share some insights and tips that were realized during the many years I assembled kits. In many cases I have pointed out alternatives so you can make informed decisions on how to solve a particular problem. I will not go into great detail on any particular subject. There are enough specialists, videos and written material available if you need more specific information on any particular subject. My goal is to give you enough information so you will realize when you need professional guidance. There is absolutely no reason for you to abandon your project if things don't go well, or to build a bad car, even if you do receive poor quality parts or an assembly manual that makes no sense at all. There are a multitude of aftermarket parts manufacturers to help you with every part of your car. There are companies that manufacture combination heater and air conditioning units, roll bar kits, interior kits, brackets and mounting tabs for seats, seat belts, suspension parts and an abundance of other bells and whistles.

If there is one general piece of advice I can give, it is to be

organized right from the beginning. The organization of any project large or small is no different. The process is really quite simple, you just break it down into smaller, easily achievable goals (which is, by the way, how I approached writing this book). For example: You might say to yourself, the first thing I will do today is to open each box, take inventory and store them, either on a shelf or in their own box. Make that task an item on your list and check it off when it is done.

Keep your organization simple and flexible. Don't let your system get too complex or be too rigid. If you won't be able to complete task "Z" by Tuesday, that's OK! I'm sure you have something else you can do by Tuesday. The simpler your system is to understand the easier it will be to use and benefit from. Write your system down, keep clear notes, and if you feel overwhelmed close the door and go relax for a while.

The most difficult part of any project is getting started. Sometimes you just don't know where to start when faced with a blank sheet of paper. Usually at the beginning of any project it is vague, a lot of questions remain unanswered, and other questions haven't even been thought of yet. So the best place to start is to sit down and write. Here is an example of a thought process you might use as a model.

• Select the car (model and manufacturer).

•Determine if you can afford to build this car. If you have spoken with the manufacturer or someone that owns one of these cars you already have an idea how much it will cost. Most kit cars (Hot Rods or Reproductions) will cost anywhere from a low of $15,000 to about $50,000 and higher, depending on the car you are going to build. If you were to buy a kit that had been started but never finished, you will usually get a good deal.

• Who will actually build this car or will you have it built for you?

• Where will you get your parts from?

• Do you have all the necessary tools to build a car?

• Do you have a suitable space to build the car?

Don't underestimate your time, either! You must realize how much time a project like this will consume! Five hundred hours may not sound like long, but that's 20 hours a week for 30 weeks! Can you afford to dedicate that much time? The first thing to be affected will be any relationship with your wife and children. If your mate is supporting you and this project, it is only fair to set some boundaries.

Do not rush any part of this, and don't let yourself become consumed or obsessed with the project. Yes, it can happen! Make good decisions for the right reasons and don't allow yourself to get caught up in the romance of the cars. If you feel overwhelmed with any part of this project, shut off the light, close the door and talk to a friend, the car will be there tomorrow.

You have an opportunity to learn and practice skills that can produce a rewarding experience for yourself and your family if you have one. During the building process you will perfect your project management skills, problem solving skills (mechanical & electrical), the art of negotiation and most of all patience. ■

GETTING STARTED

Your budget and mechanical skills should dictate the sort of car you build, but of course, your taste in automobiles will have the greatest influence. Fiberglass car bodies come in enough different makes and styles to confuse even the most avid enthusiast. You can find replicas of European and domestic sports cars, early pick-up trucks that fit on Ford Ranger chassis, '32 and '49 Ford sedans that fit original or custom chassis, '55 or '57 Chevys that fit contemporary or original chassis and many more variations. The actual body mounting may require special attention though. You can buy all the parts from one manufacturer as a pre-engineered kit, or you can buy them separately from the same or different manufacturers. Most manufacturers use the same types of parts. For example, you could buy a Cobra body from someone in Connecticut and use a custom aluminum Cobra chassis from someone in Massachusetts that uses 5.0 Mustang driveline pieces. Some manufacturers offer "Pallet" cars where they have pre-assembled your car to a certain point and you add the mechanicals such as engine, transmission, rear end, etc. So you see, almost all hand-built cars with fiberglass bodies can be considered

A '23 T bucket can be built very basic and for relatively short money, and then the basic parts can be changed for custom parts over the years. Something like this allows someone on a limited budget to get his foot in the hobby door.

kits. VW-based cars and T-buckets are the least expensive and typically the easiest cars to assemble.

REPANELS

A "repanel" might be more interesting and affordable to you. Cars such as a Fiero, Porsche 914 or Corvette can have a new skin installed to transform the car into a Ferrari, Pantera, or Lamborgini. The nice part about this method is its simplicity—the chassis and mechanicals remain intact. You simply bolt and/or bond new fiberglass panels to an existing frame. If you already own the base vehicle, this can be the least expensive method of "building" a new car.

Narrowing It Down

Let's start with body style. Do you want a coupe, sedan or roadster? A

Ferrari Spyder California replica is an example of a mid-priced car that offers more of the creature comforts like air conditioning.

This repro '56 Chevy truck body fits any full-size short bed, Chevy or Ford chassis. It's a great way to turn your ho-hum S-10 or Ranger into a classic street truck.

two-seater or room for the family? Will you drive it daily, show it, race it, or a combination of all three? Besides looking good, careful consideration must also be given to how this car will perform. Is there a trunk and is it large enough to allow you to take enough luggage for a long trip? For example: When my wife and I chose our car we had an infant, so the number of models to choose from was narrowed down considerably. We needed a car that would have room for a car seat.

Research

You will need to do some homework. After all building a car requires a significant investment, of both time and resources. And, the reputation of the kit car industry has been spotty in recent years, due for the most part to a few bad companies (most of them long gone) that cast a pall on the entire industry.

Once you have chosen the car you want, you'll need to determine how many kit manufacturers there are. For popular models, this could mean quite a few. In the case of the Cobra, the choices number in the dozens. You can get an idea by checking out *Kit Car Illustrated, Kit Car, Street Rodder*, and by visiting Crown Publishing's website, www.kitcar.com or www.cobracountry.com, an excellent website devoted to the kit car industry. The magazines will have advertisements with a list of manufacturers of kits and accessories. Don't forget the magazines that are devoted to specific car marques, such as Ford, Chevy and Dodge. As you thumb through them you will see advertisements for companies that deal in replacement bodies and all sorts of accessories.

Clubs—You can figure out who the good guys are and who the bad guys are by calling a few of the car clubs within your region, or by contacting any of the national clubs. These enthusiasts will know who is reputable and who isn't. Remember, many of these people have already done what you are about to do, so they have first-hand experience with a number of suppliers.

The club headquarters may refer you to some of the owners, or allow you to publish a request for information in their newsletter. Chances are, you will get a better unbiased response than you might get from the manufacturer. Ask the owners the questions listed in the sidebar on page 6.

Test Drive

While you are talking with the clubs, find out if there are any car

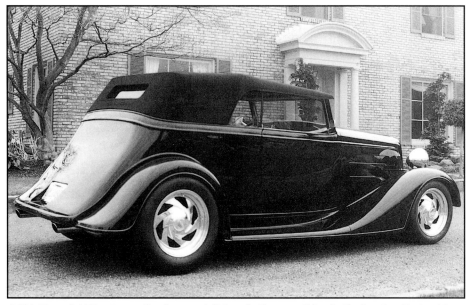

A '34 Chevrolet Phaeton replica is very stylish and stirs something in the hearts of hot rodders.

Referrals

Ask for names and phone numbers of previous customers. However, chances are most companies will be reluctant to give these out for fear of liability. If that is the answer you get, you might try giving the manufacturer your name and phone, and have them forward it to the customer requesting that you speak to them. Most car owners are all too willing to satisfy such a request.

Check It Out

After you have all the technical information you need and are satisfied, it's time to see one of their kits or completed cars up close and personal, which may require flying to the factory. Take a camera, lots of film and take pictures of any kit under assembly. These photos are handy for reference and may save you many headaches when you are trying to install a part that isn't documented well in the manual. Some manufacturers claim they will reimburse your airline tickets if you purchase their kit, so ask them! The worst that can happen is that they will say no.

shows in your area. Take the time to examine the cars first-hand. Visit the manufacturers and the cars you are interested in. Don't forget to sit in the car (ask the owner first!) and check to make sure you like the fit and finish, or if you even fit in it. If you can, try to drive, or at least get a ride in the car. Make note of how the car rides. Is it excessively rough? This could be due to stiff spring rates or suspension components colliding. Does the car shake when it hits a bump? If so then the frame structure may not be capable of remaining flat and square as the car corners or the suspension is compressed.

You will be spending a lot of your money and time building your kit. Quality should not be treated lightly.

To help you sort things out I suggest you use a note book to jot down the names and addresses of people you spoke with, notes about the cars and answers to any questions you may have asked.

GT-40 replica is one of the most expensive cars to assemble but can bring even larger returns if assembled well.

Ferrari Daytona GTC replica. If a refined touring car appeals to you the GTC is assembled on a Corvette chassis and offers all the same comfort, convenience and heart thumping performance.

Maintenance

Maintaining your car must be considered when you are selecting the kit. For example, filling the gas tank requires that the filler be located in a place where a pump nozzle and your hand will fit. If it burps and splashes back, will the overflowed gas be a problem? Make sure the engine, transmission and power steering fluid dipsticks can be reached easily without having to remove any components. A common maintenance item is the oil filter. Make sure you can change it easily. If not, then consider a remote oil filter kit. Radiator overflow bottles, suspension lube fittings, drain plugs, etc., are all maintenance items that must be designed so that they are easily accessible.

When it comes time to replace worn-out parts, you will appreciate the thought you put into how those parts were installed. Parts likely to require replacement include your battery, timing belts, ignition parts like spark plugs, spark plug wires, distributor points, ballast resister, alternator, voltage regulator, exhaust system, and shock absorbers. Make sure that all of these items can be reached without having to do anything drastic, like remove the engine.

Get It in Writing

After you have decided which kit will meet all of your requirements, it's time to get things in writing.

It's a good idea to follow up any phone conversation with a letter to or from the manufacturer. Those letters or contracts must identify all costs, such as shipping and extra handling fees, and any other points that you may have discussed. To make sure that there are no misunderstandings, everything must be in writing. Stand your ground and insist on it, and don't proceed to the next step until you get what they promise in writing. If they won't put it in writing then you should consider finding another manufacturer. Reputable manufacturers will back up their product.

BUDGETING

Before you buy your kit you must sit down and figure out how much you are going to need for the whole project, and be realistic. Remember, in order to figure out what you will need to purchase you must know what comes with the kit.

One general rule of thumb commonly applied in the kit car industry is to double the cost of the kit. This figure will get you in the ballpark. Can you afford $20,000? If you are interested in a front engine car with a tube chassis you can spend that easily. VW powered cars are a little less expensive and the higher end cars, like some 5.0 Mustang-based Cobras, can cost up to $50,000.

Build It on Paper First

To determine a budget as accurately as possible, you must get a handle on the parts, tools and services required. Once this is done you can determine how much you are going to need for the whole project. Be realistic!

There are hundreds of man-hours involved to get this '23 T-bucket from kit to driver. With careful planning, your car building experience will go as smoothly as possible. Build the car on paper first before you ever turn a wrench.

Estimate the costs on the high side so you won't be surprised if the actual cost is higher. Knowing the cost of the basic kit and additional parts will get you close enough to make a decision. The parts could total as little as $15,000 or as much as $50,000 or more by the time you're done. Machine shop time or labor of others will add up pretty quickly.

Parts List—In order to figure out what parts you will need to purchase, you must know what is included with the kit you are considering. Using that list and the cost estimating table on page 162 at the back of this book, check off the included items. The remaining items on the list need to be purchased. This will be your shopping list to take to the local parts store or mail order catalog. If you were unable to get this list from the manufacturer you can still get an idea from this chapter and the appendix, or from someone that has built a similar model. If at all possible, use the list from the manufacturer though, because it should be the most accurate.

Don't forget to price all the little extras you would like to have, such as air conditioning, cruise control, CD player or a navigation system. After that you should have a good idea of the real cost, but don't forget to add a few thousand for inflation, mistakes, shipping, and last minute goodies. A good rule of thumb is to add 5% for such contingencies.

Shopping—While it is always a good idea to shop around for the best price, be careful you don't compromise quality. You will only regret it after you start driving the car and things don't work the way they should or fail quickly. Some discount auto part houses sell some parts cheaper because they use poorer quality, imitation parts that don't stand up for long or don't operate correctly to start with.

Some of the major pieces (engine and transmission, see the chapter on engines) might be better bought from the factory or a company that reconditions the piece and will put together a package for you. Be careful dealing long distance though. It may be impossible to get satisfaction from a company halfway across the United

States, but a little easier if they are in the same state. Buy from someone that has been around for a while.

Payment—When you purchase parts, you should always use a credit card, which makes it easier to help solve any disputes if they should arise.

PLANNING & ORGANIZATION

One thing that I have learned from the years I've spent building cars is that planning and organization are critical. Although you will be ready to get started with "beginner's fever," it is best if you spend the next few weeks preparing for every phase of the car building process. This will not only make the entire project go much faster and smoother, but it will also make it much more enjoyable.

Consider all of the phases you are about to undertake: chassis, body, interior, engine and drivetrain, electrical, etc., and try to anticipate every possible turn of events having to do with that job. Reading this book from start to finish will certainly help. If it is attaching a part, buying a component, or just picking the color, think about it, anticipate, imagine what it will be like to live with that decision.

As with any large project the process is really quite simple; just break it down into smaller, more easily achievable goals. For example, your first goal might be to simply open each box, take inventory and store them either on a shelf or in their own box. This will allow you to become familiar with each part. Inspect it closely for quality of design, finish, etc., and think about how you will finish it.

Keep your organization simple, don't let your system get overly complex. The simpler and easier your

Questions to Ask the Manufacturer

• What is the normal delivery time?
• What is the back ordered part's policy?
• What are their payment terms and what is the cancellation policy?
• How long has the company been in business?
• How many kits have been produced?
• How many kits have been completed? This will give you an idea of the buildability or how easy the kits are to assemble.
• How long does the body cure in the mold?
• Along with the contracts you need to see all other documentation that comes with the car. DON'T OVERLOOK THIS PART!
• What is contained in the different kit stages and how much is each stage going to cost?
• What will you have to supply besides the donor car and the kit parts? (You must have this information and in writing because it will be difficult but not impossible to calculate your cost to build the kit without it.)
• What is included in each stage and what will be required from you to complete the car?
• Does the fiberglass need trimming, i.e. wheel, air scoops, door openings, hood and trunk openings, headlights, etc.? If so, are there instructions or templates provided?
• How is the body constructed? What type of fiberglass is used and how is it applied?
• How are the areas that will hold the weatherstripping on the passenger compartments and trunk designed? Are they designed in such a way that if the gaskets leak, the water will be channeled away and not allowed to enter the compartment?
• Is core mat or any other form of stiffening/stabilizing material used in the fiberglass?
• Does the wiring harness come with connectors (attached or not) or do you need to supply them yourself? (If it is up to you, then get a list from the manufacturer.)
• What parts are OEM type parts and what parts must you get from the kit manufacturer? If you ever wreck the car, where will the replacement parts come from?

Questions to Ask Owners About the Kit

• What was the worst part about building your car?
• If you were going to do it again, would you change the way you did any part of it?
• Were you able to stay within the budget you had estimated?
• Did you get everything that you bought from the manufacturer?
• How was the factory to deal with?
• How long did it take to build your car?

system is to use, the more likely you will use it and benefit from it. Write your system down, keep clear notes, and if you feel overwhelmed close the door and go relax by the pool or in the backyard for awhile.

Parts Management

As soon as the boxes arrive from the manufacturer, take inventory of everything! Check for any damage, and contact the shipper and manufacturer immediately if anything is missing or damaged. The longer you wait the more difficult it will be to get this situation corrected. If anything is missing, get an explanation and check to make sure that you haven't been charged for those parts. If you have been charged for them, get that corrected as soon as possible or come to some sort of an agreement. If any parts are short you need to determine if you can get them from someone else or if it is a part only available from the manufacturer.

After taking inventory, consider the following points with any of the parts that were not included with the kit. This is all part of the planning process.

New Mechanical Parts—Will the local parts store give you a volume discount? Visit your local auto parts stores, and show them the large number of parts you intend to purchase. They might surprise you and give you the jobber price, which is what most garages pay. Will they be new or reconditioned parts? The hot rod aftermarket matured decades before the kit car industry, and as a result, there are many new-old reproduction parts available. The antique car restoration aftermarket also has many parts developed. There are a number of parts suppliers that specialize in things like switches and trim pieces for foreign and British cars. If you haven't found the parts

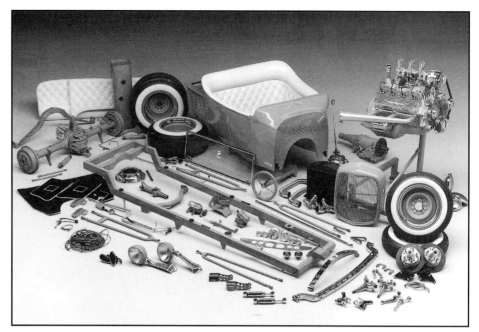

A '23 T-bucket kit. Some cars are very basic and require very few parts and some manufacturers will provide virtually everything needed to complete your car. But you must have a plan to manage the parts, and you must consider all aspects of the overall design when selecting parts that haven been supplied by the manufacturer.

you are looking for yet, you haven't looked in the right place.

Chassis Parts—Select the appropriate suspension parts. Will they be new or rebuilt? Will the control arms, springs, shocks, or sway bars be painted, plated or powder coated?

Brake System—Select the appropriate system and parts for your car. Where will you get the brake lines from, what material will you use, do you have the necessary tool to form and flare them, etc.

Fuel System—Where will you get the tank, gas cap, vent tube, charcoal canister, etc. How will you bend the new fuel and vent tubes?

Engine, Transmission and Rear End—Select the appropriate units for your car. Where will you buy them, who will deliver them, how will you handle and store them, how will you lift them for installation?

Exhaust System—What style will meet your expectations? Where will it come from and how will it be routed?

Tires and Wheels—What size tire

and wheel did the manufacturer intend for you to use? Include mounting and balancing in the purchase price.

Body—Do you need to do any assembly, trimming or fiberglass work on the body before you mount it to the chassis?

Mounts—You will need motor, transmission and body mounts.

Insulators—You will need rubber or polyurethane insulators for the steering box, column, suspension parts, exhaust system, etc. Some of these may come with the parts when you buy them.

Bracing—You will most likely need to design, fabricate and install some sort of brace or bracket on your car, the kind and location will be dictated by your car. Factor in fabrication and installation costs if you are not proficient with welding.

Doors, Hood, Trunk and Roof—Where will the door handles, hinges, and latches come from? Don't forget to look at the door hinges—do you need to fabricate stops to prevent the door from swinging open too far.

Cars like these Allard replicas will come with many of the parts, but not all. Before you jump into a classic car reproduction, check to make sure that you'll be able to get authentic reproduction parts from aftermarket manufacturers. In the case of these cars above, consider replacing some components with more current, safer ones for racing, especially in the area of brakes and suspension.

How will the trunk and hood be held open? Do you want a simple prop rod, a motorized lift or a gas spring?

Instruments—Do those come with the kit, or will you need to buy them separately, from the manufacturer or aftermarket? How will you light them at night, what will you use for a light switch?

Controls—Where will you get your steering column, shifter, parking brake assembly, etc.?

Wiring—Does the wiring harness come with the kit, are the connectors included (attached or not) or do you need to supply them yourself? Will it mate to your different components?

Store the Parts—Store your parts away until you are ready for them. Some parts are better left in the boxes until you need them and others may need modification prior to installation. Sort and store them accordingly.

You will need space to store your parts, lots of space. Shelf brackets and rough cut lumber are relatively inexpensive, so take the time to put up enough shelving to store all of your parts and supplies.

As you build the car and empty the boxes, flatten them out so they will fit under the car on the floor to catch any coolant and oil spills that will occur before everything is buttoned up for good. You can also use the boxes for painting your small parts on. Masking tape and a grease pencil will be handy to mark on the outside exactly what is in the box and where it is to be used. By the time you get around to using it, you won't remember what was important about it or where it went.

Donor Car Parts—You could buy a complete donor car, bring it home, take the parts off and then try to dispose of the remains, or you could approach a junkyard with a proposition. Using the list of donor car parts provided by the kit manufacturer, head for your nearest junkyard and try to get a volume discount for all the parts you will need. The pricing should be better than if you go back each time you need one part. For an agreed upon sum, you get to take all the parts you need from the yard. This method could work to your advantage,

especially if you need parts from more than one donor car. The disadvantage is making repeated trips to the junkyard, but at least you don't have to buy and store more than one donor car out in the street, yard or whatever. Many homeowner associations in developed communities won't allow that anyway.

The second option requires having the junkyard deliver a donor car to your house. You can then strip the parts at your leisure. Don't forget to get receipts and/or titles from the donor cars, because these may be required when it comes time to register the car.

As you strip the parts from your donor car, don't forget all those little odds and ends. Take note of all the little clips, brackets, nuts and bolts that the manufacturer has used to construct the donor. It may not have dawned on you before but you will also need that sort of thing. Don't just blindly remove the parts and don't let someone else do it for you. As you remove the heater, for example, be sure to note how it was secured in the car and take all the little parts that went with it. As you remove the nuts and bolts, install them in the holes where they came from, don't leave them and don't just throw them into a can or box. If you have a video camera you could take a few minutes of video in case you forget how it was installed on the donor car. Believe me, you will be happier if you do this for yourself.

Documentation

It may not seem important now, but as you assemble your car, perform routine maintenance, or repair worn-out parts, the time will come when you will need information about them. It may come from installation instructions, a factory or aftermarket service manual or a book on a

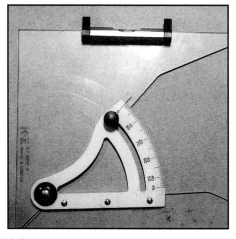

Adjustable protractor and string bubble can be useful in determining the operating angles of items like your hood or trunk.

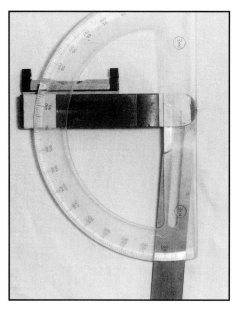

This angle finder and string bubble can be used in tighter places to determine angles. Place the blade against the part being checked, and adjust the angle finder until the bubble is centered. Then place the protractor over it to determine the angle.

specialized subject. I am sure you have heard the expression that the job isn't complete until the paperwork is done. Well, building a car is no different. You should gather as much information as possible about your car and the parts you are using. Save every piece of documentation so you can build your own owner's manual after the car is completed. Record every casting number and serial number from the engine, transmission, rear end, and any other serial number you come across. Record them in a notebook and store for safekeeping.

Donor Car Information—I recommend that you buy a service manual for the donor car. If it is out of stock or not available, try some of the listings in *Hemmings Motor News*. Save this information and add it to your owner's manual. Save every receipt and installation instruction. Keep copies of everything, including the receipts from the junkyard.

Owner's Manual—You may remember everything that went into the construction of your car for a few months, but I guarantee that with time you will forget. The last section in this book is titled "Owner's Manual," guess what that is for? Cut it out, copy it or just fill it in, but record that

information. Use it to keep the as-built information on your car. When the car is complete you will want to have an owner's manual in the car with you. When it comes time to buy parts or service your car, you will be glad you have it. So, remember, as you gather your parts and documentation, record every model, part number or casting number and serial number from the engine, transmission, and rear end, etc., in your car's new owner's manual.

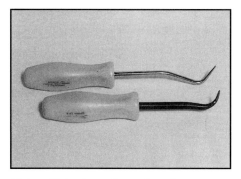

Picks with hooks on the end can be a lifesaver as you are fishing wires through your doors or the firewall.

Tools

The final step in the budgeting process is to factor in the cost of tools and equipment you will need to complete the project. This is an item often overlooked by first-timers. They budget so closely for the parts that when it comes time to purchase a die grinder, they can't afford one.

I don't care what the salesman told you, you will need more than just a few basic hand tools to assemble your car properly. Life will be a lot easier if you have a few extras in addition to your basic hand tool assortment. I have provided a list of suggested and optional tools and a place for you to add prices. Your wife may think that this list is a little excessive, but we all know that you can never have too many tools. Tools are another area where you shouldn't try to save a few dollars; poor quality (inexpensive) tools are generally made with poor quality metals and will bend, lose their edge or worse, break as you are trying to tighten a nut or bolt. Spend the extra money for good tools!

General Recommendations—A small air compressor will come in handy to dry parts as you clean them, fill tires, and power (relatively) inexpensive air-powered tools. Some air saws are shaped like a pistol and

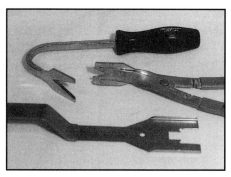

Panel poppers are used to remove door panels with conventional door panel clips. You slip the blade under the door panel so it straddles the clip and pry it up until the clip comes out of its hole. These panel poppers allow you to get into those stubborn places and the door handle clip remover is sometimes the only way to remove door handle c-clips.

You must use a tubing bender when forming any tubing for your car. Any kinks in your fuel lines, brake lines, or even transmission cooling lines can restrict the flow of fluids or weaken and fracture the tubing. Benders are sized for each specific sized tubing and using the wrong size bender for your tubing is inviting trouble.

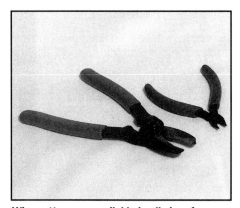

Wire cutters are available in all sizes from large enough to cut battery cables to small enough to cut unneeded wires from the back of connectors. You'll find more on electrical tools and their use in Chapter 10.

are better than an electric saber saw for making clearance notches and trimming the edges of fiberglass panels during the fitting stage of assembly. Because of its shape, it will fit into tight places. A small spray gun and air-powered sanding tools will be welcome when it comes time to block-sand the body, blowing things off, and painting small odds and ends.

A disc grinder is good for preparing fiberglass before bonding, smoothing fiberglass after it has hardened, preparing the edges of steel to be welded as well as smoothing them out afterward. If your welding skills are anything like mine, you'll need a disc

grinder to remove the terrible weld bead you just laid down. Select a grinder that will also accept abrasive cutting wheels, which are good for trimming light gauge metal brackets or cutting heavier steel.

A torque wrench that reads in foot pounds will be required for most of your engine assembly work; occasionally you will need an inch pound wrench, but one may not be worth purchasing. Remember, bolts or nuts that are not tightened enough may vibrate loose, while over-tightened ones may break. Improperly tightened components may cause damage or accelerate wear. "Blown out" gaskets and broken head bolts are typical examples. Improperly tightened head bolts may result in poor compression, and over-tightened bearings may bind, etc.

Warning: Suspension and brake hardware must be torqued to specified settings. If not tightened properly they may vibrate loose, while over-tightened ones may break.

A MIG (Metal Inert Gas) welder is faster and in general requires less skill than a TIG (Tungsten Inert Gas) welder that produces a nicer-looking joint. MIG and TIG are preferable

over Arc because they leave a nice clean weld with no messy slag to clean up after, but an arc welder will do when it comes to making those heavy-duty brackets.

I've mentioned these tools just to give you a partial list. Use the tool checklist in the Appendix to help you compile the tools you'll need.

At this point, you should have a pretty fair idea of how much your kit car or street rod is actually going to cost. To be sure, you will need a cash fund for small purchases that crop up right in the middle of a job, but unless you really make a costly mistake (like blowing the motor on startup because you were too excited to put in oil), the 5% overage cost should cover these and other small mistakes.

FASTENERS

Most likely, your kit will not include fastening hardware. This includes nuts, bolts, washers, Dzus fasteners, hinges, adhesives, cotter keys, etc. Put some thought into selecting the hardware you are going to use on each item before you finally bolt that item on. Use the same size per part. As you choose the various nuts and bolts, consider how easily they can be removed when the part needs to be serviced or replaced.

Hardware is right up there at the top of the list with brake and suspension components as an item where quality should be considered ahead of cost. Buy the best hardware you can afford. The reasons should be very obvious. If you use cheap hardware, the chances of failure increase. Most "inexpensive" hardware is inexpensive for a reason, and material quality is usually one of the reasons. Use aircraft grade hardware in high stress components, such as suspension pickup points. Use good quality hardware everywhere else. The

Bolts come is all sorts of sizes, strengths and head styles. Flat head, pan head, phillips head, hex head or socket head. Choose your hardware type carefully; socket head is neat to look at but may require you to carry additional tools. Flat head is simple but the flat screwdriver will easily slip out of the slot and could cause damage or injury.

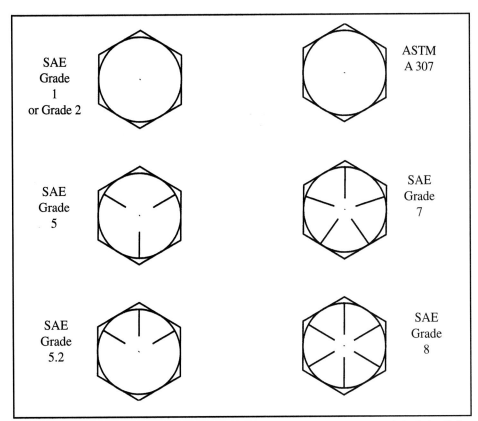

SAE Grade 1 or Grade 2	ASTM A 307
SAE Grade 5	SAE Grade 7
SAE Grade 5.2	SAE Grade 8

The heads of most bolts carry "grade markings," which indicate the strength of the bolt. If the heads of your bolts have no markings, they could be junk bolts or low to medium carbon steel grade 1 or 2 bolts. Consult Table 1 in the table section to make sure that these bolts will carry the load they will be exposed to.

hardware from the original manufacturer of your donor car is usually good stuff.

Caution: If some of your hardware is coming from a wrecked car, don't use any that has been subjected to a hard impact. If the hardware has been weakened it could fail; inspect all used hardware carefully.

Recommendations

There are many types of nuts and bolts that can be useful when building your car.

Bolts

Socket head or Allen head bolts are neat to look at and are good for trimming out your engine or for a buried bolt where a hex head may be tight. Six-sided hex head is a good standard bolt head. Torx hardware is fine for production automobiles, but you want to use hardware that can be removed if you get stuck away from your toolbox.

Nuts

There are many types of nuts available, standard hex nuts, nylock nuts with nylon inserts to prevent loosening due to vibration, flex nuts with a light deformation to the top, castle nuts for use with cotter pins or safety wire. Choose the correct nut for the application. Tee nuts (a nut with a large flat surface) can be welded to panels. Pem nuts are threaded inserts that are pressed into an undersized hole. If none of these will do the job then a piece of flat stock (metal) can be drilled, tapped and attached to whatever it is you are trying to bolt to, preferably on the other side, so the load is spread over a larger area.

Washers

Wherever you have a bolt passing through fiberglass or other soft material, you must spread the load out across a larger surface. Large pattern or fender washers, as they are sometimes called, will do nicely. The larger the washer, the more force will be required to cause the fiberglass to fail and the nut to pull through.

Lock Washers—Because kit cars tend to ride a little stiffer than production autos and have less insulation from the chassis, we find that more vibrations are transmitted through the fiberglass. Therefore it is wise to use some sort of locking device on your nuts and bolts. This can be a split lock washer, a star

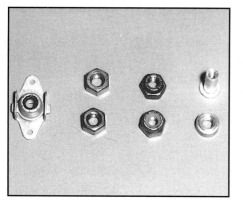

The type of nut you choose is also important. Depending on the location, a threaded insert similar to a pop rivet may be better than a floating nut with a nylon locking insert. Standard nuts are better suited to items that will be serviced routinely.

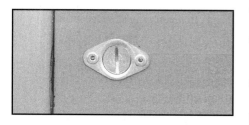

Here is an example of a quarter-turn fastener used to secure an engine compartment side cover. Quarter-turn fasteners are ideal for panels when access may be needed quickly and access to the back may not be possible.

washer, or locking nuts. Regardless of the installation torque, you need to lock the hardware together. If you don't prevent the hardware from loosening, it will happen.

Liquid Thread Lockers—There are two general types; the kind applied to the bolt before the nut is added, and the kind applied after the hardware is tightened. With the latter, the material flows over the threads and "wicks" into open spaces between nut and bolt. These thread lockers come in different "strengths" for different applications and size of hardware to be retained. There are even retaining compounds for retaining press-in parts such as bearings and bushings. Even though these are locking compounds, most can be removed with a bit of heat. In areas exposed to high heat, higher heat rated thread lockers are available.

The type of washers used can be critical. Large pattern flat washers are ideal to spread loads on weaker materials. Lock washers, external star, internal star, and split lock are intended for hard materials and standard non-locking nuts. Lock washers must not be placed directly against something soft like fiberglass. A flat washer must be used to keep the lock washer from digging into the soft material.

Adhesives

There are many pieces that can be bonded in place instead of bolted. Before you bond something in place be sure that it is not something that will require removal or replacement. Plan ahead and locate it so it can be removed or serviced if need be. Consider the location and the temperatures and humidity that the adhesive will be expected to survive. Generally the quicker the adhesive cures, the more brittle and less forgiving it is to minor movement or vibrations. Fiberglass Resin (Epoxy and Polyester) along with some chopped matte can be used as an adhesive for fiberglass parts. Epoxy resin should be used if bonding to metal.

Hot Melt Adhesives—While excellent for quick and temporary bonding, these should be used carefully. Some of these adhesives can not tolerate a very high temperature. They are very good for bonding cardboard for templates and things that will lay flat, like trunk carpeting. Always check the recommended temperature range.

Solvent-Based Adhesives—These

Bonding Pieces

After aligning the pieces to be bonded, clamp them together and if possible, pass a drill through the mating surfaces in two places so they can be bolted in place while the adhesive cures. Remove the pieces, rough and clean the surfaces with a solvent so the adhesive will bond. Fiberglass pieces may have residual mold release on them and require cleaning so the adhesive will adhere. Apply the appropriate adhesive (your parts store should have a wide variety for different materials and applications) and bolt the pieces together. If access to the other side of the piece is impossible then use a few self-tapping screws. After the adhesive has cured, you can remove the screws or bolts (be sure to coat the screws with something like wax or soap) and glass-over the mating surfaces.

include contact cements and weatherstripping adhesive, and are good for a wide range of temperatures and applications such as weatherstripping, interior panel installation and carpeting.

Sealants

Any silicone or latex household caulking will work well to prevent water and air leaks into the cockpit, providing no grease or mold release is left on the fiberglass. Be sure to wipe the surfaces to be sealed with a solvent.

If you find you have to seal the windshield you should consider either butyl rubber or urethane sealant (both are non-hardening and available from a glass dealer).

Any tool that has to do with a potentially hazardous operation, such as jacking up your car, should not be skimped upon when purchasing. The two floor jacks you see here are both rated at two tons of lifting power, but which one would you feel safer using? The large six-inch head of the jack on the right is much more apt to keep your car from slipping off the jack than the little three inch head on the one on the left. Don't be cheap when it comes to your safety.

Gaskets—Usually the gasket or weatherstrip kits that come with your car will do the job nicely but you still need to check for proper compression of the gasket when the door or trunk is closed. When you think you have the doors installed and aligned properly tack the gasket in place temporarily. To check for proper compression place a piece of paper over the gasket and close the door. You should have tension on the paper but still be able to pull the paper out without tearing it. If you don't have any tension on the gasket, this could be the location for a water leak or draft. This is the time to make adjustment to the gasket mounting surface by building it up for more compression, or grinding away material for less compression. After the placement is correct the proper door panels outline can be determined. Take your time doing this, don't overlook any possible areas that might leak water during your weekly washing or if heaven forbid, you get caught in a rainstorm.

THE GARAGE

Determine where you will assemble the kit. If this was a perfect world you might be able to build your car without a garage, but it isn't. Anyone that tells you otherwise has never done it or has something to gain. You must have a dedicated work space with power and lights. The part of the country you live in will dictate your heating or cooling requirements. If you have dry storage for your parts, you can do it in a single stall garage but you will wish for more space within an hour of starting. A more realistic minimum is a two-stall garage, and of course, the more space you have the better. The further away the garage is from your home, the less time you will have to work on it. If you have to drive for a half hour just to tinker with the car, it will get old very fast. The closer it is to your home the more likely you will be to pop in for a half hour or so and those little half hours add up.

You need to make provisions for painting your larger parts before they are mounted on the car. Some sort of a bar or rack hung across the door jam of your garage may work for you, or a box with an air conditioning filter that will trap the paint overspray might be better. You can put a fan in back of you so the fumes are blown out the door. Remember, protect yourself! Wear protective clothing, eye gear and respirators when painting in a closed space.

Is your shop ready? Does it have enough electrical capacity or are you going to be tripping circuit breakers or blowing fuses if you try to use two electrical items at once. Is it clean, dry, warm, well lighted and ventilated? Now is the time to take care of these items if not. A good place to start is to inventory your supplies, tools and storage space, etc.

Garage Safety

Every year thousands of people are seriously injured and even killed in household accidents, a large percentage of which occur in the garage or shop. To prevent injury always practice "The Common Sense Laws of Mechanics." For instance, if you have a nut to loosen, don't even think about using an open-end wrench to break the nut free, use at least a boxed end (enclosed end) wrench or a socket. Six point sockets will grip better than a twelve point socket can. When you do try to break the nut free, use an open palm instead of an enclosed fist around the wrench handle. This way, if the nut unexpectedly breaks free, or if the wrench slips, your knuckles won't get busted.

The work space itself has to be conducive to working on your car too. Don't try to raise your car with a floor jack on an inclined driveway; don't set up jackstands in the grass; don't paint a part for your car with your wife/girlfriend/buddy's car parked two feet away and the wind blowing towards their car, etc. I know these all sound like "duh, I think I know better than to do that," but if you think back, I am sure there has been a time where we have all worked in less than safe conditions because we were too cheap to buy the right tool, in too much of a hurry to enact the appropriate safety measures, or just plain weren't paying attention. So check out the following safety guidelines before you go any farther into this book.

Safety Guidelines

• If the job requires a tool you don't own, beg, borrow, buy, or rent the right tool. Specialty tools are just that, special, and regular tools will not accomplish the same job. Regular tools will just damage the fastener, or part, and possibly cause personal injury.

• When working under your car always, and I mean always, have it in Park for an automatic, or in a forward gear for a manual transmission, the parking brake set, high capacity jackstands locked in place and in the correct location, and tire chocks in use at opposite wheels.

• When working on electrical repairs or modifications, disconnect the battery's negative cable to prevent electrical damage or sparks.

• Don't smoke when working on your car, even if you're not working on part of the fuel system. Cigarette ashes and embers can smolder and start an interior fire or damage the paint.

• Take breaks often. Every project has a frustrating moment that will get you throwing wrenches into the street. Take five minutes, replenish your

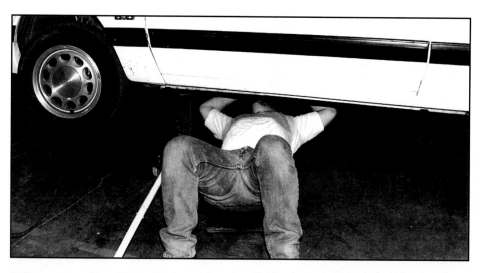

While we are on the subject of jacks and jackstands, don't ever consider this: working under a car with just a jack. A five minute clutch cable adjustment can cripple you or even kill you if the floor jack fails or someone bumps it. It will only take another minute to grab a jackstand and be safe. The two most common types are the "pin" style and ratchet style. The pin jackstands can only adjust to a set number of heights, and the head is usually not designed to fit the center of the vehicle. The ratchet type is cast steel rather than stamped (stronger), and the head allows for centering, such as on a rear axle. Get the stronger ratchet kind if possible.

body fluids, take a deep breath, and try a new approach to the problem. Frustration is where accidents start and stupid things happen, like dropping a bolt down the engine's intake manifold.

• If you have a friend come over to help, find out what their abilities are before you give them a job they can't handle. Chances are they won't say anything to you about their inability out of embarrassment, and then injure themselves or damage something in the process.

• Always read the instruction manual over several times before attempting the project. This will mentally prepare you for the job at hand, as well as give you time to rent any specialty tools, set up shop time at a machine shop, or get the parts you need before hand. Just think how many times you have pulled a car apart for some work, then found out the local parts house won't have the part you need until the middle of the week.

• Keep a well-stocked first aid kit

within a few steps of your work area, preferably hanging on the wall of your shop or garage next to a water source. I know it sounds gross and cold hearted, but you don't want to bleed all through the house trying to get to a bandage in the upstairs bathroom.

• Some background music is nice to break the silence when working on your car, but don't have it so loud it annoys the neighbors or people nearby can't hear you call for help if needed in an emergency.

• Speaking of people nearby, try to schedule your work when there will be someone home. If you need emergency help, or even someone to run and get you a part, there is someone there within earshot of your voice.

• Finally, don't work on your car under the influence of alcohol or drugs. The more impaired you are, the greater the risk of injury or making a mechanical mistake that will come back to haunt you later. Save the cold ones till after you're done for the day. ■

CHASSIS TIPS 2

Even if you were able to go to the factory and inspect the parts for your car, take the time to inspect the chassis! Even if the manufacturer told you he built the chassis on a jig, you should always check to make sure. You will probably never know how square the jig was to begin with, and the problem is serious enough that you need to check for yourself as added insurance. Your primary concern should be to ensure that all the suspension points are located correctly.

You should consider as you look at your chassis whether or not it is strong enough to withstand the type of driving you intend to do. A highway cruiser does not require the rigidity of a chassis that will be autocrossed or club raced. At a minimum, your chassis must be flat and square. This is not difficult or time consuming to check, so don't skip this step. All that is required is a little measuring.

CHASSIS INSPECTION

In order to inspect the chassis thoroughly, you should elevate it so you can inspect it without crawling around the floor on your hands and knees. Set the chassis on something

The manufacturer of your car will have a jig for the chassis to be assembled and welded on. Here is an example of a manufacturer that is serious and has developed first class tooling. The accuracy of your chassis will reflect the accuracy of the chassis jig.

stable like jackstands, sawhorses or a dolly. You will need a tape measure, large and small levels, C clamps and a ball of string.

Note: You will need the chassis level for other measurements so you might as well level it as soon as you raise it. You can kill two birds with

one stone by making a dolly with casters that securely support the chassis high enough for you to do all the measuring and assembly work at a comfortable height. Be sure that the stock is strong enough and the casters are rated to support the weight of the finished car.

Chassis designs are not limited to simple box tubing ladder frames. This multi-tube space frame offers more rigidity and less weight than a conventional box tubing chassis.

This is an example of a simple T-bucket frame before it is painted.

Perhaps the first and most important thing to do is examine all the welds. This is an example of a weld with little penetration. Notice how the weld seems to be sitting on top of the steel rather than being a part of it.

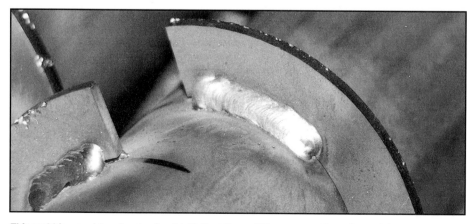

This weld is considered a good weld. Notice the weld has a smooth surface with a nice semi-circle pattern similar to fish scales. Looking inside the tube reveals good penetration.

Welds

Check all of the welds. A good weld will have a smooth, linear bead, and not just be a glob of welding rod. The edge of a good weld should make a smooth transition to the metal. The weld should have a pattern similar to fish scales or semi-circles along its entire length. Under no circumstances should a weld have any cracks in or near it. The weld bead should be around 1/4" to 3/8" wide. If any welds look suspicious, have them examined by a competent welder. Failure to catch a weak or fractured weld could be catastrophic.

The frame structure, steering geometry and suspension design are areas where considerable engineering work must be done. If the manufacturer of your car has done his homework you should have nothing

Once you are satisfied with the integrity of the chassis, support it on jackstands at a suitable height.

When you check your chassis for twist, stretch strings from corner to corner. The strings should cross in the center within 1/4", preferably just barely touching.

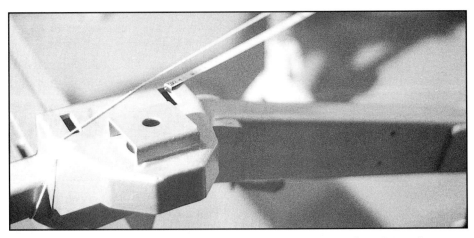

In order to check your chassis for squareness, select suspension mounting points and measure from corner to corner. These measurements should be within 1/4".

If you are working where the assembly will take place, now is a good time to ensure that the chassis is level. A long framing square will work best for this.

to worry about. If you find any problems in any of these areas, contact the manufacturer immediately. If the manufacturer refuses to help resolve the problem, call a chassis shop or someone knowledgeable in these areas and get it fixed anyway.

Twist

With the chassis raised, leveled and secure, stretch two strings from suspension mounting points on opposite corners of the chassis. For example: an upper control arm mounting bolt hole on the front of the chassis to a suspension mounting point at the opposite rear corner. It's not critical which mounting points you use, just make sure you use the same point on each side. Remember, you are looking for a difference in measurements. The strings will cross somewhere in the center of the chassis near the transmission mount. They should just touch where they cross each other or come within 1/4" of just touching.

Square

To determine if the chassis is square, use a tape measure to check from those same suspension mounting points. Again, measure from the front corners to the opposite rear corners. You're looking for the distances to be

Measure diagonally to the opposite corners of the chassis. The suspension mounting points should be accurately located.

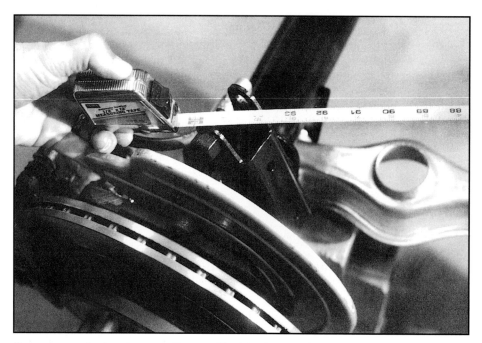

If your suspension is not square, the car will not track correctly. If the rear axle is not square, the car will track sideways.

identical within 1/4" (some race chassis dimensions are held to 1/16"). If the measurements are way off or the strings are further apart than suggested, the chassis has some problems. This should be correctable though, so seek qualified help! Start by calling the manufacturer of your chassis. Most body shops will also have frame straightening capabilities, so check your local Yellow Pages.

STEERING RACK

The mounts for your steering rack should locate the box precisely in relation to the rest of the front suspension (pivot points). If not, you could end up with bump steer (read on for an explanation of "bump steer"). For the purposes of inspection, you only need to temporarily install the steering rack, but the information here is for final installation and proper alignment.

When you connect the steering column to the steering rack input shaft you may find that the shaft or a universal joint comes close to or interferes with the headers. You need approximately 1/2" here to compensate for motor mount flexing during acceleration, etc. If you have less than that, you might be able to adjust (roll) the steering rack to get the needed clearance. One way to do this might be to add wedge-shaped shims between the mount and the rack. This will roll the rack forward or rearward, which will in turn raise or lower the input shaft. Be careful how much you roll the rack. Unless you can rotate the box around the tie rod axis you will be raising or lowering them as you add shims.

Caution: If the steering universal joints come close to the headers, they must be protected or shielded from the heat. If you allow the joints to become overheated the lubrication could cook, causing the joint to become stiff and/or seize. A universal joint boot over the joint will protect it from contaminants such as dirt and water. The boot must be protected from any extremely high heat, however.

If the steering rack is being forced to the side during hard cornering the factory rubber bushings can be replaced with polyurethane bushings. Any movement or gross misalignment here could create bump steer also.

If the manufacturer of your kit has done his chassis design and fabrication correctly then everything will work well. However, if they haven't, then you may end up with a car that doesn't like to go where you point it or does strange and dangerous things when it hits a bump or goes around a corner and the suspension compresses or rebounds.

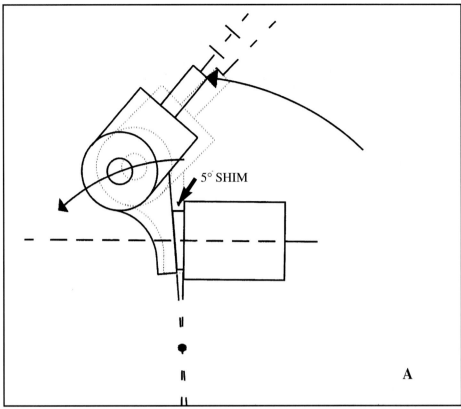

This illustration demonstrates the effect of adding a 5° shim to roll the steering rack forward. Note how the input shaft moves forward and up while the tie rod moves forward and down. The point where the two planes of the shim cross determines the point that the steering rack rotates around.

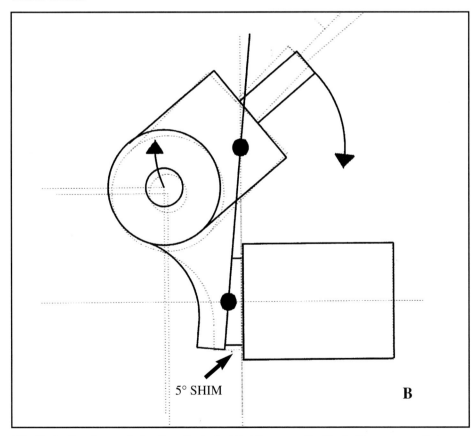

This illustration demonstrates the effect of adding the same 5° shim but in a manner that causes the steering rack to roll to the rear. In this case the tie rod rotates up more than forward and the input shaft rotates down and back equally.

Steering Rack Location

If you find that you need to move the input shaft of the steering rack, try rolling the rack or spacing it away from the crossmember, by adding 5° wedges or spacers. In the two examples at left, we will use the same wedge. The wedge is made from round stock and is about 2 1/4" in diameter. The wedges taper from a low of about one quarter inch to a maximum of just under one half an inch.

In illustration "A" we added a 5° wedge between the mounting flanges and the crossmember in order to gain clearance for the steering shaft.

In the illustrations note how the different parts of the rack move. In the first example, the 5° wedge is installed so the rack rolls forward. The result of this is that the rack pivots at a point about 4" below the mounting bolt, and every part of the rack rotates around that point. The input shaft moves approximately 0.8" forward and the tie rods move forward a little more than 0.5" and down almost 0.2". This 5° change will cause the input shaft to rise almost one tenth of an inch for each inch it is above the pivot point. If you only need 0.5" of clearance and the end of the input shaft is more than 3" from the obstruction, this may do the job for you. This will depend on your chassis and steering rack of course.

In the second example, B, we add the same 5° wedge so the steering rack rolls to the rear. The pivot point is now about 4" above the mounting bolts. The input shaft moves rearward and down almost 0.2" and the tie rods will move about 0.15" and about 0.1" of an inch forward. Again, depending on how much clearance you need, this could do the job.

If you think rolling the steering rack will help your situation, simply loosen the mounting bolts and move the

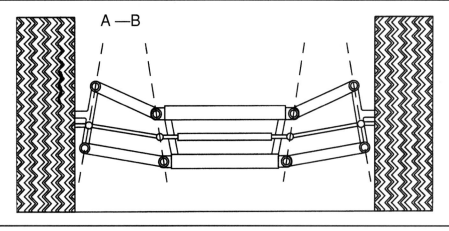

If you draw lines (A & B) from the upper control arm pivot axis to the lower control arm pivot axis, the lines should intersect the inner and outer tie rod ends.

input shaft forward or back enough to clear the problem. You may need to just space the rack from the crossmember to gain the needed clearance. Measure the gap at the top and bottom of the cross member, and be sure to allow for clearance at all parts of the rack and tie rods. The diameter of your wedges (or shims) should be large enough to provide a large enough surface for the rack mounts to sit securely on.

You may consider making temporary spacers out of PVC or similar easily workable materials and try them before making them out of metal. Be sure to check for bump steer before finalizing any changes in the location of any front end parts.

Warning: Be very careful when it comes to modifying front end parts, their mounting methods, and locations. If you have any doubt, check with a professional chassis builder.

BASIC SUSPENSION GEOMETRY

You must have a working knowledge of basic suspension geometry to complete your chassis inspection. You should understand the concepts of camber, caster and toe

alignment settings. Detailed explanations of these concepts are beyond the scope of this book. In the following sections, I will address some basic suspension geometry and its relationship to the installation of your suspension.

Bump Steer

One of the first concepts you'll need to be aware of prior to final-installing any parts is "bump steer." This is the tendency of the car to change direction or feel skittish as the suspension works. Contrary to common belief, bump steer is not

caused by worn parts, but is the result of suspension parts that are not aligned correctly.

The upper and lower control arms, as well as the steering rack, must be mounted exactly as they were designed in order to work correctly. If the suspension mounting points are not located in the correct location, the toe alignment will change as the suspension works up and down.

For an example, I will use the Mustang or Pinto front suspension with rack and pinion steering, and a solid or live rear axle (not independent). With such a design, the front tires should move up or down a minimum of 2 1/2" to 3" (5" to 6" total at the tire) with very little camber and toe change (less than .120"). Being independent, one tire should be able to move up and down without affecting the alignment of the other tire very much, .030" is considered acceptable.

Inspection—The upper and lower control arms, spindles and steering rack with tie rods must be in place. The bolts don't need to be torqued but must be at least snug. Adjust the tie rods so the spindles are pointing straight ahead. Using a carpenter's

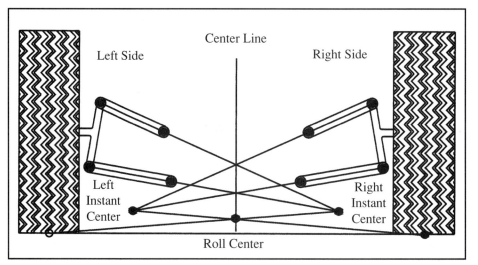

To locate the roll center of your chassis, using graph paper, draw your suspension to scale. Extend lines as shown from the left side to the right. Where these lines meet will be the right instant center. Repeat this on the right side to locate the left instant center. Extend a line from the instant centers across the car to the center of the opposite tire. The point where the lines cross the center line will be the roll center.

This space-frame chassis incorporates a removable upper crossmember. This brace ensures that the chassis will not flex under hard cornering. The forces from one side will be fed into the chassis. Without a similar type brace the chassis could flex, causing the suspension to move.

level make gross camber and toe adjustments to get the spindles parallel. Look at the suspension and chassis from the front, top and sides. You are looking for anything unusual, such as a control arm hanging differently. Both sides should look the same from all angles.

With both the lower control arms level and the steering rack centered, look at the steering rack and the tie rods. The tie rods should be parallel to the lower control arms (from the ball joint center to the lower mount pivot centers). If the tie rods are not parallel, the steering rack may want to be moved up or down.

Next, with the steering rack centered (left and right), look down from above. The tie rods should be straight or angle slightly to the front but not angled toward the rear.

With the lower control arm still level, adjust the upper control arm so that the brake rotor bolting surface is straight up and down, and both of the upper ball joints are at the same location, front to rear. Slide the upper control arm in and out, forward and rearward, as necessary. The important

thing here is that both sides are as close to identical as possible. A small carpenter's level may be helpful.

Now, holding one side (suspension) level with a jack or blocks, raise and lower the other side. Using a tape measure, measure from one rotor to the other. Some movement is expected but if it's no more than .015", then everything should be OK. If you see a lot of movement then you need to inspect the suspension and steering rack mounting points for proper location.

Set the steering rack straight ahead. Look at the chassis from the front, draw an imaginary line or hold a straight edge up to the suspension pivot points from the inner pivot of the upper control arm to the inner pivot of the lower control arm. The inner tie rod joint will be somewhere between the upper and lower pivots and the line should pass through it (or pretty darned close to it).

Note: On some kits, the front track was purposely narrowed by mounting the upper and lower control arms closer together than was intended. The result was that the inner tie rod

ends are too far out, and the tie rods end up being too short. The result is that the tie rods and control arms don't swing through the correct arcs any longer, and bump steer is the result. If you find the inner tie rod ends are too close together or too far apart, the steering rack must be modified to correct this. If you scan car magazines, you will see ads for machine shops that can modify your steering rack.

FRONT END

It would be a good idea to check the range of adjustment on your front end. To check the camber adjustment range (with the suspension still at the static ride height), clamp a level to the spindle. As you slide the upper control arms in and out you can watch the camber change. The spindles must be able to move from positive (out) to negative (in) camber.

Caster—To check the caster adjustment range, clamp the level to the rotor bolt surface. A piece of angle iron held in place with lug nuts could provide a suitable clamping surface. You should also be able to rotate the upper control arm so the top of the spindle will move forward and back of vertical.

If you have found any problems with your inspection, contact the manufacturer before you do anything else. If the manufacturer refuses to acknowledge and repair the problem, then your only alternative other than legal action is to go to a race car chassis shop and have them correct these problems.

Front End Rigidity

If you are building a car that will be club raced or autocrossed, you need to examine the bracing of the front spring and shock mounts. If the frame is not properly braced you need to

This brace looks nice, and will keep the shock towers the same distance apart, but has two major flaws. It is not triangulated back to the firewall, and the ends are free to rotate around the removable bolt.

When upgrading your suspension with stiffer springs and shocks, the chassis or body can flex. This upper brace ties the shock towers together with the firewall, adding a great deal of rigidity to the front end of the car.

consider adding an upper spring perch brace. This brace ties the left and right side of the chassis together, which in turn will distribute the forces over the entire front end of the car rather than concentrating them in one spot. The brace should be made of large diameter thin-wall tubing and needs to extend across the chassis from one shock tower to the other. If possible, a third leg should extend back over the engine and tie to the chassis. Do not use rod ends or Heim joints! Rod ends or Heim joints will allow the ends to rotate around the mounting bolt, reducing the effectiveness of the brace. This brace must be bolted in place in order to be effective, so design your mountings to lock in place for maximum rigidity and be

removable for engine servicing or removal if necessary.

REAR END

Your rear axle must be aligned to the front wheels and suspension. After you have located the rear axle and snugged the mounting hardware, measure from the axle centers to a front suspension mounting point to make sure that the axle is square to the front suspension.

Note: Do not measure to the front spindles. Without the front end aligned, these points may not be located correctly. Check to see that the axle is centered (left to right) in the chassis by measuring across the chassis from a point on the axle to a point on the front part of the chassis. Now is the time to make any corrections to the mounts. Attention to these details will help ensure that your car will track straight down the highway.

Axle Dampers and Leaf Spring Wrap Up

You will only need an axle damper if your car experiences leaf spring wrap up.

If your rear end is sprung with leaf springs, you should spend a moment looking at what provisions were engineered into the chassis design to minimize spring wrap or wind up such as a link between the chassis and the rear end housing. Spring wrap up is just as the term implies. It is the result of the leaf springs flexing as you apply the gas or brakes.

Example: Let's assume that you have your car on a lift and you set the parking brake so the rear wheels are locked. Put a socket and breaker bar on one of the lug nuts and apply pressure first one way then the other. Watch the leaf springs as you do this and you will notice that the springs try

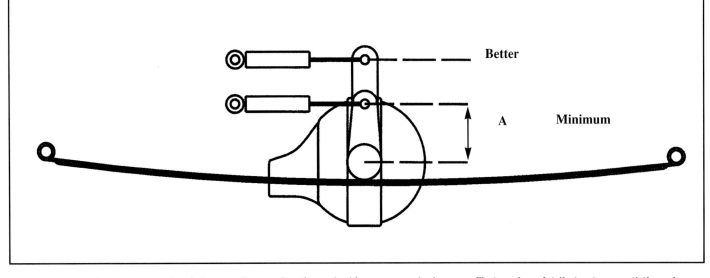

If you determine that your rear axle winds up under acceleration or braking, a rear axle damper will strongly resist (but not prevent) the axle from rotating forward or rearward. The damper must be mounted horizontally and a minimum of 7" (A) above the axle; 12" would be better.

to distort into an "S" shape as the axle housing tries to rotate around the axles. Imagine what happens as you drive your car and what happens if you accelerate or brake really hard. As the tires lose traction with the surface, the spring snaps it back to its normal shape. The tire may start to hop up and down, gaining and losing traction and the spring keeps twisting and snapping the axle back to where it is supposed to be. This effect is sometimes called "axle hop." Traction bars will take care of this but most hang down below the springs close to the road. Adding additional springs will reduce this tendency, but will stiffen the spring rate, causing the ride to be harsher. An axle damper may be a better answer. An axle damper looks like a shock absorber but is valved differently and mounted horizontally. Its purpose is to resist the rotation of the axle housing and minimize spring wrap up. Depending on how much horsepower your engine will be making or how aggressively you will be driving, a second damper may be necessary.

The damper must be mounted horizontally to prevent affecting the normal up and down movement of the axle and not move the dampers' rod in or out. The body or chassis mount must be strong enough so as not to flex or bend. The further away from the center of the axle (A) the better, but it should be 7" at a minimum, 12" is better. If it is less than 7" it may be necessary to use 2 dampers. The damper can be mounted facing forward of rearward.

Fuel Tank

The manufacturer of your car may offer a tank that has been designed to fit a special space or they may have designed the chassis around an existing production tank, or an after-market fuel tank. If you use a tank that relies on tabs that have been welded to the tank, consider adding straps that will cradle the tank. I (personally) don't recommend relying solely on the welded tabs to carry the load. The whole welding process causes the metal to "work harden." The metal becomes more brittle and subject to fatigue and ultimately cracking. At about 8 pounds per gallon, a 20 gallon tank has about 160 pounds of fuel sloshing around inside. If you look at any production auto you will note that the tanks are almost all

strapped into place. It may not be necessary but straps are cheap insurance.

Tank Vent

The tank must be vented! You must allow for internal pressure changes, gas expansion and contraction. Due to the temp changes, as gas is consumed by the engine it will create a vacuum in the tank, so if it is not vented to the atmosphere your engine could starve for gasoline. The vent can be routed in a number of locations including inside the fill neck if your cap is the vented kind. The minimum vent size should be 3/8" ID, but a larger vent won't hurt and if you fill your tank at a truck stop the increased venting capacity might be welcomed.

Note: It is not uncommon for truck stop fuel pumps to pump gas at a faster rate than your local gas pump. Truck drivers don't want to be hanging around waiting for the tank to fill.

Note: If you use a charcoal canister in your system, it must be mounted in the engine compartment, not the trunk!

Your fuel tank must have a vent and some sort of overflow. Here is an example of how a vent and drain tube were secured to the chassis.

Radiator

When it comes to selecting the proper size radiator for your engine, there appears to be no basic formula such as number of square inches of surface required per cubic inches of motor displacement. This is another area (like brakes) where the engineering required to select the correct parts is better left to the experts. The car manufacturer should have figured this out in advance. If not, a radiator shop should be able to help you out. At a minimum, the radiator should be rated (by application)for a car with that size motor. If you have the option, buy a radiator with more capacity than you think you need (for the obvious reasons).

Mounting—Installation and removal of the radiator with the body mounted is another often overlooked item, and the radiator shrouding is probably the second.

Before you start, take a moment and open the hood on your daily driver and examine how that radiator is mounted. As you mount your radiator you need to consider things like

transmission cooling line routing and connections (if you have an automatic transmission) and, body clearance.

First, examine the mounting brackets supplied with the kit to be sure that the mounting hardware is of adequate number, size and will not be hidden by other body parts. Will you be able to remove the radiator either from above or below the car without having to remove major body parts? Avoid loose nuts at all cost, there is a

very good chance that your shrouding will prevent you from getting a wrench on the other side without removing the shrouding. The mounting bolts should thread into something secure, like a threaded hole, nuts brazed to the brackets, "Tee Nuts" or some other blind fastening method. Using loose nuts and bolts will make mounting and removing difficult at best and is an invitation to damage or injury. ■

Painting Your Chassis

Before you paint your chassis, weld or braze a few threaded studs to the chassis for your electrical ground network, 1/4" - 20 or 28 should be sufficient. Just make them at least 3/4" to 1" long. Place one near each head and tail light, one near the motor where the ground strap from the motor will be and one near where the voltage regulator will be mounted. This will ensure that you will be able to ground the entire electrical system properly.

OK, now you can paint, but only after having double-checked the chassis and are confident that everything is correct. The following are the types of paint available. You decide which is best for you. The choices are listed in order of "good, better, best."

Enamels—These are the least expensive, good for the street (non-show). A good quality metal primer and enamel color is adequate. Just degrease, de-scale, prime and paint.

Epoxy or Catalyzed—These paints are medium priced. They are harder, and more chip resistant, but more difficult to apply.

Powder Coating—This is the "cost no object" option. While these are probably the best coatings available today, the size of the parts you can powder coat will be limited by the size of the oven that the service bureau has. Remember, powder coating is baked at about 400 degrees. You may be fortunate to have an oven in your area large enough to handle a chassis. Cost is comparable to catalyzed paints but there is no "drying time" to contend with.

Color—Consider a gloss grey or other light color for your chassis paint. A light color will show any leaking fluids almost immediately, and if it is a gloss, it will wipe off easily. I would rather see a drip on my chassis before I discover a puddle on the garage floor.

If your chassis develops a crack at a weld, the crack will be more easily seen than with a dark color and tell-tale rusting will show up very quickly. Parts that may be rubbing together will sometimes give off steel shavings or dust that will also show up very quickly. Black will hide all of these potentially hazardous situations.

SUSPENSION TIPS

3

Suspension is defined by HPBooks' *Automotive Dictionary* as "a system of springs, shock absorbers and locating linkages used to support a vehicle's structure and powertrain on its wheels." If the manufacturer of your chassis did his design and fabricating work correctly, your car should be well mannered and stable on the highway. However, if he didn't, you could have a car that is a handful or even unsafe.

The front tires on your car should remain parallel (when straight ahead) or the same angle relative to each other, when they move up and down as a car goes over dips or bumps in a road. The vehicle should track straight and true or hold its line through a turn even as the suspension works up and down. This chapter has some tips and techniques designed to help you install and set up your suspension to achieve this goal.

BUSHINGS

The manufacturer of your donor car will have used rubber insulators in a number of locations. These insulators are there to reduce the shocks and vibrations transmitted from the road

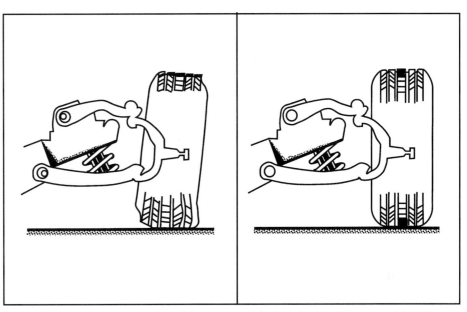

During cornering, the bushings are subject to tremendous loads. As you can see at left, the lower control arm is forced inward and the upper control arm is forced outward with rubber bushings. Polyurethane bushings (right), resist this deflection and maintain the alignment of the front end pieces because the material is firmer.

to the car and its occupants. I urge you not to leave any of them out. Rubber bushings are used throughout a car's suspension. Depending on your driving requirements, you may want to upgrade these with aftermarket types.

The factory rubber bushings for the strut rod, control arm and sway bar are designed to provide a compromise between a good ride, sound and vibration isolation and reasonable

durability. The soft rubber factory bushings will allow the parts to move during hard cornering as the (softer) rubber compresses and distorts. You can substitute stiffer polyurethane bushings and insulators. If you use softer factory rubber bushings, the car will ride smoother and quieter, but may not perform as well in corners. Polyurethane bushings will improve cornering, but at the expense of ride harshness and road noise.

Polyurethane control arm bushings resist compression and degradation from the natural elements. Replacing the soft OEM control arm bushings can make a drastic improvement in the way your car will handle.

Polyurethane strut rod bushings will minimize caster change due to the lower control arm shifting rearward during hard braking.

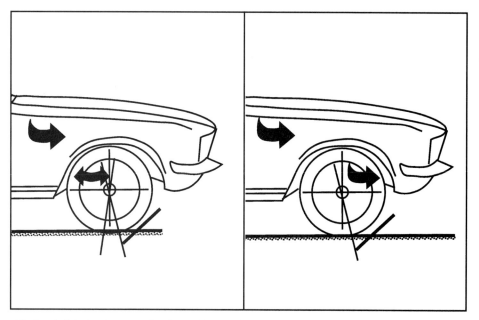

Strut rod style front suspension (sometimes referred to as drag strut), relies on a large rubber bushing to resist any forward or rearward movement of the lower control arm. If the lower control arm is allowed to move back under hard braking, the steering axis will attempt to go from positive to negative which will change the amount of caster.

Rubber Bushings

If you choose to use OEM rubber bushings, these may only be available from a dealer, or possibly a manufacturer that specializes in restoration parts for the particular brand of your donor car.

Polyurethane Bushings

The harder urethane bushings can be purchased from a number of aftermarket suppliers locally or by mail order. Stiffer bushings will more precisely hold the suspension parts where they are supposed to be.

Because polyurethane bushings do not compress or distort, they will deliver tighter crisper handling. Polyurethane is not susceptible to deterioration from elements such as oil, road salts, ultraviolet or dry rot. Polyurethane, because it is harder, will transmit more noise and vibration to the body and occupants, however.

Generally, polyurethane bushing assemblies (preassembled by the manufacturer) as used on control arm pivots will come prelubricated. If yours are not, be sure to lubricate them before installation using a Teflon-based lubricant. Sway bar, shock absorber, and drop link eye bushings or any other bushing that will rotate around a pin should be lubricated. If you don't lubricate them, your suspension will not work as smoothly as possible, and you could end up with squeaks as the suspension moves.

If you are replacing existing rubber bushings on a car you have been using for awhile, be sure to remove any scale or rust on stabilizer bars and shock mounts prior to applying any lubricant.

Strut Rod and Control Arm Bushings

The front wheels and lower control arm assemblies will try to roll under the car as you brake or turn the car. The strut rod bushings are intended to keep them properly located. If you are using a heavier engine and larger tires than the rubber bushings were designed to handle, the deflection and movement in the suspension parts could be enough to induce a change in steering axis (caster change). The more precise these can be held in alignment, the smaller change will be experienced. As a result your suspension and brakes will come closer to delivering their maximum potential; the tires will also remain more accurately aligned and firmly planted on the road.

Leaf Spring Bushings

As with all suspension bushings, any uncontrolled movement in the leaf spring bushings can affect your take off, cornering and braking. Stiffer bushings will allow the loads to be transmitted to the suspension and not absorbed in the rubber bushing first.

Note: The placement of your leaf springs (slightly angled together toward the front and the height of the front mounts) has a bearing on the

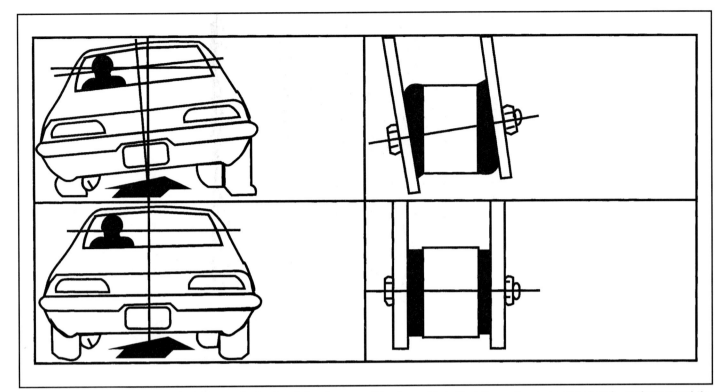

Soft leaf spring bushings (top) will deflect under load and absorb some of the forces that affect the performance of a chassis, anti-squat and the roll center for example. The rear axle will move around during acceleration, braking and cornering. Firmer polyurethane bushings (bottom) will retain their shape and allow the forces to be better transmitted to the chassis, which in turn generates increased stability.

Soft sway bar bushings will allow the body to roll abruptly. The suspension pieces move rapidly and loads are not transferred into the chassis smoothly. The result of this will be a car that may feel twitchy or unstable as you enter a turn (for example). Firmer sway bar bushings will transfer any rolling motion immediately to the chassis, which will allow the suspension to work as it was intended. Firmer sway bar bushings are said to have the effect of increasing size in sway bar diameter one size.

Rear Control Arm Bushings

If your car has a four link or four bar rear suspension and you experience wheel hop, polyurethane bushings may be in order to prevent the suspension from moving around instead of transmitting the load to the chassis.

Sway Bar Bushings

Soft rubber sway bar bushings will compress and distort before the sway bar begins to twist and transfer the force into the suspension. Installing polyurethane bushings will eliminate the "slop" and the result is the sway bar will begin to affect the body roll and minimize roll steer sooner, resulting in a crisper more solid feel when cornering.

SHOCKS & SPRINGS

Remember in the introduction of the book I urged you to take time to think

amount of roll understeer and anti-squat the rear suspension will contribute. Some schools of thought recommend using spherical rod ends or soft rubber bushings on the front and urethane bushings on the rear spring eyes. The front of the springs must be allowed to move freely without binding so the axle can twist as the body rolls around its roll center.

This street rod has its coil-over shocks mounted at a reasonable 15 degrees. You will notice that the car is lowered causing the lower control arm to angle down toward the center. The greater the angle the lower the car's roll center will be, resulting in increased cornering power.

This roadster's coil-over shocks are installed at an incredible angle, about 50–55 degrees, resulting in a whopping 60% loss in dampening and close to 70% loss in spring rate.

about how you are planning to drive the car. You are now at the point where you will need to select your shocks and springs. Do you expect the ride to be "boulevard soft" and supple, "buckboard hard" and precise, or somewhere in between? The average enthusiast will be looking for a compromise between ride comfort and handling. The shocks and springs you select will have a major impact on the ride and performance you will get from the car.

Theory

A shock absorber's whole purpose in life is to resist (not prevent) the up and down movement of the suspension. Without shock absorbers, the springs of your car would compress and extend uncontrollably, causing the tires to bounce and skip all over the road surface. Such a car would be almost uncontrollable. A

shock that offers too much dampening may prohibit the springs from moving the suspension fast enough to follow the road surface. By resisting the suspension movement, the shock dampens the bumps and vibrations the chassis and body experience. The movement that a shock absorber is subjected to is measured in *travel* (distance) and the rate of change in speed is called *acceleration*.

Shock Selection

When it comes to specifying the correct shock for your street car, your primary concern will be the amount of damping and the amount of stroke or travel that the shock is expected to go through. Adjustability and other features will be secondary. It is important to select a shock absorber that has a greater amount of travel than the suspension. If the shock bottoms or tops out because it doesn't have enough travel, the handling will be adversely affected and the shock will be destroyed quickly.

Shock Mounting

In order to take full advantage of the shock's capacity to control bumps and vibrations, it should be mounted as close to the tire as possible. If not, a position that is as close as practical and an increase in spring rate and shock dampening would be specified. This is because the shock absorber rate is affected by the leverage ratio in the same way a spring or anti-roll bar is.

Leverage Ratio—What is leverage ratio? "The amount of travel that the shock has for each inch of travel at the wheel." To clarify this let's assume the right front tire of your car experiences a bump with a travel of 1/2". If the lower A-arm length (from pivot axis to ball joint) is 12" and the shock is mounted to the A-arm 6" to the inside from the ball joint, then the shock will move half as far as the tire. The shock will still control it over the 1/2" but it will only move 1/4". Its dampening force will be reduced to 1/2 its resistance due to the leverage loss. So

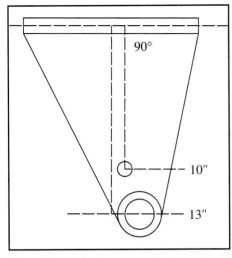

When determining the lever ratio for a shock or spring, always measure the distance at a 90 degree angle from the line of axis of a lower "a" frame.

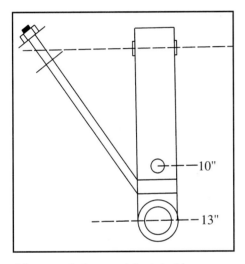

A lower control arm and drag strut is measured the same was as a traditional style "a" frame.

This is an example of a coil-over shock installed at about 10°. This suspension may be custom fabricated and uses polyurethane bushings but is still based on the Mustang II suspension geometry. The spindles and ball joints are the only OEM Mustang parts. This suspension should work nice and smoothly.

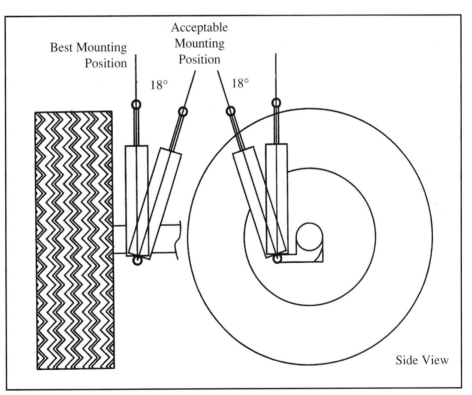

The installation angle of a shock absorber or coil-over shock is critical regardless of which direction it leans. Shocks or coil-over shocks should be mounted as close as possible to the wheel and as near vertical as practical.

the closer the shock is to the ball joint, the greater amount of the motion the shock can dampen. When taking any measurements to determine leverage ratio, the distance from the ball joint, spring mount, or shock mount must be taken at 90° to the pivot axis.

The effectiveness of the shocks or coil-over shocks is proportional to their installation and operating angle. So take a moment and examine the mounting points for the shocks, both the front and the rear.

If your shock is installed straight up and down, there will be very little change in that angle as the suspension extends and compresses, but if the shock is installed at an angle, the angle will increase as the suspension compresses and decrease as it extends. The further the shocks/springs are mounted from vertical, the greater the leverage loss and the less effective they become as the angle changes when the suspension compresses. This is true regardless of whether the shock is

SHOCK LOSSES

Loss of shock absorber dampening control and spring rate when mounted away from a vertical position

Angle from Vertical	Shock Damping	Spring Rate
5	1% loss	1 % loss
10	2% loss	3 % loss
15	5% loss	7 % loss
20	10% loss	12% loss
25	15% loss	18% loss
30	20% loss	25% loss
35	27% loss	33% loss
40	35% loss	43% loss
45	43% loss	50% loss
50	51% loss	59% loss
55	59% loss	67% loss
60	67% loss	75% loss

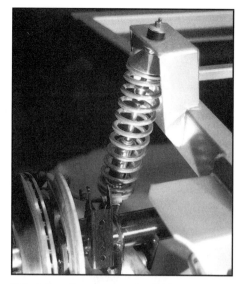

This Cobra chassis uses the 8.8 rear end from a late-model Mustang. Notice the angle of the coil-over shocks. This chassis can also use the Mustang springs and shocks. Being able to use stock OEM parts lowers the cost, both initially and down the road when it comes time to replace something.

Notice the installation angle on the rear shocks of this T-Bucket. They look to be less than 10°. Also note the location and neatness of the brake lines. This car uses radius rods to locate the rear axle.

leaning in, out, forward, or to the rear.

A shock absorber will not change the roll stiffness but its mounting angle will affect the roll resistance. Roll stiffness is the resistance that the springs and shocks generate because of the angle at which they are installed. The closer to vertical and further apart the rear shocks are, the more they will resist body roll as the car corners and the weight tries to transfer to the outside of the turn. The more the tops of the shocks are angled toward the center of the car and each other, the less roll resistance they will offer.

If you are confused, think of it this way. Wrap both hands around a broom handle about six inches apart. With your elbows spread to equal the distance between your shoulders, hold the broom handle up in front of you and have someone try to pull one end down. It probably did not take very much effort on their part to move the handle. Now spread your hands out so your hands are even with the width of your shoulders and repeat the test. It shouldn't be as easy to move the handle. You didn't get stronger, you just changed the roll stiffness.

The chart above demonstrates the amount of dampening control and spring rate loss as the installation angle from vertical increases. A greater angle will require you to use a shock with more dampening capability and a spring that is stiffer to compensate for the increased losses.

Relocating Shocks

How do you know if your shocks need to be relocated? Regardless of whether your car is finished or not, you must position the suspension at its final ride height. If you have coil-over shocks installed, you may be able to adjust them down until the chassis is at ride height. If not, install turnbuckles on the shock mounts and adjust them so that the suspension parts (rear axle and upper and lower front control arms) simulate the final

The car was supported under the axle and the chassis leveled so the static ride height could be determined. The chassis was then supported on jackstands and the old coil-over shocks were removed. Using the jack, the axle was then raised and lowered to its extremes. The total travel was noted in addition to the static ride location.

A new shock was selected based on the weight of the car, the amount of suspension travel and static ride height. A piece of tubing was drilled with holes to simulate the mid point length (static ride height) of the new coil-over shock. Brackets were temporarily mounted and the tubing clamped into place in order to set the angle and design the lower coil-over shock mount. Note the cardboard template for the lower shock mount.

the unit. Refer to the chart or the manufacturer to determine if these angles are OK.

A front coil-over or shock should be mounted as close to the lower ball joint as possible and extend through the upper control arm to the chassis mount. It should have an inward angle at the top only enough to clear the upper control arm as it moves through its travel. If the top of the coil-over is not within 3" (center-to-center distance) offset from the lower ball joint, it will be necessary to move up one or more levels of spring rate or dampening capacity on the springs and shocks. If you find that you need to move the mounting points for your shocks or coil-over shocks, consider the following procedure.

Before you start any measuring, double check and make sure the suspension's at the desired (static) ride height. Use a straightedge, protractor or level to determine a suitable mounting angle and location that will allow you to mount the shock as close to the wheel and as close to vertical as practical.

Note: If you have to relocate your mounts, you should consider using the longest shock that will fit. The more shock/suspension travel you have, the softer spring rate you can use. This will allow your suspension to work better over the irregularities in the road surfaces and reduce or eliminate the possibility of bottoming or topping out the shocks.

If the shock location and angle are correct, perform the following procedures.

Front—Using your jack, raise the suspension until the lower control arm is approximately horizontal. To determine the length of the correct shock for your application, measure the distance between the upper and lower shock mount. That length is the "static ride height." The shock that

ride height. Using a digital level (available at your local hardware store or lumber yard) or a protractor and bubble level, determine the current installation angle of your shocks.

A simple tool can be fabricated by gluing or bolting a protractor to something straight and long enough to reach between the shock mounts.

Hold a small bubble level so that it is level and intersects the center of the protractor, and read the angle off the protractor. This is the approximate installed "static" angle of your shock. Raise and lower the suspension to the maximum allowed by any suspension stops or the limits of the components and note the maximum angle seen by

Before final welding, the location and angle of the coil-over shocks are checked. The angle is verified using the angle finder with a string level secured on top. The angle finder was held against the spring and the upper part adjusted until the bubble is centered. The angle is then read using a protractor. As the spring is compressed it will swell and its diameter will increase, so be sure to build in at least 3/8 inch between the spring and any other part.

you select should have 50 - 60% of its rod showing at "static ride height."

Example: a shock with 7" of travel should have 3.5 – 4.2" of its rod extended.

Note: If you plan to autocross your car and you have coil-over shocks on the front of your car, consider replacing the lower mount with one that has two alternate holes (about 5/8" apart horizontaly). This will allow you to change the spring rate quickly and at no cost. The inner position, about 5/8" further inboard, will reduce the spring rate by about 10% over the outer location at the ball joint. This could come in handy to "fine tune" your suspension if you autocross the car.

Rear—If your rear end is located with a four-link setup, check to see if you can set the ride height so the bars head uphill from the rear axle to the chassis just a few degrees. By setting the angle of the four bars up slightly, you add anti-squat to the rear suspension. This tends to counteract the tendency for the car to squat under acceleration. Too much anti-squat, however, could cause the tires to hop

or chatter under hard braking or cause the rear end to roll steer in the turns.

Note: If your rear end is located by leaf springs, using turnbuckles in place of the shocks will allow you to compress the springs enough to bring the chassis to its ride height.

Compress the springs until the axle is centered in the fender opening and measure the distance between the shock absorber mounting bolts. Don't forget to check the angle that the shock will be installed at to ensure

that it is not excessive. If either of these is not correct, now is the time to change it.

Rear shocks must be mounted as low as possible. Never mount them on top of the axle because the higher position will require stiffer spring rates to control body roll.

Note: Mount the shocks as vertical (fore and aft as well as side to side) as practical. Angles up to 18 degrees are okay, but avoid exceeding 24 degrees from vertical. Any angle greater than that will change the leverage factor and require stiffer shocks and springs to end up with the desired rate at the wheels. The closer together the upper mounting points are, the less roll resistance the car will have.

Note: With the car empty and at static ride height, the distance between the upper and lower shock mount should be such that the shocks are slightly more than half (about 60%) extended.

CHECK RIDE HEIGHT

Once you are satisfied with the installation of the shocks and springs, temporarily replace the shocks with turnbuckles or a piece of steel angle iron. Your goal here is to locate the

This Cobra chassis has been assembled using a Jaguar rear end, OEM style fuel tank, polyurethane bushings and adjustable sway bar lever arms. The coil-over shocks are installed at about 12 degrees which should produce a decent ride. Notice the Watts linkage to locate the rear hubs (arrows).

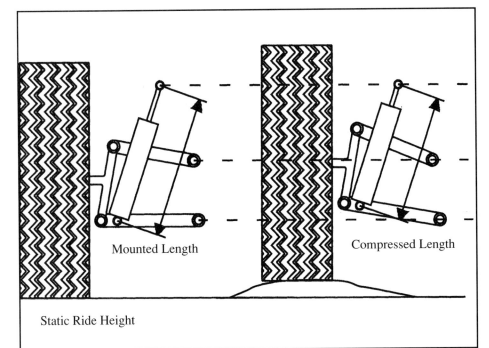

Mounted Length

Compressed Length

Static Ride Height

Care must be taken when considering "bump stops" to ensure that when your (front) wheel rises, the stop is contacted before the shock "bottoms out" to prevent internal damage.

The rear end travel is measured with only the shock installed. Notice the bumper at the top of the shock to protect the shock valving.

With the shock compressed the distance between a major chassis member and the axle is carefully measured. This will be the location of the rear suspension stop and a mount will need to be fabricated. In this case the distance measured 3 inches.

chassis at the proper ride height so you can locate things like exhaust pipes, fuel and transmission cooling lines and other components properly. Before you pat yourself on the back, check one more thing. With the shocks and no springs in place (if you are using coil-over shocks) raise and lower the chassis and double-check to

make sure that everything is clear and no parts are in danger of being crushed, bent or torn off. Don't forget to raise each side to simulate body roll. Double check to see that the ball joints don't run out of travel; if there is a danger of this, suspension stops

must be considered!

Don't forget to allow clearance around the shocks and springs. Coil springs will expand as they are compressed. Longer springs are more prone to this, so allow at least 1/2" for clearance if you can. If you don't have the room and can't shim or move the mount, check periodically for signs of contact.

If your car will be using coil-over shocks then spend the extra money and order spherical bearings for the mounts. Urethane bushings will do but are not as good. The extra load exerted on the bushings of a misaligned shock or the car's weight in a coil-over installation will cause a rubber bushing to fail. If you have separate springs (leaf or coil) rubber shock bushings should be fine. However, if you find that your shock mounts are not perfectly aligned one over the other, then bearings are in order. As a misaligned shock mount moves closer together, the angle becomes greater just like a shock that is installed at an angle. Bushings will tolerate a little misalignment but will bind if the angle becomes too great.

Note: If you use spherical bearings in a non-coil-over application, the bearings will rattle because the spring is not applying constant pressure on them. This will most likely drive you crazy after a while.

Suspension Stops

Don't forget suspension stops on the front and rear. Although you can run the car without them, if you should hit a pot hole or bottom the suspension, you could blow the valves out in a shock and turn it into scrap. The cute little rubber bumpers that come on the shaft of most coil-over shocks will not do the job. They are travel indicators, not compression bumpers! There is too much leverage generated at those points. If your chassis doesn't already

33

The suspension stop we chose measured about 2 1/8" so the mount would need to make up the remaining distance plus about 1/2" more to provide some compression before things get close.

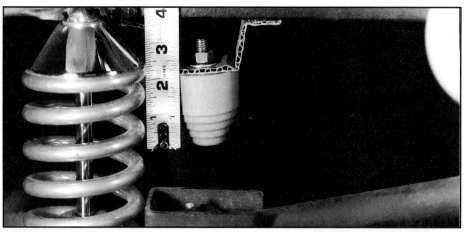

This temporary mount made of cardboard positions the stop about 3 1/2" from the chassis member. 1/2" of compression is considered an absolute minimum but with bumpers on the shocks also, we felt comfortable with that amount of stop compression. Using cardboard as a template allowed us to make sure that everything would work as intended.

have them you should fabricate some. The size and location of these will depend on your application. Suspension stops must always be mounted so that they will be under compression if the suspension comes in contact with it. Never mount them so the stop is in shear (pushed to the side). That type of mounting arrangement will fail quickly.

Check with the manufacturer of your shocks to see if any internal protection is built in. For example, Carrera shocks have an internal hydraulic lock that is designed to withstand *rebound* shock and therefore the suspension doesn't require a *rebound* stop.

Size—How big should the suspension stops be? If you do have your shocks mounted, move the suspension to fully compressed as limited by the shock.

If you don't have your shocks yet, you can use the shock absorber manufacturers' measurements for the extended and compressed lengths. Note the distance between the suspension member and the chassis that is directly above for the upper stop and below (if applicable) for a lower stop.

Caution: When the shock absorber is fully compressed, stop! Do not apply any further pressure. Doing so could damage the shock internally.

Rubber or urethane bumpers are

suitable materials just as long as the stop is long enough to prevent the shocks from ever being compressed or extended to their extremes; a minimum of 1/2" longer than the dimension should be adequate to prevent bottoming the shock. Rubber bumpers will compress more than urethane, so choose the materials and thicknesses carefully. If you are the type of driver that doesn't pay attention to bumps and pot holes, thicker stops may be in order.

Warning: When determining where your suspension stops should be you need to consider the angles that your driveshaft or half shafts will be exposed to also. The movement of those shafts should be limited to prevent the joints from bending more than three degrees.

Note: If you used turnbuckles to set the static ride height, leave them in until the car is finished. Remember, by holding the car at its static ride height you can make sure that everything will be located so as not to collide with any suspension pieces. Hopefully, this will get you close enough so you don't have to go back and move something. Do expect to make some minor ride height adjustment at some point during construction, however.

COIL SPRINGS

The process by which you select your springs will be the same regardless of whether your car is a hot rod, reproduction, or custom. It is all based on the same information, i.e., maximum vehicle weight, unsprung weight, leverage ratio, shock travel, sprung weight, and bump travel.

The manufacturer of your car should be able to tell you what spring rates are used, regardless of whether the car has separate springs and shocks or coil-over shocks. If not, then you have a bit of work in front of you.

Selecting the correct spring for your car is not an easy task. The angle of installation, leverage ratio, length of the shock and its travel must all be factored into the selection. If the spring is too long you could have coil bind as the coils compress and they come in contact with each other. This is a job better left to the manufacturer.

Springs are rated by the amount of weight required to compress the spring 1 inch. For example: a 200 pound spring will compress 1 inch if 200 pounds of load is placed on it; 2 inches with 400 pounds, etc.

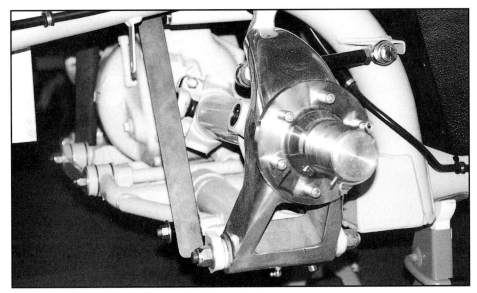

Once the shocks and spring mount locations are verified and welded, replace the springs and shocks with your static ride height spaces. The spaces can be heavy wall tubing (round or square), angle iron or adjustable shackles. Notice the clips that are securing the wiring harness.

Weigh In

If your car is complete, take it to a scrap yard, trucking business or moving company to get a total vehicle and axle weight. Axle weight is the weight on each axle. If you can't do that then you will have to estimate the weight. Get in touch with other owners of your type car and find out what spring rates they used. The supplier of your coil-over shocks may have a chart that will help you determine your car's weight. Carrera shocks has documented the weight of over a thousand cars and is well prepared to help you estimate your car's weight.

Calculating Spring Rate & Length

In order for the manufacturer to select the correct spring for your car, you have to identify a number of specifications.

• Determine the car's maximum front and rear weight (with driver and fuel).

• Determine the *unsprung weight,* i.e., the weight of suspension pieces. These are the pieces that are not supported by

the car's springs, such as the axle or spindles, brakes, springs, half the shock and spring, wheels and tires (front and rear).

• Determine the leverage ratio: This is the amount of travel that the shock has for each inch of travel at the wheel.

• Determine the suspension travel. This is the total travel of the suspension at the wheel.

• Determine the *sprung weight.* This is the weight of the vehicle minus the parts of the suspension that are supported by the springs, i.e., axle weight (half the vehicle weight, in this case the front axle weight) minus the weight of the axle, brakes, wheels, tires, half the spring and half weight, divided by the leverage ratio.

• Determine the "bump travel." This is the shock travel x .6 +.5" safety factor. This is done to add a margin of safety to prevent the coils of the spring from binding if the suspension is bottomed or compressed against the stops.

For this exercise we will assume

you are building a mid-30's Ford coupe with a total weight of 3000 lbs.

• 1400 lbs front and 1600 lbs rear.

• Mounted (static) length of the shocks is 10-7/8 and the angle will be 16 degrees both front and rear.

• Extended length of 12-3/8", compressed length of 8-3/8" resulting in a stroke of 4."

• Shock leverage ratio of 10"/13". This means that the lower control arm is 13" from the ball joint to the control arm pivot and the shock mount is 10" from the control arm pivot. (Remember, this measurement is measured at a 90 degree angle from the pivot axis.)

• Spring leverage ratio of 10"/13" because the car has coil-over shocks. If the car had separate springs mounted in a different location this ratio might be different.

With this information you can now select a shock absorber with the proper dimensions and springs of approximately the correct rate. The shocks should be selected and mounted with approximately 60% (+ 1/2") of the rod exposed at static ride height.

And one final thought here! When you select the manufacturer and style of your shocks or coil-over shocks, consider what will happen when it is time to replace them. Shocks that have the same spacing as those from a particular production car will allow you to replace them from any manufacturer. Also, coil-over shocks that have integral spring mounts will be more expensive to replace than coil-over shocks that have removable spring mounts. ■

BRAKE TIPS

4

When it comes to your braking system, you can't be too cautious or thorough. If your brake system fails due to a component failure or improper selection of parts, the results can be devastating, and permanent. If you are the least bit unsure about what you are doing, seek the help of a brake component manufacturer or supplier. Advice from friendly neighbors or the kid at the parts store often isn't the best way to go when it comes to something so important.

The average braking system is composed of a master cylinder, proportioning valve, tubing (steel and rubber), calipers and rotors on the front and most likely drums on the rear. As with every other part of this project you have quite a few options.

BUILD IT ON PAPER

Sit down and design your brake system on paper first. Decide if you want power assisted brakes, and determine the size rotors and drums you are going to use. Will you have four-wheel disc brakes? Do you want mechanical ABS?

This Mustang 8.8 rear end is fitted with SVO high performance 11" brakes. These calipers also have a cable actuated parking brake feature.

Increasing Performance

Braking performance can be improved a number of different ways. These include increasing the "total swept area," or increasing the pressure and its distribution within the system. The front wheel brakes can be upgraded with larger rotors and calipers with two or four pistons. However, four piston calipers are not necessary for the street or anything driving short of competition. You

could change the master cylinder for one with a different diameter or length of stroke, change the pedal ratio, exchanging the rear drums for larger drums or better still, installing rear disc brakes.

Some aftermarket suppliers offer increased braking performance with engineered brake packages consisting of larger rotors, calipers and other assorted parts. Some are better than others, some require additional parts fabrication or caliper shims and some

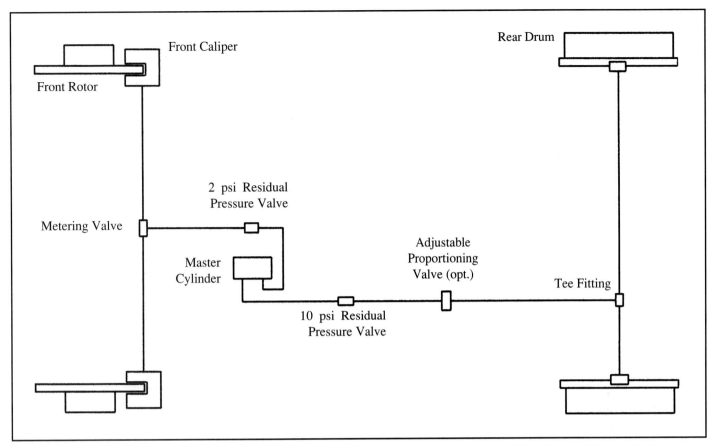

It is highly recommended that you build your brake system on paper by laying it out in a simple schematic like this one. These are typical locations for metering valves, proportioning valves and residual pressure valves (2 psi front and 10 psi rear) in a disc/drum brake system.

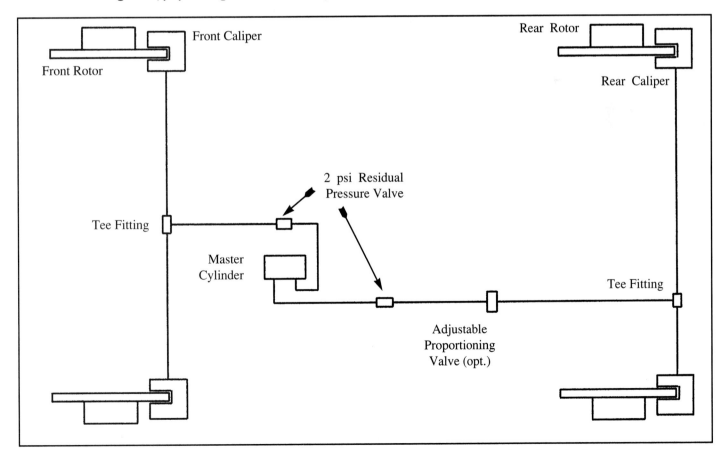

These are typical locations for metering valves, proportioning valves and residual pressure valves in a four wheel disc brake system. Note that the residual pressure valves are both 2 psi units for the front and rear.

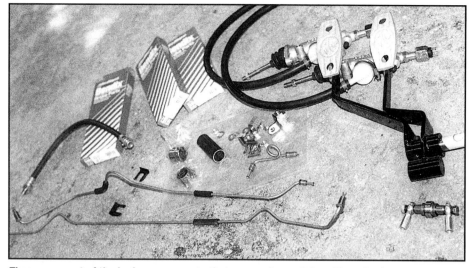

These are most of the brake components that are used on a Cobra. These basic components are the same as you would use on a T bucket, Ferrari, 34 Phaeton or any other car. The major difference though is the pedals mount low under the floor as in some hot rods. Most later model cars have pedal assemblies hung from the steering column or firewall area. Notice the brake lines are smoothly bent with no sharp bends to restrict the flow of fluid.

These are standard Ford and General Motors master cylinders. Caution: The front reservoir of a General Motors master cylinder feeds the front and the rear reservoir feeds the rear. Ford is opposite; the front of Ford master cylinders feeds the rear brakes and the rear feeds the front. Don't get them mixed up. This is the kind of thing you need to know when using donor car parts.

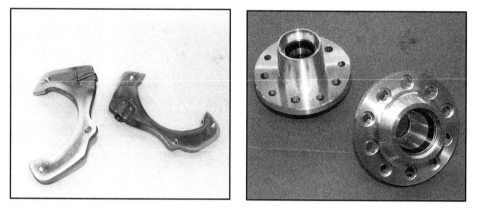

These brackets (left) and hubs (right) are from a "big brake" kit that contains rotors, hubs, calipers, bearings, seals and hardware that allows you to install 11" rotors and GM calipers to Mustang II spindles. This kit will produce a 65% improvement in braking. E.C.I. Manufacturing, (Engineered Components, Inc., Hot Rod Brakes and Brackets. P.O. Box 841, Vernon, CT 06066. (860) 872-7046.

come with everything you need.

Caution: If you choose to upgrade your braking capacity, be careful and shop around. When it comes to mixing parts, the diameters of the master cylinder, wheel cylinders and calipers are critical. Other items affecting the operation of your brakes include the proportioning valves, residual pressure valves, distribution blocks, brake pedal leverage, the size and width of the tires, the weight of the car, and the weight distribution fore and aft. All of these items must be considered as well.

The tire diameter and width alone will change the leverage on the brakes, which in turn affects the force needed to slow and stop the car. When you consider all of these variables, you can appreciate why it is a good idea to design the brake system on paper first, before any money is spent.

If you go shopping for custom brake parts, make sure you know the total vehicle weight and its distribution, front and rear, as well as the size of the tires. If you deviate from the factory donor car parts and "customize" your braking system, make sure you determine and record the diameters of the master cylinder,

wheel cylinder pistons and caliper piston diameters. Knowing this information will make it easier to make corrections to your braking system if it is not just right.

Donor Car Brake System

In many cases, you can use the brake system (non ABS) from the donor car without any problems. Usually, the donor car will be (or was when it was new) approximately the same weight or heavier than the car you are building, so you should have adequate braking capacity. You may find that the braking bias may be off due to a difference in weight distribution. This may require you to install an adjustable proportioning valve. For a street-driven cruiser I don't think you would notice the difference. If, however, you are using larger tires and a heavier engine and you tend to drive a little more aggressively, then you may find yourself with brakes that are marginal.

If you are reusing brake components from a donor car always rebuild the parts. Never take the

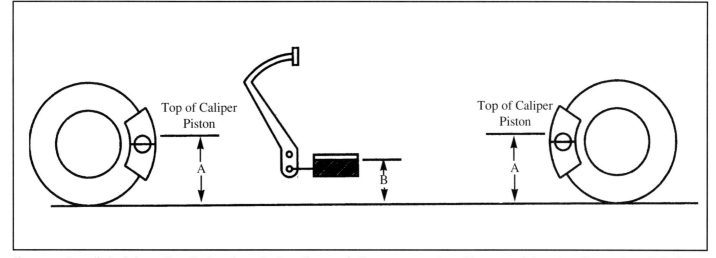

If your master cylinder is lower than the top of your brake calipers as is the case on most pre-50s cars or Cobra where the master cylinder is under the floor, you could use a residual pressure valve to prevent fluid from siphoning back into the master cylinder. Residual pressure valves are not necessary on all drum systems.

This is a typical GM master cylinder with a vacuum power booster. Notice the vapor trap on the booster; these are important because they prevent any potential damage caused by gas vapors collecting inside your booster.

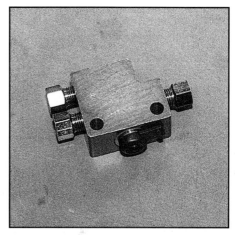

This front disc metering valve is important. It prevents the front brakes from actuating first; the rear brakes must actuate first.

condition of these parts for granted.

Warning: Always use new brake tubing and flexible lines. NEVER reuse steel tubing or flexible lines. The steel lines will most likely kink if you try to re-bend them to fit the contours of your chassis. Rubber lines deteriorate over time and the constant flexing can cause them to come apart inside. If this should happen, pieces of rubber can come off and block the flow or return of pressure. This could prevent a wheel cylinder or caliper from releasing. The rest I will leave to your imagination.

BRAKE SYSTEM COMPONENTS

Control Valve Assembly—The brake system in your Mustang donor car had one of these units. The brake lines from the master cylinder (front and rear) connect to it. The control valve assembly contains a pressure differential valve and a metering valve.

Pressure Diferential Valve (portion)—This contains a small valve that will slide and close the front or rear portion of the system if pressure is lost to the other half of the

brake system. These valves are supposed to be self centering after repairs have been made. This is where the "Brake Failure" light switch is located.

Note: If you think you are not getting proper flow to the rear or front half of your system, you can verify this by checking the "brake failure" switch with a meter. Ford will not have continuity if the valve is centered. Chevrolet is the opposite and will have continuity if the valve is centered.

Metering Valve—This valve is used in the front disc of a disc/drum brake system. It provides a "hold off"

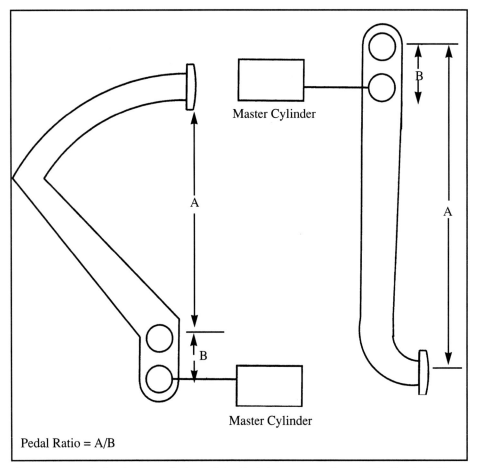

Pedal Ratio = A/B

If you have any doubt about your brake pedal ratio, it is easy enough to check. Simply divide the distance from the pivot to the center of the pedal (A) by the distance from the pedal pivot to the point where the master cylinder connects to the pedal (B). The ratio should be 5 or 6:1. You can alter this ratio slightly to accommodate different size master and wheel cylinder sizes. At left is a floor mounted pedal vs. one mounted from the firewall.

Proportioning valves are mandatory to prevent the pressure from building too quickly to the rear wheel brakes when the brakes are applied and prevent the rear wheels from locking. Residual pressure valves (the smaller valves) maintain a minimal amount of pressure at the wheel cylinders and prevent fluid from siphoning from the calipers and wheel cylinders back to the master cylinder. Notice the different AN and SAE style fittings, both can be used with mild steel and stainless steel brake tubing.

function to allow the rear drum brakes to actuate first. This function is very important in making the system function in the correct sequence in a rear wheel drive car. The rear brakes are always actuated first. This function is built into most factory type disc/drum combination valves. Make sure you have a metering valve in the system either as a stand alone valve or as part of a factory control valve assembly.

Brake Pedal Ratio—If you divide the distance from the pedal pivot to the point where the master cylinder connects to the pedal by the distance from the pivot to the center of the pedal, you will know your pedal ratio. This ratio should be between 5 or 6 to 1. The longer the pedal is from the pivot to the foot pad, more force can

be generated with the same effort. The disadvantage is that the pedal will need to travel a greater distance to generate the pressure.

Proportioning Valves—These are placed between the front and the rear brake system (disk or drum) and provide for control of the rate of pressure build-up, not the amount, to the rear brakes. The rear brakes will still see full master cylinder pressure. The reason you would control the rate of pressure rise is to compensate for the reduction of weight on the rear wheels due to forward weight transfer during braking. Not all cars will need one of these valves. It depends on your application. (All the more reason for buying an engineered brake system for your car rather than buying the pieces based on price.)

Adjustable Proportioning Valves—
These allow for fine tuning of the rate of pressure rise to the rear brakes if you have a lock-up problem. If you have a lock-up problem, experiment with the setting of the valve to eliminate lock up for all but all out panic stops.

Residual Pressure Valves—These may be used in both disc/disc systems and disc/drum systems.

2 psi Valve—This valve is used in disc brake systems only and is required when the master cylinder is at or below the height of the calipers. Its purpose is to act as an anti-siphon valve preventing the brake fluid from siphoning back into the master cylinder when the brake pedal is released. Even if the master cylinder is at the same height or slightly above the caliper, put one in anyway. If you don't and you park on a hill, fluid will siphon! This valve is cheap insurance.

Note: You will know if you need one of these if you need to pump the brake pedal a couple of times before you get a good (hard) pedal.

10 psi Valve—This valve is used in a drum brake system to prevent air from being ingested into the hydraulic

These vapor traps are small and inexpensive. They are installed anywhere in the vacuum line between the intake manifold and the brake booster. Vapor traps prevent fuel vapors that may be present because of a "lumpy" camshaft from entering the brake booster.

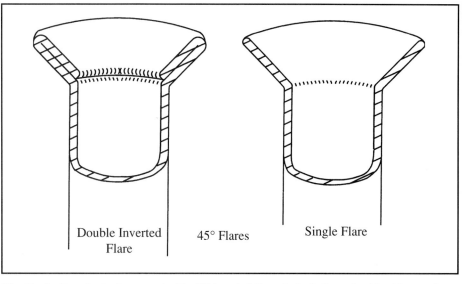

Double Inverted Flare | 45° Flares | Single Flare

Steel brake lines typically use a double 45° inverted flare. A single flare should not be used on your brake lines. It may not seal at all and is certainly not strong enough to resist fatigue fracturing and could fracture over a period of time.

system when you release the brake pedal. Typical wheel cylinder seals only seal when there is pressure behind them. Rapid release of the brake pedal creates a vacuum in the system that can cause the seals to relax and pull air into the wheel cylinders. Maintaining 10 psi in the system at all times prevents this. Some disc/drum master cylinders have a 10 psi residual pressure valve installed internally, some don't. If you're not sure, call an expert, they can tell you how to check. Also, some new style wheel cylinders have cup expanders which negate the need for a residual pressure valve. Either way, if you are not sure whether you have one or not, put one in. The effect is not cumulative and will not hurt if you have two. Don't worry about brake drag. It takes roughly 75 psi to overcome the return springs.

Vapor Trap—This little device is used on cars with power brakes (vacuum assisted) and prevents gas vapor from collecting in your brake booster (can). If your camshaft has very much overlap and pumps fuel mist back through the carburetor, or your booster can is lower than the intake manifold, you should install one of these.

Brake Lines

Your choice of brake lines is critical. Give some careful thought to the type of lines you are going to install. This is one area where quality is worth the extra expense. As mentioned before, never reuse old brake lines from a donor car.

Mild Steel—Mild steel is the material that brake lines have been made from for decades. It can be purchased in bulk rolls, usually about 25-ft long, or in shorter pre-made lengths. Using the proper tools, it is easy to form and flare. Mild steel offers the ability to be repaired easily, even on the road. Mild steel could even be coated with powder coat, paint or my favorite, cold zinc galvanizing, which is available in a spray can.

Stainless Steel—Stainless steel is a little more difficult to work with and will cost you 50%—60% more than mild steel tubing. The stainless alloy is harder and a little more difficult to work with. While this material will give you an excellent finish for a show car, it is not necessary for a street car. Because the stainless alloy is harder, an inexpensive flaring tool will not do the job. It is virtually impossible to double flare without a

proper machine. It can be double-flared, but you must find a shop with a machine to do this and someone with who knows how to operate the machine.

Typically, stainless steel tubing will be used with "AN" fittings. These use a ferrule and a nut with single 37° flare. An "AN" style adapter fitting must then be screwed into the standard fitting hole and then the tubing and the AN fitting is screwed into the adapter.

The standard fittings for mild steel tubing have a flare angle of 45° and will not allow the direct connection of 37° stainless steel tubing. Stainless steel tubing can be double flared with a 45° flare, but as I indicated, it does require a special machine. So, you can use stainless tubing and regular SAE style 45° fittings if you like.

Stainless steel tubing is usually sold in straight lengths and not in coils. This shouldn't pose a problem, unless you were plumbing something really long.

Flares Types—Make sure you know what type of flare your brake lines need, i.e., 45° inverted or double flare for mild steel tubing, a "Bubble

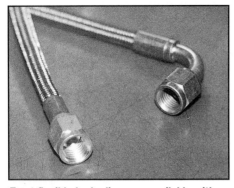

Front flexible brake lines are available with stainless braided covers and AN style fittings that are DOT approved.

This roadster uses a DOT-approved braided flexible brake line. Note how the brake line has been formed close to the axle.

Flare" as used on metric systems with mild steel tubing or 37° single for stainless steel tubing.

Warning: Single flares are not as strong as double flares and are subject to fatigue cracking, which could lead to fluid leaking at a minimum. Do not allow anyone to talk you into using single flares on your brake tubing.

Tubing Requirements—You will need about 25' of tubing (this is a standard length per box) and 2 fittings per line (the average total is 14) plus 3 flexible brake lines (2 for the front and 1 for the rear) in order to plumb your average 102" wheelbase chassis. Don't try to form or flare the tubing without proper tools. If you kink the tubing, don't use it, throw it away. The kink will restrict the flow of fluid and pressure, which will disturb the braking balance. Buy, rent or borrow a tubing flaring set, tubing bender and tubing cutter (some parts stores will rent this equipment). Don't cut the brake tubing with a saw. Use a tubing cutter. The chips from a saw could lodge inside the tubing and travel to and cut a seal in a wheel cylinder or caliper.

Flaring tools and benders generally come with instructions but tubing cutters may not. When cutting, be sure to tighten the tubing cutter on the tubing only until it starts to indent or cut the tubing. Don't overtighten the cutter. Spin the tubing cutter around

the tubing, periodically lubricating the pin that the cutting wheel rotates on. When the cutter becomes easy to spin, tighten a little more and repeat these steps until the tubing is severed. Before you attempt to flare the end, remove any burrs on the inside as well as the outside of the tube. Blow the line out with compressed air to ensure that no metal chips remain in the tubing.

Rubber vs. Braided Stainless Steel—What are you going to do with the car, drive it or show it? If you are going to drive it, remember that rubber lines have served the industry well for decades (don't forget that your daily driver has rubber lines). But if you are going to show the car or compete it, braided steel lines may be better for you. Don't forget that those braided lines may require the extra AN fittings to mate them to regular 18-27 inverted flare threads of the regular parts.

INSTALLATION TIPS

At this point the chassis should be a roller with all of its suspension and possibly the power train installed. With the body off the chassis, it is a

relatively simple matter to form the tubing within the contours of the chassis. But even if the body is on, follow a few simple guidelines.

Installing Brake Lines

Route the tubing away from where the exhaust system will run or where the tubing could be crushed by a jack or a suspension member and don't forget to consider the possibility of having to repair or replace the tubing. On the inside of the chassis rail is usually a good place. An intricate shape could cause you to waste some tubing before you get what you need so you may find it easier to visualize the shape if you use a coat hanger or other soft aluminum wire and bend it to shape first.

If you haven't installed the master cylinder, control valve assembly or proportioning valve, start forming the tubing at the rear axle and front suspension and work towards where the control valve assembly or proportioning valve will be. Be sure to install the brake lines that lead to the front and rear into the correct ports of the control valve assembly and the master cylinder. The front and rear are different. In the control valve

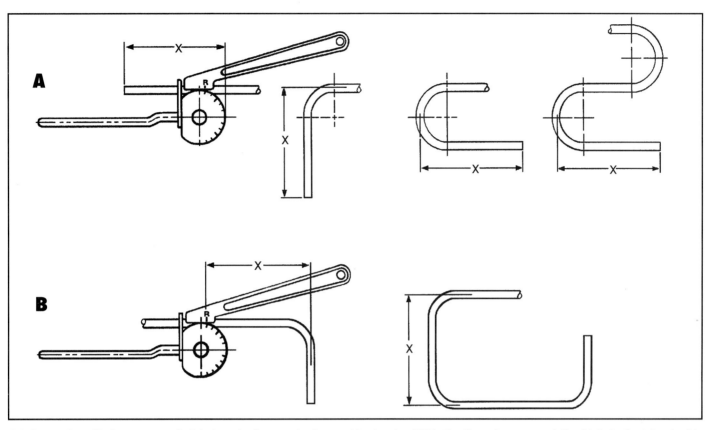

This illustration will give you some insight into the fine art of using a tubing bender. "X" is the dimension you need. To obtain it, the tube should be placed in the bender as illustrated in Figure A or B. A pencil or ink mark on the tubing will help your accuracy.

When you install your steel brake lines, don't forget to secure them to the chassis. In this case the manufacturer has welded a sheet metal tab to the chassis for this purpose. A piece of rubber tubing is placed over the line to isolate it from the chassis while still allowing it to move around as necessary.

assembly, there are 2 ports for the front and 1 for the rear. Usually the pressurization rate is restricted to the rear brakes to minimize rear wheel lock up and creating a potentially dangerous situation. By the way, this is also an excellent time to run the fuel (supply and return) lines.

Bending Brake and Fuel Lines— Bending your brake lines is actually a simple matter if you are willing to take your time.

• First, measure carefully and deal with each section separately. If you try to measure the entire length and all the bends, you will not be happy with the results.
• Always bend the tubing in the same direction. Start at one end and work toward the other end, measuring and bending as you go. If you work in from both ends toward the center you will end up with extra tubing somewhere in the middle.
• As you bend tubing and it is drawn around the bender, it will stretch. The tighter the bend the more stretch.
• Expect tubing to spring back about 3 degrees for a 90-degree bend, so expect to overbend it a little.

• To help make sure your bends go in the correct direction, draw a line with a pencil on the outside of the tubing where the bend should be. When you hold the tubing in the bender make sure that the line is opposite to the bend.
• Clamp the tubing in the bender securely to prevent the tubing from creeping as it is bent.
• A piece of soft wire (about 1/8" dia) can be used as a template or guide before bending any brake line.
• Be sure to clamp your brake and fuel lines to the chassis. Make sure the tubing is supported at all times. Clamp close to the bends and about 18" to 24" apart. If the tubing shakes and vibrates, it could cause the fittings to loosen and leak or fracture the tubing.

Caution: On Ford master cylinders, the front reservoir feeds the rear brakes and the rear reservoir feeds the front brakes. Chevrolet is the opposite: the forward reservoir feeds the front and the rear feeds the rear.

Flexible Brake Line Brackets— The manufacturer should have mounted the brackets for the flexible lines on the chassis and they should be located properly. However, do spend a moment and check this. Mount the hoses, and move the suspension through its entire range. Watch the hoses as the suspension travels to its extremes. Ensure that they are not stressed. If a hose is pulled tight, relocate the brackets as necessary to prevent this from happening. If you have any reservations, now is the time to change the location of these brackets before you cut and bend the steel lines.

Bleeding

When it comes time to bleed the system, start by disconnecting the tubes from the master cylinder to the control valve assembly. Install "bleeding tubes" in the master cylinder so you can purge it of air. Your bleeding tubes are easily fabricated from scrap tubing and fittings. Flare one end while the other end is bent in a loop so that it empties back into the master cylinder reservoir. Locate the ends as close to the bottom of the reservoir as possible, so that when you fill the reservoir with fluid, the ends will be submerged. This will prevent air from being sucked back into the lines. Pump the master cylinder until all the air is purged. Remove the bleeding lines and reconnect the master cylinder to the control valve assembly. You can remove most of any remaining air using a vacuum pump and jar at each wheel. Be careful that you don't apply too much vacuum. You could pull air by the cups in the wheel cylinders or around the bleeder itself.

TROUBLESHOOTING

Symptom: Losing your pedal (i.e., it goes to the floor, not misplaced), could be caused by:
• Fluid boiling due to wet fluid or foot drag.
• Undersize brake system.
• Wrong-size residual pressure valve.
• Incorrect or faulty master cylinder.
• Leak in caliper of hydraulic lines.
• Inadequate cooling ducting.
• Pedal linkage failure.
• Excessive spindle deflection in corners.

Solution:
• Flush out entire system with fresh Wilwood Hi-Temp 570 racing brake fluid. Install a dashboard brake temperature light.
• Refer to the caliper portion of the catalog to select the correct caliper for your application.
• Use no larger than 2 lb. residual pressure valve.
• Repair or replace master cylinder.
• Check for leaks in caliper and lines.
• Reposition air ducts to center of the rotor and caliper.
• Check pedal assembly
• Check spindles for warpage.

Symptom: Your brakes drag, which could be caused by:
• Bad master cylinder.
• Incorrect residual pressure valve.
• Rotors warped.
• Calipers not square to rotor.
• Line lock shut off during braking.
• Tapered brake pads.
• M/C has internal residual pressure.
• Flexible lines have deteriorated and rubber is blocking a line.

Solutions:
• Switch or replace master cylinder
• Use no larger than 2 residual pressure valve
• Replace rotors
• Re-align brackets or shim calipers
• Open line lock and shut off during non-braking
• Replace pads, check caliper alignment to rotor
• Remove residual pressure valve

Symptom: Your car will not stop (well), caused by:
• Glazed pads and / or rotors.
• Pads too soft. Replace with harder pads or grind and/or sand glaze on rotors.

(continued next page)

Symptom: You have to push too hard on pedal:

Symptom: You have to push too hard on pedal:
• Too large a master cylinder diameter.
• Not enough pedal ratio.
• Pedal mounted at bad angle.
• Wrong pad material for your applications.
• Wrong brakes for your application.
• Frozen pistons in calipers.

Note:
• Master cylinder push rod should not be off more than 5° in any angle.
• If the rotor is not glowing orange, do not use hard pads. If glowing orange, do not use soft pads.

Symptom: Caliper Leaks
• Caliper seal old or dried out
• Nick or ding on piston or cut seal

Symptom: Spongy pedal or bottoms out:
• Air in brake system
• Calipers not bled with bleed screws straight up
• Wrong size master cylinder (too small)
• Faulty master cylinder
• Calipers not mounted square to the rotor
• Calipers mounted equal to or higher than master cylinder
• Calipers flex excessively
• Pedal ratio too great.
• Excessive spindle deflection in corners causing piston knock-back

Symptom: Oscillation feedback in pedal
• Excessive rotor run out
• Pad material buildup on rotors
• Calipers loose
• Rotor faces not parallel
• Cracked rotors
• Excessive front bearing clearance

Notice how the brake tubing is secured and formed with smooth bends to the shape of the chassis. This allows the chassis to provide protection from jacks and jackstands, etc. You should also notice the radiator hose is clamped to a crossmember to prevent it from moving around and becoming damaged.

Documentation

Remember to record all of the brake components that go into your car. If you are using custom brake parts, record the bore diameters of your components. I've provided space for that information in the Owner's Manual (on page 164) just so it won't get lost.

SUMMARY

Caliper or Wheel Cylinders Pedal Feel
Larger piston bore = softer, longer travel
More pistons (multi-piston caliper) = softer, longer travel
Fewer pistons (smaller bore) = harder, less travel

Master Cylinder Pedal Feel
Increase bore diameter = harder, with less travel
Decrease bore diameter = softer, with more travel

ABS SYSTEMS

Transplanting an ABS system from a late-model donor car is something that is difficult if not impossible at

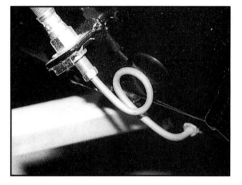

This loop is called a "service loop" and should be formed at each end of the tubing just in case you need to renew the flare. This would prevent you from having to replace the entire length of tubing or splicing in a short section.

this time because each system is tailored to each application. Vehicle weight, tire size, etc., are just a few of the "many" variables that are factored into the final design. Change any one of those and the system will not function correctly. Depending on a transplanted ABS system could cost you your life. Currently, there are two types of systems, mechanical and electronic.

Mechanical

Mechanical ABS systems have been around for decades and have been refined from a crude large coffee can-sized object to the current version, which is approximately the size of a

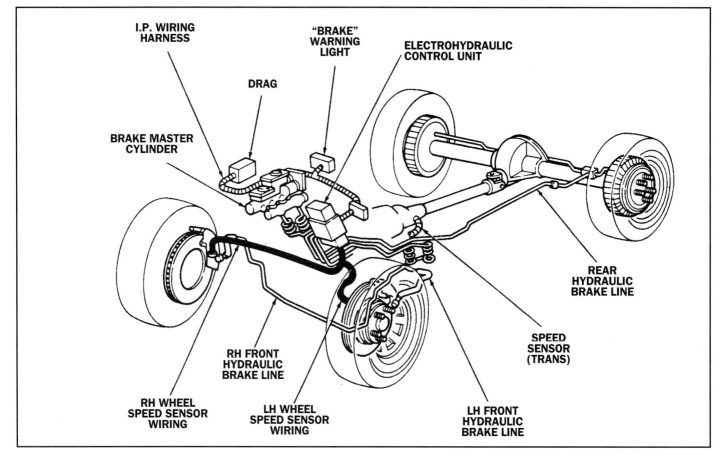

At this time, there is no simple method to transplant an electronic ABS system into your project car. One look at the schematic of a typical 4-wheel ABS system and you'll see why.

baby food jar. The systems operate by adding a high pressure gas chamber to the hydraulic system. The chamber is generally sealed with a diaphragm to separate the gas from the hydraulic fluid. The pressure of the gas chamber, in some cases, is adjusted by applying pressure on the diaphragm with a bolt or screw. During the normal braking operation, as the brake pedal is depressed, the caliper or wheel cylinder pistons extend and the friction material contacts the braking surface. At that point if the pedal is pressed harder, the pistons can't move any further and the pressure in the system and dome increases. The greater the force applied to the pedal, the greater the hydraulic pressure within the system and the greater the pressure on the friction surfaces and the gas dome. As the pedal is pushed harder, the hydraulic pressure will increase until

it matches the gas pressure in the dome. The gas, because it is compressible, will continue to compress preventing the pressure on the friction surfaces from becoming great enough to lock the wheels. The amount of pressure required to lock the brakes is dependent on a number of things like the weight of the vehicle, swept area, diameter and width of the tires, and brake bias. As long as the pressure is below that of the dome the brakes will operate normally, even to the point of locking the wheels under the right situations.

The principal by which this type of system works is due to the compressibility of the gas in the pressure dome. Pressure spikes generated from hitting the brake pedal too hard and run out from the rotors or drums are absorbed by the gas compressing in the dome, minimizing the possibility of locking the wheels.

The effectiveness of these types of systems is dependent on vehicle weight, tire size, traction and speed. As you can imagine the faster a car is going or the heavier its weight the more force is required to lock the wheels. If the car is light or moving at a low rate of speed, it will require less pressure to lock the brakes. Your vehicle will fall somewhere in between.

Electronic ABS

At the time of this writing, there is no simple way to transplant an electronic ABS system into your car from another due to the fact that those are engineered systems. Every facet of that car is considered just as we talked about when it comes to designing your brake system parts. Vehicle weight, tire size, etc., are all considered when designing an electronic ABS. ■

ENGINE TIPS

5

Choosing an engine and transmission is dependent on a variety of factors. Your budget, personal preference, intended use, and type of car are all factors that need to be considered. Of course, some kits are designed to work only with a specific engine and drivetrain, so there is no choice. But when you have a choice, how you intend to use the car will greatly influence your decision, much the same way when it comes to suspension and chassis. Do you want a car that your family can use daily, to the store and on trips, with great fuel economy? Or do you want a sporty race car for spirited Sunday drives? My guess is that like the majority of car owner/builders you will select the "somewhere in between" area. So if and when I give examples they will be relative to a small-block V8 (300–350 cid) that will be driven on the street most of its life.

ENGINE SELECTION

What engine is right for you? Chevy, Ford, Dodge, or Jaguar? Should you get a four cylinder, V6, V8, or even a V10 or V12? Should you invest large sums of money into a

This is a carbureted small-block Chevy 350. Its distributor is located at the rear of the engine and can sometimes interfere with the firewall. As the world's most mass produced engine, there are plenty available in scrapyards, and plenty of inexpensive aftermarket parts. They are also powerful, and easy to work on. If you have a choice, give the small-block a close look.

super modified crate motor, build something in your garage or just buy a stock motor?

V8 Considerations—V8 engines offer more horsepower and torque at a lower engine rpm than a V6, but they do require more room, more fuel, more of everything. If you're not

concerned too much about economy, and want neck-snapping performance, a stock-block V8, either Ford, Chevy or Chrysler, is the way to go. In addition, these engines are very easy to find used (more than 100 million small-block Chevy engines have been built since 1955), relatively easy to

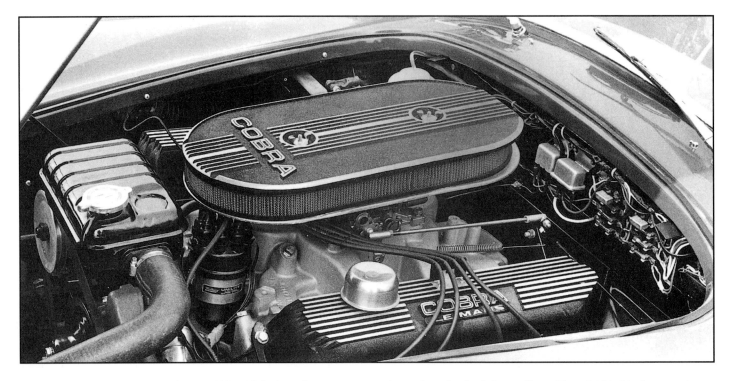

This carbureted big-block Ford 427 and 460 cubic-inch engines are very popular engines for the Cobra replicas. Chevrolet big blocks seem to find their way into most hot rods. Both are good engines but again, the Ford parts may be harder to come by and therefore a bit more expensive.

work on, and parts, both stock and aftermarket, are readily available. The selection of parts for the small-block V8 Chevrolet is near infinite, with Ford trailing somewhat and Chrysler a distant third.

V6 Considerations—But that doesn't mean you can't get satisfactory performance and better fuel economy from a V6, either, especially some of the later model (about '88 and up) Chevy and Ford engines. The '90 Chevy V6 is an excellent engine. There are also many turbocharged V6 engines available in scrapyards as well. V6 engines can be tuned and modified for high output horsepower and torque, although often at a higher rpm than a V8.

Four-Bangers—A dual overhead cam four cylinder, or an engine like GM's Quad Four, is a good choice for a small engine. However, give careful consideration to the horsepower output of your engine vs. vehicle weight. You wouldn't want to go to all of the effort of building something like a Cobra replica, only to have it

get beat at the stop light by a Hyundai.

New vs. Used

You can select an older engine more like the engine that came in the original car, or a contemporary engine with computers, catalytic converters and fuel injection. Older engines can be built with camshafts and carburetors like old engines; these are much easier to keep in tune for the novice and can be worked on with a minimum of tools and test equipment, unlike the contemporary engine that requires sophisticated electronic equipment.

EPA Laws—These laws vary from state to state, and could greatly affect your decision to install a pre-emissions engine in a late-model car. In some states, the motor must meet the emission standards for the year that the original host car was first assembled in, but in others, the engine must be brought up to current code. If this is the case, you may be forced to use a contemporary motor and all the

emissions equipment that goes along with it.

Older engines can be purchased from a variety of sources, from your local auto sales flyer to nationally produced vintage journals. A number of aftermarket engine builders manufacture engine blocks from the same specifications as the originals. In some states this qualifies that engine as being of that vintage regardless of when it is manufactured. For example the aluminum Ford 427 from the Ohio area is built to original late '60s specs, so it is considered a late '60s 427. Factory rebuilt engines (if they use an original block) would be an original engine. When you order an engine, make sure that you know what you want and get what you ordered. Check the casting (identification) numbers carefully.

Newer Engines

As you know, each year new and more wonderful engines are designed and produced. Engines are becoming more powerful and more efficient.

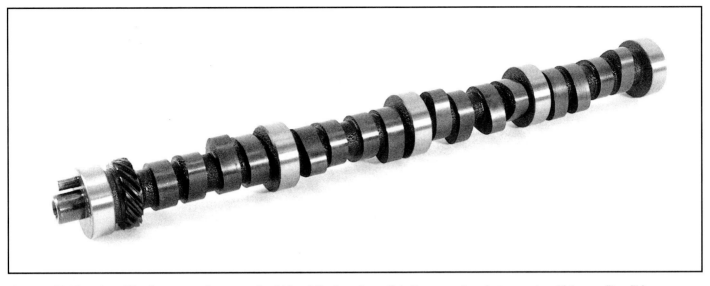

If you're thinking of modifications, swapping cams should be at the top of your list. However, changing a cam to a higher profile will increase power within the limitations of your engine. The more radical the cam, the more modified components (heads, exhaust, fuel) it will need. The cam manufacturer is the best source for choosing the right cam. Be prepared to give them all details of your engine and car.

The good news is you can select anything that will fit into the chassis and engine compartment. The manufacturer of your kit will know what the chassis and engine compartment were designed around but you don't have to stay with a Ford or Chevy, for example. If you want to use a late-model engine, I suggest the best way to secure all the necessary parts would be to buy a complete wreck. This can be done with any "Auto Recycler," maybe even the one that supplied your donor car.

Be sure that you strip all components, such as the wiring harness, computer modules, fuel tank (most contain the fuel pump, for example) and all associated hardware. It is easier to store these parts than to go looking for them after the donor car is gone.

ENGINE MODIFICATIONS

Generally, the more modifications you make to an engine, the more expensive it becomes to build, maintain, operate and insure. If your engine is supposed to comply with emissions standards, then some modifications may prohibit the engine from meeting them. So choose your modifications and parts carefully. You must involve all the different manufacturers of the different parts. For example, your cam choice should be made knowing what type of intake and exhaust manifold will be used, and what type of transmission and rear end gears will be used. You must also know what size tires will be used, how much the car weighs and how you will drive it. So do it on paper first, talk to the different manufacturers and ask lots of questions.

There are many different ways to increase the torque and horsepower output of your engine, and there are scores of books written on this subject. While it is beyond the scope of this book to go into details, some general tips apply.

Camshafts

Changing a camshaft to one with a "higher profile" may increase power, but only within the limitations of the rest of your engine. In other words, don't install a cam that must also have modified cylinder heads, more fuel and air, etc., to work effectively. "Too much cam" can make the car unpleasant to drive around town because the powerband will be too high in the rpm band. The engine may not have enough manifold vacuum to keep the engine running at a reasonable rpm, and it may have trouble maintaining idle speed. To determine your cam needs, there is no greater source than the camshaft manufacturer. Popular aftermarket camshaft manufacturers include Crane Cams, Competition Cams, Iskendarian and Edelbrock. These can be found in any number of high performance car magazines. Also, high performance cams are often available from the OEMs as well. Ford SVO, and The Chevy Race Shop, are factory high performance divisions with custom-tailored cam profiles. Check with the local dealer of your engine.

Before you contact the cam manufacturers, describe your engine on paper. The tech people will need to know engine displacement and number of cylinders; bore, stroke and compression ratio; rocker arm ratio; carburetor size or fuel injection type; ignition, heads, and the type of intake and exhaust manifolds. They will need to know your emissions

Adding roller rockers is a simple, cost effective method to add a few horsepower.

requirements, whether or not an engine computer will be used, and how the engine will be run most of the time. How will the engine be used? Will it be a manual or automatic transmission (stock or have a shift kit); 4, 5 or 6-speed, have an overdrive top gear or really short first gear? And don't forget to describe the rear end gears and rear tire diameter. You need to consider what rpm the engine will be seeing at 60 mph, your average cruise speed. The more information you can provide, the better suggestion they can make for a cam to fit your needs.

Whatever you do, do not let the kid down at your local auto parts store sell you a cam. The selection is often beyond the knowledge of the average parts counterperson, and they are not generally familiar with the details of every cam manufacturer. Of course, if you're just buying a replacement stock camshaft, the auto parts store is okay.

A factory camshaft, like most of the other parts, are a compromise in their design. They were designed to meet the expectations of a wide number of owners. You can select a cam that will be an improvement over the factory stock cam in a number of areas and

not have any bad points such as lumpy idle or poor fuel economy.

When you talk about camshafts, terms like duration, overlap and lift are used to define the specifications of a cam.

Duration—Measured in crankshaft degrees, duration refers to how long the valves are open. A cam with less duration (around 200 degrees) will yield greater fuel mileage and low end torque and the powerband will be in the lower rpm range. The powerband can be thought of as a point (from 1500 to 4500 rpm for example) where the engine produces optimum torque and horsepower. Torque and horsepower do not happen simultaneously. Torque is produced at the lower rpm ranges and horsepower is produced in the higher rpm range. This means the torque powerband (where the engine makes most of its usable torque) will be in the lower rpm range and therefore will be more usable on the street with an automatic transmission because the motor will pull smoother at a lower rpm than an engine with a higher torque band. The more duration the cam has, the higher the powerband moves up—about 500 rpm for every 10 degrees.

Overlap—This is the situation that occurs when the intake and exhaust valves are both open at the same time. The more overlap the cam has the more power it will produce in the higher rpm band. Less overlap will provide less scavenging at low rpm (as the engine would see on the street).

Lift—This number is how far the valves are opened, or lifted off their seat. The greater the lift the more air/fuel mixture can be drawn into the cylinder. The size and shape of the ports in the heads ultimately determine how much air and fuel can be drawn into the cylinders, so be careful that the amount of lift (lobe lift x the rocker arm ratio = valve lift) is not more than the heads or the exhaust headers can flow. If you install a camshaft with a lot of lift, or add high lift rocker arms, you must check the clearance between the valves and the pistons to ensure that they will not collide.

In general, you should consider a cam that produces a "flat" torque curve, for the street. This is what will make the car easier to drive. The motor will be more tolerant of being driven at a low rpm in high gear. A cam that produces a curve that is narrow will not respond well at the lower rpm band and will be difficult to drive in frequent stop and go situations. You will need to keep the engine turning at a higher rpm just to keep it running and it won't like being lugged.

Roller Rockers

If you are interested is picking up a little "free" (relatively inexpensive) horsepower, roller rockers are an area that may interest you. There is an awful lot of friction at the tip of the rocker arms as the valves are depressed. If your cam has more lift and duration than the stock cam, the

In addition to the size of the grille opening, the amount of air that will flow through a radiator depends on things like the shrouding inside the grille opening and the amount of turbulence. Anything that can be done to seal the radiator to the grille opening, and therefore reduce the turbulence, will go a long way to improving the heat removal capability of the engine's cooling system.

Notice how far the fan is from the radiator. Without any shrouding, this engine is likely to overheat if forced to stand still on a hot summer day. Also notice the alternator mounting; it is tilted forward, which could cause the v belt to wear out prematurely or jump off. All pulleys should be aligned with each other.

geometry may be off, so the engine is a good candidate for roller rockers. Roller rockers come in all sorts of styles. Basically, the difference in roller rocker arms is that some only have a roller tip and some also have a roller pivot. At a minimum, roller tip rockers should be considered to reduce the friction and side loading applied to the valve stem tip.

Regardless of which style you choose, as you are assembling your engine, inspect the rocker arms to ensure that the rocker arms do not bind on the mounting studs.

COOLING CONSIDERATIONS

Radiator

What is the basic rule of thumb for sizing a radiator? There is none, at least that is what the experts tell me. Walker Radiator tells me that the best

thing to do is buy a radiator that was intended for an engine of the same size you are using.

Fan—An electric fan should be mounted so it pulls air through the radiator. It must be shrouded so that the air will not leak around the edges. Electric fans mounted in front of the radiator will block the air flow, reducing the amount of heat removed by the air passing through the radiator core.

Shrouding—Airflow through the radiator will be greatly improved if there is a pressure differential in front of and behind it. Simply stated, if you have a negative pressure behind the radiator you will have better airflow than if the air inside the engine compartment can't get out easily. Forming a shroud between the grille opening and the radiator will help create a positive pressure. It will direct as much air as possible through

the radiator as smoothly as possible.

Consider for a moment that the front of the radiator is the "high pressure" side, and the engine side is the lower pressure side. The air must move through the core. While the car is at rest, the fan moves air through; at speed, it is the movement of the car through air.

Think of the shrouding as a funnel. Starting at the grille opening, any shrouding inside the nose should be smooth and direct the incoming air into the radiator. If this area is not smooth, turbulence can stall or inhibit the smooth flow of air. The radiator must also be sealed to the body or inner fenders to force the air through the radiator and not allow it to leak over, under or around. If your fan is mounted between the engine and the radiator, you also need shrouding

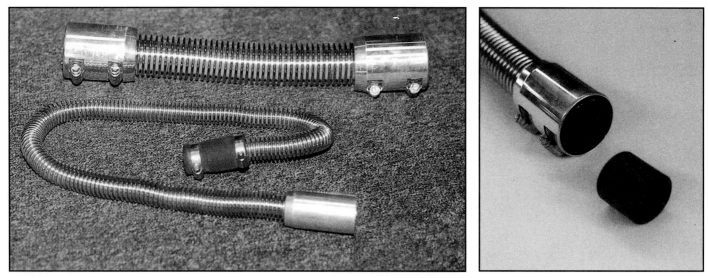

Radiator and heater hoses don't need to be ugly or plain. Inglese manufactures this ribbed flexible tubing called cool flex. This tubing can be cut and formed to fit just about every application. Because this tubing is ribbed copper it will also act like a radiator. As the air in the engine compartment flows over the ribs some heat will be transferred from the hot coolant. The cool-flex tubing has adapter sleeves (1 3/4 and 1 1/2 inch) so it will fit almost any application. It is also available in 3/4 and 5/8 for heater hoses.

between the radiator and the fan to prevent air from being drawn around the outside of the fan blades instead of through the radiator. This is mandatory in order for air to be drawn through while the car is sitting still.

If you have the grille opening sealed to the front of the radiator, and the radiator is sealed to the body, you will have a positive pressure in front and a negative pressure behind the radiator. Hood scoops that are open to the engine compartment will reduce the negative pressure in the compartment, resulting in a reduced pressure differential and lower airflow through the radiator. The upside to having a hood scoop that is open to the engine compartment is that it will deliver cool air to the engine compartment. This cool air will also be turbulent and any cooling effect may be offset by the reduced heat transfer from the radiator.

Water Pump—If you have a problem with your engine overheating or boiling over, or if after you shut your motor off you hear a bubbling or percolating sound, you could have air trapped in your engine. Anything you can do to increase the volume of water pumped through your cooling

system should flush or blow out the trapped air. Some manufacturers, such as Flow Kooler, offer water pumps that will pump more coolant at a higher pressure. Sometimes an open impeller will cavitate at higher rpm and not pump as much water as it could if it were closed. Pumps that cavitate can cause your motor to have "hot and cold spots" that can lead to excessive wear. Flow Kooler sells kits to close your open impeller which can

reduce or eliminate the cavitation. Do not remove any fins from the impeller in an attempt to enhance the heat transfer from the motor to the coolant. Move the coolant through the motor and let the thermostat control the flow.

Thermostat—Some people recommend that you remove the thermostat so your engine will run cooler, but I'm not one of them. Although the engine will run cooler

Any of these openings in the front of this Cobra body are in the high pressure area and are preferred locations for any fresh air need. The lower opening feeds cool air to the oil cooler, the two small openings next to the grille can feed air to the brakes or the passenger compartment and the large opening feeds the radiator. Passenger compartment fresh air can also be taken from inside the grille opening.

You may choose to use tubing to connect your engine and radiator. Metal tubing will outlast rubber and can be painted, powder coated or plated.

Note the radiator shrouding on this race car. The shroud makes a smooth transition from the opening under the bumper to the radiator. All bends are smooth and gradual.

Depending on your car and the amount of space you have in the engine compartment, you may be able to draw air for your carburetor from under the bumper. If this is appealing to you, place the scoop opening forward in the high pressure area.

when the air temperature is cool, you will never get any heat into the engine and your heater. The purpose of a thermostat is to bring the engine up to temperature quickly and operate within a narrow temperature band. Different parts of your engine, depending on the material and its mass, will expand and contract at different rates. If the temperature is allowed to swing wildly, those materials will expand and contract, causing abnormal wear. The thermostat will remain closed so the coolant will not circulate through the radiator but stay within the engine until the engine heats up. The thermostat will open at a specific

temperature and once open will modulate (open and close) as the temperature varies from hot to cold, allowing the coolant to be routed through the radiator and cooled. If you have an overheating problem, and other steps have not cured the problem, selecting a larger diameter thermostat can have a dramatic effect. Robert Shaw Co. offers thermostats that will flow a substantial amount of water.

Troubleshooting—If you find the engine overheats at idle or in traffic, examine the shrouding between the fan and the radiator. It must be sealed so air will not leak around the edges. If this is okay, examine the fan, its cubic feet of air capacity (CFM rating or engine size), the radiator's capacity to remove heat, the thermostat diameter and operating temperature range, and water pump. High volume pumps and larger diameter thermostats are available. If the engine overheats on the highway examine the air inlet and any shrouding between the radiator and the body. If these are okay examine the area under the nose; a chin deflector or scoop can help here to scoop up extra air from the road.

CARBURETORS

Depending on the engine you select, you will have a choice between carburetion or fuel injection. There are various types with pros and cons to each. Obviously, if you are using a Mustang 5.0-liter V8, you won't want to swap Chevy's TPI system. Superchargers and turbochargers have special requirements and would require additional research beyond the scope of this book. For now, we'll focus on some basics about carburetion and fuel injection to give you a better understanding of how these systems operate.

Although the trend is to go with fuel injection, there are times when you can't beat the simplicity and value of a carburetor. Simply put, carburetors rely on air moving through venturis to create a vacuum, which in turn pulls the gas from the fuel bowls into the airstream. As a result, they can be finicky on modified engines that don't produce very much vacuum at idle. The more the engine is modified, the more tuning a carburetor needs in order to work correctly. The advantage is that they often work out of the box for stock or mildly modified engines, they are

Carburetors come in all sorts of sizes and configurations, from single 2 or 4 barrel models to multi-carburetor assemblies. This small-block Chevy engine is fed by four Maserati two-barrel units.

inexpensive and have a high comfort factor for the enthusiast that is not comfortable with electronics or fuel injection. The downside is that they often can not be retrofitted to later model engines that are fuel injected. If you are installing a carbureted engine of vintage years, then consider the high performance replacements below.

Selection

The major brands of performance carburetors are Holley, Rochester, Edelbrock and Weber. There is much to be said about each brand, but going into details are a bit beyond the scope of this book. Detailed information on the merits of the various makes and models can be found in HPBooks' *Holley Carburetors, Manifolds &*

Fuel Injection; Rochester Carburetors; Weber Carburetors; Small-Block Chevy Performance; and *Big-Block Chevy Performance.*

But one general piece of advice I can pass on is how to determine the correct carburetor size for your engine. I say pass along, because the following information on carbs, manifolds and GM fuel injection is excerpted from Dave Emanuel's *Small-Block Chevy Performance,* available from HPBooks.

When awareness of carburetor airflow capacity became commonplace, bigger was typically equated with better, and "too much" was just barely enough—even the largest available four-barrel was not capable of over-carbureting a highly modified small block. Two of the biggest early-model Holley 4150's provided a total airflow capacity of only 800 cfm (600 cfm four-barrels were not offered until 1958), and many factory dual four-barrel options utilized even smaller carburetors. It is interesting to note that dual four-barrels first appeared as original equipment on the 265 small block of 1956—just one year after the engine's introduction.

By comparison, the largest standard flange Holley four-barrel currently available flows 850 cfm and the larger square-flange "Dominators" flow up to 1150 cfm. Obviously, with the general availability of such grandiose carburetors, bigger no longer necessarily equals better. In fact, more often than not a smaller four-barrel is preferable to an extremely large one. While a 600 cfm unit with vacuum secondaries may not offer the glamour of an 850 double-pumper, the former will provide better driveability, greater fuel economy and crisper throttle response than the latter. It's also considerably less expensive.

Air Capacity—Choosing a performance carburetor therefore

This small-block Ford is fed by two side-draft Weber carburetors. Weber's carburetion systems are available for small- and big-block Ford and Chevrolet engines.

Holley's 4500 Dominator carbs come in 1050 and 1150 cfm sizes. But make sure that your engine can handle it. When it comes to carbs, bigger doesn't always equate to better. Too much carb and you'll have a poor performing engine. Use the guidelines below to help you estimate the airflow requirements of your engine.

amounts to somewhat more than purchasing the largest model your budget allows. The first step is to determine the maximum airflow potentially demanded by the engine that is to receive the carburetor. On the surface, this appears to require no more than converting cubic inches (engine size) to cubic feet, multiplying by maximum rpm (to determine the engine cfm requirement), and selecting a carburetor that offers a corresponding airflow capacity. However, intended usage, engine efficiency, engine operating range and the total number of throttle bores must also be taken into consideration.

The basic mathematical formula for relating engine size and rpm to carburetor airflow capacity is:

Carb. cfm=
Engine cid x Max. rpm/3456

By way of example, consider a 350 cid powerplant with a maximum engine speed of 8000 rpm. By working it through the above equation, the cfm works out to 810 cfm. Therefore, a carburetor with an 800 cfm capacity would appear to be ideal.

Volumetric Efficiency—However, no adjustment has been made for volumetric efficiency (V.E.). Simply stated, volumetric efficiency is how many cubic inches of air and gas are consumed by an engine every two revolutions. Theoretically, a 350 cid engine with a 100% V.E. will consume 350 cubic inches of air and gas every two revolutions. However, except for well-prepared race engines, few small blocks reach 100% V.E. Volumetric efficiency is not constant throughout the rpm range, although it is usually highest at the engine speed where maximum torque is produced. According to Mike Urich, former vice president of engineering at Holley Carburetors and co-author of

HPBooks' *Holley Carburetors, Manifolds & Fuel Injection*:

"An ordinary low-performance engine has a V.E. of about 75% at maximum speed; about 80% at maximum torque. A high-performance engine has a V.E. of about 80% at maximum speed; about 85% at maximum torque. An all-out race engine has a V.E. of about 90% at maximum speed; about 95% at maximum torque. A highly tuned intake and exhaust system with efficient cylinder-head porting and a camshaft ground to take full advantage of the engine's other equipment can provide such complete cylinder filling that a V.E. of 100%— or slightly higher—is obtained at the speed for which the system is tuned."

Urich goes on to recommend that you assume a V.E. of 85% for high performance street engines and a V.E. of 110% for all-out, highly tuned racing engines. As an example, consider the 350 racing engine running at 8000 rpm:

cfm =
(350 cid x 8000 rpm)/3456 x 1.1 V.E.
cfm=891

Theoretically, a carburetor with an 850 cfm capacity would be ideal. The 1.1, by the way, is 110% converted to a decimal. To calculate the street carb cfm, use the above equation only multiply by .85 (85% converted to a decimal) to arrive at a theoretical cfm.

These percentages of volumetric efficiency really mean that instead of consuming 350 cubic inches of air and gas every two revolutions, a 350 engine will use that percentage thereof. In other words, an engine with an 85% V.E. will only use 297 cubic inches of air and gas every two revolutions (350 x .85).

Vacuum controlled secondaries, like the ones on this Holley 600 cfm model, are smoother and more consistent—if tuned properly.

The laws of physics prevent these percentages from changing very dramatically. Intake manifold efficiency, valve and port size, camshaft timing and exhaust manifold configuration are a few of the more readily identifiable factors affecting the volume of intake charge that will reach a cylinder prior to the power stroke. Since the low pressure created by a piston moving downward in a cylinder (during the intake stroke) is not sufficient to draw in 100% of the volume required to completely fill that cylinder (with the piston at the bottom of its travel), the effect of inertia is needed to keep the incoming air/gas mixture flowing after the piston has started moving upward (during the initial stage of the compression stroke). The inertia or "ram" effect increases with rpm, which is one of the reasons that internal combustion engines produce maximum horsepower in the upper rpm ranges.

Vacuum vs. Mechanical Secondaries—The only other basic consideration with four-barrels is how the secondary throttle is activated. Vacuum control offers potentially smoother operation and in theory "sizes" the carburetor to the needs of the engine. If a vacuum actuating mechanism is properly tuned, maximum air velocity through the carburetor will be maintained at all operational levels. This is theoretically possible because secondary throttle opening responds to engine demands. Therefore, a 780 cfm carburetor may never flow more than 650 cfm, if that's all the engine requires.

Mechanical secondaries offer the advantage of allowing the driver to control precisely when the secondary throttles are opened, however, vacuum control is typically advised for street, RV and recreational boat use, while mechanically operated secondaries are found in virtually all competition applications, the notable exception being off-road racing, because the inconsistent terrain doesn't allow the driver to maintain a smooth, constant application of power.

Recommendations

Regardless of horsepower figures produced on a dyno, engineering theory or mathematical formulas, the bottom line is the ability of a carburetor to function in a "real world" environment. In many cases a carburetor is expected to compensate for inadequacies in the intake system. Some people mistakenly believe switching carburetors will correct certain problems (poor low speed response or lack of top end power) that are actually caused by other factors.

For example, the combination of a big-port intake manifold, large-diameter headers and a super-lumpy camshaft will not allow any carburetor to meter fuel with optimum efficiency. Not only will fuel economy be poor, reduced vacuum at idle (created by long cam overlap and weak low-rpm exhaust scavenging) will delay activation of fuel flow through the main nozzles. This makes for poor low-speed throttle response, disappointing torque and possibly an off-idle stumble. Switching to a smaller carburetor is frequently viewed as a means of improving low-speed operation. The reasoning is that velocities will be higher if venturi and throttle bore diameters are reduced. That's true at wide open throttle, but at part throttle, the effect is minimal. About the only advantage offered by a smaller carb is quicker activation of the main metering system. This may reduce the size of the performance "hole" but it will still be there.

Therefore, there is more to carburetor selection than mere size consideration. In spite of all the theories and reasoning behind proper carburetor selection, in the real world things usually boil down more to a matter of price and availability. With Carter and Edelbrock carburetors, only a few models are available, so it's

Dual-plane manifolds are more the norm for high performance street applications. The long runner design is conducive for low speed torque.

pretty much a matter of selecting the carb that provides the desired airflow capacity. With a Holley the selection process is more involved, but not much. Part number 0-1850, which is rated at 600 cfm, and part number 0-3310, which is rated at 750 cfm, are "universal" carburetors that are produced in large volumes. Consequently, they're cheaper than other carburetors with similar airflow ratings. Other Holley carburetors with identical airflow capacities differ only in air/fuel calibration, linkage arrangement or choke mechanism. Since these carbs are tailored for engines of specific model years, they're easier to install and rarely require a change of jets. Emissions-type carbs will also clean up exhaust pollutants compared to a universal carb. The only real drawback is price: carburetors designed for specific applications are produced in relatively low volumes so they're more expensive than a universal carb of similar specifications.

Just about any street-type small block of 330 cubic inches or less will be well-carbureted by a 600 cfm four-barrel; small blocks of 350 cubic inches or greater displacement are equally well-served by a 750 cfm carburetor. Super high performance engines and race engines usually benefit from larger capacity carburetors with mechanical secondaries, such as those with cfm ratings of 750, 800, 850, 1050 and 1150 cfm. A variety of other carburetors are also available for specific applications.

However, before selecting a carburetor, check the emissions regulations that pertain to your vehicle so you don't run into problems if a governmental agency decides to check your vehicle's emissions levels.

INTAKE MANIFOLDS

The application for which an engine is designed dictates the specific rpm range in which power must be concentrated. Selection of intake manifold type should therefore be predicated upon a given design's ability to enhance performance at specific engine speeds.

All intake manifolds perform the same basic function, specifically that of providing a passageway between the carburetor and the intake ports of each cylinder. The configuration of the Chevy small block, like that of most V8's, dictates that the passage connecting the manifold plenum to the cylinder head either travel a rather tortuous winding path, or take the shortest, most direct route. Both arrangements provide advantages and disadvantages which to some degree determine specific performance characteristics. In essence, each intake manifold configuration offers the potential for increased power within a particular rpm range while sacrificing performance somewhere else along the horsepower curve.

Dual-Plane Manifolds

Since passenger car engine designers are primarily concerned with low-speed driveability, they have always utilized the dual-plane design. Such manifolds are essentially two-in-one affairs, each plane or manifold half routing air and fuel from a separate plenum area to an individual group of four cylinders. With each half of the manifold isolated from the other, runners are grouped so that 180 deg. of crankshaft rotation separates the intake cycles of cylinders fed by the same half of the manifold—hence the label "180-deg. manifold." The 180 deg. separation of cylinders, and relatively long runners which are required to snake around obstacles (like other runners), are the dual plane's greatest virtues. They are also the reasons that the design is conducive to the production of ample low-speed torque. At higher engine speeds, however, these assets become liabilities as the manifold runners are too restrictive to handle the volume of air required to produce maximum horsepower at 5500+ rpm. The high-rise design alleviates some restriction

TPI PRIMARY COMPONENTS

ECM—Electronic Control Module. This is the brains of the outfit. Essentially, the ECM receives all sensor input and performs all the calculations required to establish fuel flow rates. The ECM also controls ignition timing.

PROM—Programmable Read Only Memory. This means that once programmed, a computer can read it, but can't alter it. The PROM or chip holds all the data that the ECM needs to match a given set of sensor inputs to fuel and ignition control outputs. Aftermarket PROMs can be programmed to include conditions not recognized by a standard PROM. All it takes is the right programming to make computerized controls capable of handling just about any engine requirement. Starting with the 1994 model year, removable PROMs were no longer included in the PCMs found in Camaros, Firebirds and Corvettes. Instead, *electronically erasable programmable read only memory* (EEPROM), also called "flash" memory, is used. With these systems, new calibrations can be downloaded into the EEPROM without removing it from the PCM.

MAF Sensor—Mass Air Flow. These sensors were incorporated in 1985-89 TPI and 1994 and later LT1 systems. This sensor monitors the amount of air flowing through by sensing the voltage of heated wire it contains. At wide open throttle, maximum air flow will exert a strong cooling effect and voltage through the wire will be close to the five-volt maximum in order to maintain temperature; at idle, with not much air movement, only about .4 volts are required to heat the wire.

EGO Sensor—Exhaust Gas Oxygen. This sensor measures the amount of oxygen in the exhaust and alters fuel flow so that the air/fuel ratio is maintained at *stoichiometric*, which is the chemically ideal ratio of 14.7:1. One of the problems with standard EGO sensors is that they must be located relatively close to the heads so they reach operating temperature. Heated EGO sensors are the solution and are used on many original equipment and custom installations. A heated EGO sensor is mandatory when an engine is equipped with headers because the sensor is too far downstream and the exhaust is too cool for proper operation.

MAT Sensor—Manifold Air Temperature. As its name implies, this sensor keeps track of the air temperature within the manifold. This information is sent to the ECM so that calibrations can be finely tuned.

TPS—Throttle Position Sensor. In addition to throttle position, this sensor also sends data concerning the rate of throttle opening. This rate is used to calculate the degree of air/fuel enrichment required for acceleration (in a carburetor this function is handled by the accelerator pump). TPS position is physically adjustable, and a volt meter is normally used to determine the proper position.

Coolant Temperature—The name for this sensor is self-explanatory, but the output of this sensor has a pronounced effect on performance. Both air/fuel ratio and ignition timing are altered depending upon coolant temperature. Lower temperatures result in richer mixtures and more aggressive spark timing. High temperatures have the opposite effect.

Knock Sensor—This is a device that protects the engine from destruction. The sensor itself is like a small microphone. When the ECM "hears" detonation, it temporarily retards timing.

IAC—Idle Air Control. This device incorporates a small electric motor that controls an air bypass valve (a separate air channel not controlled by the throttle plates). If the idle speed established by throttle position is too high or too low, the PCM moves the IAC to open or close the bypass valve as required to achieve the desired idle speed.

MAP Sensor—Manifold Absolute Pressure. This is another way of stating manifold vacuum. The MAP sensor is essentially an electronic vacuum gauge that tells the ECM the amount of load under which an engine is operating. The ECM alters air/fuel ratio to accommodate varying load conditions, just as a power valve or metering rods perform this function in a carburetor. Speed/Density systems rely heavily on MAP sensor input to calculate the fuel curve.

Limp Home Mode—Of course, with all these sensors, something can very well take a wrong turn so TPI systems incorporate what's known as a "Limp Home" mode. In the event of a major system or sensor malfunction, the ECM automatically slides into "Limp Home" mode whereupon it holds timing to about 22 deg. and establishes a relatively rich air/fuel mixture. The whole idea of "Limp Home" mode is to protect the engine from damage while it is being driven a short distance. Some custom wiring harnesses (designed to allow installation of TPI systems in vehicles not originally so equipped) force activation of "Limp Home" mode. This isn't desirable, nor is it necessary. Proper harnesses are available from a variety of sources.

The Tuned Port Fuel Injection on this small-block Chevy can be adapted to any car. A number of aftermarket wiring companies can provide harnesses to adapt it to any car that has never had fuel injection.

problems by allowing the runners to curve more gently, but it can't completely eradicate the inherent characteristics of the dual-plane configuration.

Single-Plane Manifolds

Conversely, a single-plane manifold is ideally suited to supplying great volumes of air to the cylinders. With eight large runners connected by the most direct route to a single plenum, this design offers comparatively little airflow restriction. The large open plenum offers an additional advantage in that it supplies a large reservoir of air/fuel mixture (the open plenum) from which the cylinders may draw, and this has the same effect as installing a larger carburetor. For high rpm operation, this arrangement is ideal, but the large plenum/short runner combination intensifies the problems of low air velocities at lower engine speeds; with insufficient velocity, cylinders don't fill with intake charge as well as they do with a dual-plane manifold, so low-speed torque is significantly reduced.

Another problem with the single-plane design is "mixture stealing" by adjacent firing cylinders. In the Chevy small-block V-8, at least two cylinders positioned next to each other fire in one-two succession. An example is number 7 cylinder firing immediately after number 5 cylinder. The first cylinder of the adjacent pair "steals" some of the intake charge that should go to the second, and at low engine speeds this can significantly reduce power output. At higher rpm levels, air velocities are such that each cylinder receives a full charge, but with the inherent low speed problem, a single-plane manifold can lead to objectionable off-idle performance, especially in heavy vehicles and those that are geared for good economy on the highway.

General Recommendations

Laying down specific manifold selection guidelines is a difficult, if not impossible task, since the number of variables pertaining to engine/chassis combinations are virtually unlimited. However, there are some broad guidelines that will keep you out of trouble. Edelbrock, Holley, Chevrolet and Weiand offer dual-plane high-rise manifolds that are ideally suited to stock and modified engines. These models produce strong low and mid-range power and allow an engine to pull strongly up to about 6000 rpm. They represent the best all-around choice for any high performance street engine. Most street engines run out of camshaft, cylinder head or carburetor before they ever get to the rpm at which a single-plane manifold makes maximum power. There are exceptions, but on many dyno comparison tests, the dual plane outperforms the single plane up to about 5000 rpm. If you shift at 5500 rpm, that doesn't give you much of an rpm range to take advantage of the increased top-end power.

FUEL INJECTION

The difficulties in modifying, adapting and tuning electronic fuel injection systems have largely been resolved by the aftermarket industry as well as the OEMs. Fuel injection systems allow for much more precise metering of the air/fuel mixture.

Throttle Body Injection

TBI is a halfway transition between carburetion and fuel injection. Rather than rely on uneven engine vacuum to supply the air/fuel mixture, the throttle body injects fuel into each throttle bore, pulsing on and off to deliver the correct amount of fuel into an intake plenum. GM used TBI on small-block V8's from the mid-1980s onward, and there are several aftermarket units that bolt on in place of the carburetor.

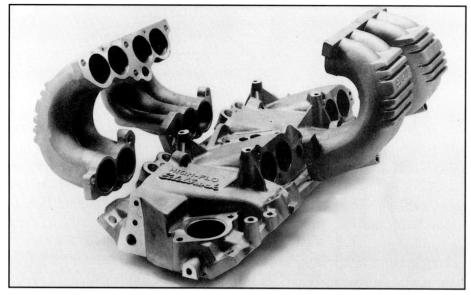

Edelbrock has a high performance replacement for Chevy's stock TPI manifold.

Port Injection

Port injection systems are the most accurate method of fuel delivery. Rather than rely on the shotgun approach like a carb or TBI, each intake port has its own injector, generally located just outside the intake valve. The injectors are all tied together by a manifold, sometimes called the fuel rail, which, naturally, supplies the fuel. The injectors are programmed to "pulse" only when the intake valve is open. Such systems are the most expensive and complex, but they are generally worth it. For stock or mildly modified engines, you can find the factory systems from scrapyards at reasonable prices. However, complete bolt-on systems are available from a variety of aftermarket manufacturers.

Tuned Port Injection

The outstanding performance of factory small blocks produced during the late 1980s and early 1990s is largely a result of Chevrolet's Tuned Port Injection (TPI) system. The first TPI systems (installed on 1985-1989 model year engines) employed a mass airflow sensor to monitor the volume of air entering the manifold. A heated wire serves as the actual sensing device and air flowing past the wire cools it, altering its electrical resistance. Higher airflow has a greater cooling effect. The ECM monitors the resistance and adjusts fuel flow accordingly.

In 1990, Chevrolet switched to speed/density systems which rely on programmed information rather than measured airflow to determine fuel flow. Although speed/density systems offer increased performance potential because they eliminate the Mass Air sensor, which is somewhat restrictive, they are more difficult to work with when making engine modifications. Since there's no Mass Air Flow sensor to tell the ECM what's going on, custom PROM calibrations become much more critical since they're in total control.

With both types of systems, a variety of other sensors feed input to the computer so adjustments can be made for changes in manifold air temperature, throttle position and engine coolant temperature. When the system goes into "closed loop" operation, an Exhaust Gas Oxygen (EGO) sensor is used to monitor the oxygen content of the exhaust. Based on input from the EGO sensor, the ECM makes the adjustments required to keep the air/fuel mixture at the chemically correct ratio (14.7:1).

Ford

If you are powering your car with a 289 or 302 cid motor, you can use the complete injection unit from a late-model 5.0-liter V8. You can use the factory control system or use an aftermarket system such as the one built by ACCEL. If you plan on using a 351 cid engine, Ford SVO has an

Ford's electronic fuel injection will work with 289, 302 and 351 cubic inch engines. These systems can also be installed in older chassis.

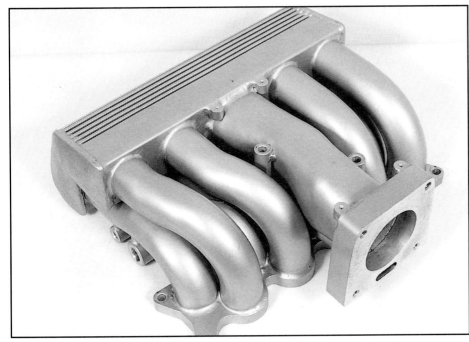

For the Ford 5.0-liter engine, Ford SVO makes a replacement GT-40 intake manifold that offers a significant performance increase.

intake manifold and all the necessary parts to allow you to use the 5.0 parts on the 351. The following parts are necessary to install the 5.0 injection system on your 351 cid motor.

GT-40 lower intake manifold for the 351W: M-9461-A58

GT-40 upper intake manifold: M-9424-A51

Main underhood harness (2 oxygen sensors, MAP Sensor, EGR, TIB and TAB solenoids, fuel, AC and EEC pwr. relays): M-12071-C302

Sensor and Relay Package, M-12071-D302

Engine Harness and Controls Package, M-12071-E302

Mass Air and Computer Conversion Kit (5 speed): M-12071-F302 (automatic): M-12071-G302

Computer-Compatible Distributor Kit ('87 or newer with 5/16 hex oil pump drive). E7TE-12127-D

SVO Cobra injector kit (24 lb./hr injectors, 70mm mass air meter) M-9000-C52

Distributor Gear , Roller: M-12390-F
Flat tappet: M-12390-D

• If you are planning to use a roller cam or flat tappet lifter cam, the drive gear on the distributor must be changed.

• Stock 302 cid 19 lb./hr injectors may not deliver enough fuel for a modified 351 cid engine, so this may require changing to 24 lb./hr or 30 lb./hr injectors, depending on what modifications have been made to the engine. The 24 lb./hr injectors are rated for up to about 400 hp and 30 lb./hr injectors are rated for about 500 hp. 30 lb./hr injectors will require a re-calibrated mass air sensor.

Aftermarket Alternatives

There are a number of companies that offer complete multi-port fuel injection kits for small- and big-block V8 engines. Most of these systems come with their own electronic control units that can be programmed for a variety of performance applications and conditions with the help of a laptop computer. You'll be able to fine tune ignition and air/fuel delivery according to the engine rpm, temperature, throttle position, vacuum, etc.

Aftermarket port injection systems and throttle body injection systems are becoming more accepted as an

Holley manufactures a line of throttle body fuel injection systems. This system is a 700 cfm digital fuel injection system. This system can have its program modified to suit any engine, or if this engine has its camshaft changed, the fuel injection program can be changed.

Holley has developed a complete throttle body fuel injection system. Holley offers analog-based systems as well as this digitally based system. The analog systems are a wonderful replacement for carburetors. The analog based system can be installed and tuned in a weekend while the digitally based systems are intended for the more serious tuner who has an understanding of electronic fuel injection systems.

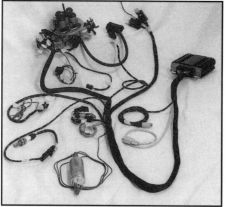

Before you start the installation process you need to become familiar with all the parts and the manual. Perhaps the best way to understand the system is to lay the harness out and plug each of the components into the harness. This procedure will give you an excellent idea of the mounting location of all the components.

You should note that the height of the 4 barrel Holley throttle body is a scant 3 inches from the bottom of the fiber insulating gasket to the top of the air cleaner adapter. The extremely low profile of this throttle body may make it attractive if hood clearance is a problem on your car.

alternative to the carburetor. The cost of a throttle body injection system is about the same as an upper end carburetor and they work well with modified engines.

If you choose one of these aftermarket systems, make sure that it comes with an oxygen sensor or a closed loop kit. This is critical because that is the part that allows the

ECU to adjust the mixture based on the amount of unburned air/fuel in the exhaust.

Holley—Holley, one of the most famous names in carburetors, has offered throttle body injection systems designed to replace carburetors on many OEM and aftermarket applications. The systems are relatively simple bolt-on kits that

come complete with all of the necessary wiring harnesses, fuel pumps, sensors and ECU.

The first models, while superior to carburetors, were based on analog technology. These units work well and are relatively simple to install and tune. Analog technology is a little slower to adjust to the changing atmospheric conditions than the newer digital technology models. Digital technology allows the ECU to perform many operations at the same time and adjust the mixture more quickly. Both types work very well with modified engines and even engines with camshafts that produce low manifold vacuum will benefit from throttle body injection.

Holley offers several choices in the Pro-Jection Throttle Body Injection series. For maximum performance applications, Holley offers the Pro-Jection 4Di microprocessor-based digital fuel injection system, available in 650 to 900 cfm ratings. These units can be interfaced with an IBM compatible computer that allows you to monitor and analyze engine parameters and adjust fuel flow and ignition curves for maximum performance.

The Pro-Jection 4D system comes with a handheld calibration module for fine-tuning the fuel system performance.

The Pro-Jection 4 analog system utilizes an analog controller to manage the fuel mixture, and the standard Pro-Jection system is available in 300 and 670 cfm rated two-barrel units that are capable of using an optional closed loop kit to control the fuel mixture.

Accel—Accel has expanded in recent years from ignition products to complete bolt on fuel injection systems, including both multi-port and TBI. Their Multi-Point Spark Fuel Management System is a port

Here is the Holley 700 cfm 4-barrel throttle body injection system installed on a Ford 351 Windsor. This particular engine has a cam with a lot of overlap and always had a very rough idle. The best fuel mileage this motor every delivered was 16 mpg. The 4 bbl, because of its tuneability (via lap top computer), smoothed the idle and improved the mileage to 18.7 mpg. Other major improvements are low end torque and throttle response. The finishing touch to this installation was the K&N air filter.

Inglese Induction Systems has modified the Weber style casting, installed injectors and created a throttle body fuel injection system that has the look of a classic race induction system. This system is intended for a small-block Chevrolet engine. Shown at bottom is a closeup of the injector. The electronics on these systems are from Accel.

injection system that is intended for big-block motors. It is capable of flowing 1000 cfm and comes complete with everything required for the installation including the intake manifold, plenum and fuel rails with injectors and all the sensors necessary.

Accel's four-barrel TBI Spark Fuel Management System is a throttle body system designed for small-block 350 Chevy engines. This system is rated at 750 cfm. These units can be reprogrammed with the (included) calibration module for other applications. The controller interfaces with the GM HEI computer, but will also work in non-HEI applications.

Accel's electronic fuel management systems are designed to allow the installation of Ford's multi-port fuel injection and Chevrolet's Tuned Port Injection systems on a previously carbureted engine. The electronic fuel management systems in both cases are pre-calibrated for typical engine configurations but can be re-calibrated using a PC or laptop computer for your specific engine configuration. For the computer phobic, Accel does offer a "Master Tuner" to allow you to fine tune their own fuel/spark management systems without having to use a computer.

Edelbrock—The Edlebrock/Weber Pro-Flo Multi-Point Electronic Fuel Injection is a complete multi-point electronic fuel injection system that includes all the necessary parts for installation on a Chevrolet small block V-8 engine. This is a Speed Density system and controls the ignition timing also. The ECU is programmed with one of six chips to fit in the calibration module. The chips are sent separately so you can select one that is compatible with your camshaft. The calibration module allows you to make adjustments to the fuel curve, spark advance and idle speed without using a PC or laptop computer. All changes are saved and stored but a restore key allows you to return to the previous settings or the original Edlebrock settings.

Howell Engine Development— Howell Engine Development offers stand alone and integrated wiring harnesses allowing the adaptation of late-model GM V8 or 4.3-liter V6 engines. These systems only require two wires to connect the harness to the battery and ignition. All of the

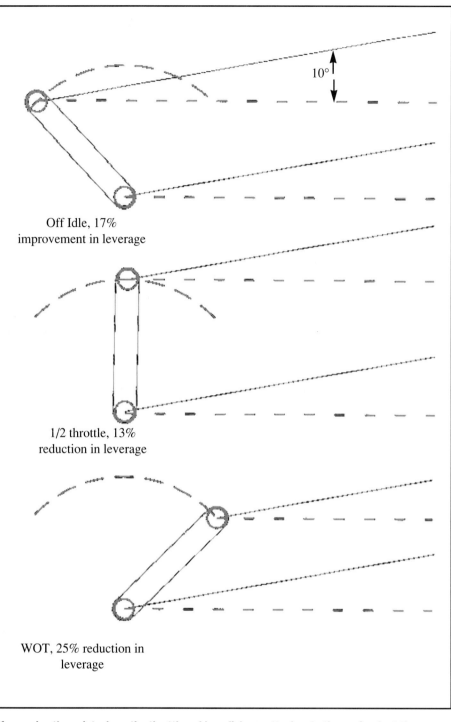

Off Idle, 17% improvement in leverage

1/2 throttle, 13% reduction in leverage

WOT, 25% reduction in leverage

If you raise the point where the throttle cable or linkage attaches to the engine (not the throttle lever) you will increase your leverage and reduce the effort to start opening the throttle. Once the throttle is "off idle" any reduction in leverage should not create any driveability problems.

Here is a closer look at the throttle cam that will be installed on this throttle body. The geometry and location of the throttle pedal and throttle linkage produced a very sensitive throttle. The throttle opening rate was so fast off idle that the car was very jumpy as you came off idle. Howell Engine Development Company manufactures this cam that bolts to the side off the throttle arm and corrects this problem.

Howell systems utilize the GM computer and oxygen sensor, and provide complete GM diagnostics capability. System faults will be displayed using a "Check Engine" or other dash-mounted light.

Howell Engine Development also markets a line of throttle body injection systems known as HP/TBI systems. These combine GM electronics, Howell wiring harness and the Holley two- or four-barrel TBI units and can be used on big- and small-block engines. These systems also offer the GM closed loop spark and fuel control. Howell Engine Development offers systems for Chevrolet, Ford and Chrysler engines.

THROTTLE OPENING RATE

When you first drive your car you may notice that the throttle pedal is hard to press at first and then just afterward it begins to move, it becomes easier; or the car seems jumpy and tends to leap forward with the slightest bit of pressure (off idle) on the gas pedal. If this happens, there is a good chance that your throttle opening rate is incorrect. Generally, there are two reasons this can happen and it is usually caused by the relationship of the throttle linkage (or cable) and its anchor point to the lever on the side of the carburetor.

If you examine the side of the carburetor and the linkage closely you will find that the linkage or cable runs uphill to the carburetor. Also, if your carburetor is like every other one, the lever on the side of the carburetor has an inherent design problem. Every lever, when pulled from a stationary

FUEL CUT-OFF SWITCHES

Most fuel injected and high performance carbureted engines have high pressure electric fuel pumps. If your car has an electric fuel pump, you should seriously consider installing a fuel cut-off switch that is activated by sudden changes in inertia, such as during an impact. If a fuel line were to become disconnected or ruptured, fuel would continue to flow as long as the pump had power and the tank had fuel.

Note: Some fuel injection systems (Holley's Pro-Jection, for example) will shut down the pump if they don't receive a signal from the distributer. However, if the motor continued to run, the fuel pump will continue to pump fuel.

Ford has used these for a long time. PNE1AZ-9341-B is for up to and including 1991; F5AZ-9341-A is for later models after that date. NAPA (National Auto Parts Association) distributes a "Universal Fuel Cut-Off Switch" (PFS100) as well that is available from just about any parts store.

These sensors do not have to be mounted near the fuel pump or tank. These are electrical switches that are wired inline with the power to the fuel pump. They contain no fuel! They can be in any convenient location as long as it is mounted rigidly on a stiff panel, within three degrees of vertical and the reset switch is accessible. If the switch is allowed to shake around, you could very well have false triggering, and most likely just at the worst time.

NAPA's universal switch is basically a single throw, double pole switch rated at 10 amps. It has 3 electrical terminals, a common terminal for power in (from the fuel pump power source), a normally closed terminal to feed the fuel pump (or better yet, power the entire fuel system) and a normally open terminal that can be tied into a signal device like a buzzer, indicator light or your car's four-way flashers. I personally like the four-way flashers because it serves a dual role. In an accident, if the sensor trips, the flasher will indicate that, and if you were incapacitated, the flashers could aid in summoning help.

If you have any concerns about these sensors, they can be checked at any time. Remove the sensor from its mount and hold it in one hand. With the engine running strike it with the other hand. The pump (and motor) will stop and your warning light(s) will start. These are re-setable and can be checked as often as you like.

To correct this, the initial opening rate of the throttle needs to be slowed. Start by raising the point where the cable attaches to the engine. This will reduce the angle and slow the initial opening rate somewhat. The midrange rate will be close to what it was before and the wide open rate will be faster.

In the example we will assume that your carburetor will have 90° of travel from full closed to full open. If the throttle arm was set so that half open was straight up and down, point A when the throttle is closed is not directly above the throttle pivot, but is about 45 degrees forward of the shaft. The result of this is that the throttle will open faster at first and then slow as point A is directly over the throttle shaft. As it passes beyond that point, the rate of opening will increase again.

As the lever swings through its arc, the amount of horizontal travel changes depending on where it is in its arc.

If you raise the point where the linkage mounts to the engine 10%, you will note that the full closed position is 10% closer to directly above the throttle shaft. As point A is pulled back, the rate that the throttle shaft opens is slower than it was before, and increases as it goes beyond over center. This arrangement will make the car feel more driveable because you are giving it less gas for the same amount of pedal travel.

There is another solution that I feel is preferable: Replacing the throttle lever with a cam will eliminate this change, sort of. If the cam is a true constant radius arc, the throttle opening rate will remain constant. However, cam profiles could be tailored to your particular situation though. Your particular throttle pedal location, lever ratio, location of the mounting point on the engine and amount or throttle shaft rotation could

point, will go through a leverage change as the effective distance from the pivot to the end changes. If you drew two horizontal lines, one at the throttle shaft and the other at the ball joint where the linkage connects, and you move the throttle through its range of operation (idle to wide open), you will notice that the two lines separate at first and then as the linkage goes over center, move closer together. This effect creates a changing ratio, pedal travel vs. throttle shaft rotation. Depending on where the throttle linkage is located (up or down) relative to the carburetor, that ratio can require a high throttle pedal effort just to get off idle. The closer the lever on the side of the carburetor gets to straight up and down, the easier it becomes. This results in your giving it too much gas to start off.

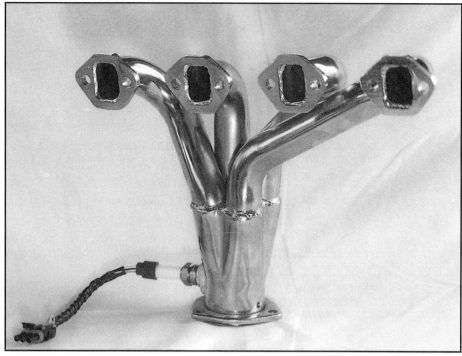

If your exhaust system does not have provisions for an oxygen sensor, one must be installed. The oxygen sensor needs to be located as close as possible to the engine and sample the exhaust from as many cylinders as possible. If your engine uses catalytic converters, the oxygen sensor must be located in front of the converters.

dictate an arc of a different profile. The arc of the cam could be larger at first and decrease as the throttle opens, thereby producing an ever-increasing opening rate as the throttle is opened.

Because of the shape of the cam changes, the opening rate changes from slow at first to faster as the cam rotates. The result is a throttle that is smooth to operate and a car that is easier to drive around town.

EXHAUST SYSTEM

The first part of the exhaust system you should consider are the exhaust manifolds. Will you use factory cast-iron manifolds or invest in a set of tubular headers? There are performance gains possible from using tubular headers but there are also some negatives. Factory exhaust manifolds, on the other hand, will last indefinitely, absorb engine noise better and generally take up less room in the engine compartment.

Factory Manifolds

These are usually a single, cast-iron "log type" pipe that all the cylinders empty into. Because of this, factory manifolds are not (generally) designed to promote optimum exhaust flow. They are used by auto manufacturers because they are easy to make and better suited for mass production. On the plus side, if cast-iron manifolds came with your engine, then you can save money by using them. Factory exhaust manifolds may also be mounting points for some accessories such as the alternator, air conditioning compressor or a power steering pump bracket. Factory manifolds should be cheap to buy from a junkyard, can be sanded and coated so they look okay and will last for quite a long time.

Factory exhaust manifolds are compact, quiet, and should clear all the engine accessories. On the negative side, they don't look as showy as headers, they are more restrictive and therefore will cost you in the performance and fuel mileage department. With all the cylinders emptying into one tube, there is a lot of turbulence and back pressure. **Note:** If your car has a custom chassis, it is possible that the chassis designer didn't have the foresight to allow for the installation of a factory exhaust system, which eliminates the option of using them.

These Sanderson block hugger headers are ideal for a chassis with limited ground and chassis clearance. For street driving and anything short of all out racing, block huggers will perform as well as full length headers. These headers are coated with a hpc coating, a ceramic coating that will extend the life of the headers and prevent some of the exhaust heat from escaping into the engine compartment.

Tubular Header Glossary

Block Huggers: Sometimes referred to as shorty headers. The primary tubes are short and are formed close to the engine block.

Collector: The collector is the larger tube that the primary (and sometimes secondary) tubes feed into. The diameter and length of the collector is determined by the displacement of the engine (how much air the motor will pump). If it is too small the exhaust will have a hard time leaving the exhaust system and if it is too large will lose efficiency.

Four Into One: Refers to a design where all four primary tubes are joined together into one collector.

Full Length: Refers to headers with long primary tubes that generally sweep down under the car.

Primary Tube: This is the tube that is welded to the flange that bolts to the cylinder head. The phrase "tuned headers" refers to headers that have primary tubes that are all the same length and are of a specific length. This "optimum" length is different for each engine and is determined by things like cam, heads, and the rpm range where the engine will be running.

Some chassis and car bodies will allow headers with long primary tubes that sweep down under the car. Others will require a "block hugger" header. As the name implies, they are short and fit very close to the block. In some cases they may even fit as tightly as a factory manifold.

Tri Y: Refers to a design where all four primary header pipes are paired into two collectors, with two large diameter secondary tubes running from these into a single collector, resulting in a 4 into 2 into 1 configuration. The Tri Y design delivers more low and mid-range torque over the "four-into-one" design.

Tubular Headers: Refers to exhaust manifolds manufactured from mandrel-bent tubing of differing diameters and lengths.

Flange Plates or Header Plates: Refers to the plate that the primary tubes are welded to, which in turn is bolted to the exhaust ports in place of a factory cast-iron exhaust manifold.

Tubular Headers

Why would you want to use tubular headers? The greatest advantage is in how well tubular headers "scavenge" the exhaust gases over factory manifolds. Factory manifolds, because of their more restrictive design, build more back pressure and reduce the speed and amount of gases that are removed from the chamber.

Second, because all of the cylinders empty into one tube, the high pressure exhaust from one cylinder can "leak" into an adjacent cylinder just before its exhaust valve closes. This dilutes the air/fuel mixture in the adjacent cylinder.

Third, due to the back pressure, the engine uses more power to push the exhaust gases and therefore less to push the car. Tubular header exhaust systems greatly reduce turbulence and back pressure by giving each cylinder its own primary tube to carry the gases away from each cylinder. The size and length of each primary tube, as well as the collector, are designed to minimize turbulence and back pressure, and maximize efficiency and performance. Remember, the more exhaust that gets out, the more air/fuel mixture that can get in, and the more engine power goes to propel the car.

Many of today's performance street cars now use tubular headers. Tubular headers reduce the likelihood of diluting the incoming gases and the engine produces a broader torque curve, meaning more torque if available over a wider rpm range. They can be chrome-plated, painted, or given a ceramic coating.

Primary Tube Diameter and Length

According to the data supplied by a number of header manufacturers (including Sanderson Headers and Doug Thorley), for a street-driven, small-block V8 (300–350 cid) with dual exhaust, shorty or block hugger headers with primary tubes of a smaller diameter (1 1/2" to 1 5/8") create air velocities high enough to scavenge the spent gases from the combustion chamber. Full-length headers will yield greater performance improvements over the block hugger only if the car is used in competition, where the engine is operated at higher rpm without mufflers, and the tubing diameters and lengths are selected for that engine. With mufflers installed, it is a tossup.

For more enthusiastic driving, tubular headers with equal length primary tubes can produce more power but they tend to be more motor specific. A primary tube length that is good for one engine may not be good for another, depending on things like cam, fuel system, ignition, etc. If the primary tube is too large, you will lose low end torque and it will peak further up the torque band. Also, for street driving, the primary tube length does not have to be of equal length.

Not many drivers will take full advantage of the power-making potential of full length tuned headers

Full length, tuned headers are neat to look at and are sometimes the best way to construct an exhaust system. If the benefits of a full length header are to be fully utilized, it must be matched to the engine (ignition, cam, etc.), gears and tire size.

unless you are planning on racing the car on weekends and need to extract every ounce of available power from the engine. In this case you might take advantage of the longer primary tube and tune them to the rest of the engine.

For a small-block (V-8) street engine, the current hot setup suggests using headers with a small diameter primary tube, 1 1/2" to 1 5/8". The smaller diameter, longer primary tube length and the Tri Y designs tend to make more bottom end torque and cause the curve to be flatter, less peaky. For a street-driven car, this is ideal.

Note: If you increase the diameter of the primary tubes, you move the torque curve up the rpm range. For the street, that's not what you want. You want to keep it on the lower end where the engine will be operating most of the time.

Headers of this design will come equipped with collectors in the 2 1/2" to 3" diameter range. The larger the collector volume (i.e., diameter and length) the more low end torque the engine will provide (this is better for

an auto with an automatic transmission) and a smaller volume collector would be better for a high winding manual transmission car. Whichever style you choose there are a few areas that require your close attention.

Tubular Header Tips

• The flange the bolts to the head should be 3/8" thick to minimize warping. Thicker tubing material will help muffle the exhaust noise and will also be less likely to crack.

• Primary tubes should be small diameter (1 1/2" to 1 5/8") and constructed of 14 or 16 gauge thick material.

• A longer primary tube length is preferred; the improvement though is minor so shorty headers are OK.

• Tri-Y design will boost low and mid rpm torque.

• Larger diameter collector will boost low rpm torque for automatic cars, smaller diameter collector is better for

standard transmissions.

If you run your headers open at the track, (in general) a shorter length collector will move the torque curve lower; longer collectors move it higher in the rpm band.

Catalytic Converters

If you are using catalytic converters, in theory, they should be as close as possible to the manifold or headers so they will get hot quickly and "light off" quickly. However, each factory exhaust system (including converter location) is engineered for each engine and the chassis it was installed in. You may be required to locate the converters the same distance from the manifolds as they were originally. If the converters don't "light off" soon enough then they may carbon up and clog. This could result in a converter fire. These internal fires can create enough heat to burn the carpeting in a production auto and will almost certainly burn fiberglass. Therefore it is very important to install a heat shield between the body or heat-sensitive component and the exhaust system. Heat shields can be reused from the donor car or made from sheet metal. Inexpensive metal tubing can be used to shield the exhaust pipe itself. Items considered to be heat sensitive are transmission cooling lines, power steering hoses, fuel lines, the oil filter and remote hoses, for example.

The older style bead type converters have a useful life of about fifty thousand miles (if the engine runs clean and doesn't load up with gas and oil). The newer style, monolithic catalytic converters (looks like a honeycomb) are the least restrictive to the point that a 3" monolithic converter (according to the catalytic converter manufacturer) will flow almost as much air as a straight 3" pipe and if not abused will last

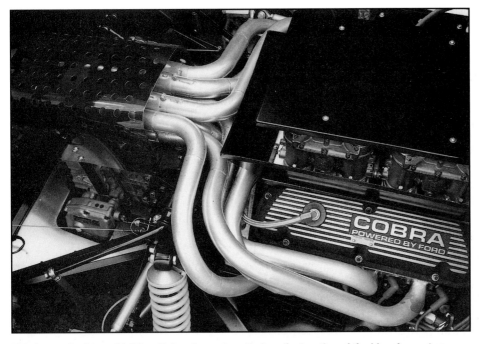

This is a typical tuned full length header system that replicates the original header systems designed for use with the racing GT40's. The length and diameter of the primary and collector pipes was selected for each particular engine and transmission, etc.

indefinitely. Three inch pipe will flow enough air for 650 hp.

Note: Don't forget to check with your local Registry of Motor Vehicles to determine what your responsibility is regarding emissions equipment on your car. The EPA has specific guidelines regarding exhaust systems and Catalytic Converters.

General Tips

Crossover Pipe—A crossover pipe is a pipe that connects the two exhaust pipes together. It is sometimes called an "H" pipe. It should be the same size pipe (within 1/2") as the collector and the rest of the system and be located as close to the engine as possible, about 21" to 24" from the collector. The crossover ties both sides of the motor together and the pulses from one bank help the other bank scavenge the other pulses coming down the pipe. Remember, design and install everything with service in mind. Install the crossover pipe with flanges to facilitate removal. You may want to service or change the trans-missions in the future.

Be aware of the heat that will be generated by the crossover pipe. You should put the crossover near the tailshaft rather than under the transmission pan (which is the wrong place to have it).

Pipe and Muffler Location—Now the rest of the system should be installed with consideration given to replacement, ground clearance and practicality. You have a number of options here. You can purchase the system that the kit manufacturer offers (if any). If your car is a classic and you are trying to make it as authentic as possible, then that will dictate the type of system you use. The kit manufacturer or a company that offers reproduction parts may have a system to meet your needs. If authenticity is not an issue, the manufacturer's system may still be best, because it should fit within the constraints of the body and powertrain. However if none of those are important and you will be taking the car to a muffler shop, then I urge you to consider another alternative. Before you turn the muffler technician

loose to bend up pipe to fit, have him try to fit a set of exhaust pipes from an existing performance car such as a Corvette, Camaro or Mustang. You may have to trim or add a little to the pipes, but if you can get a set of these pipes to fit your chassis with little or no modification then you have just allowed yourself to use a replacement stainless steel system or a system with a lifetime warranty. If that doesn't work then you still can have a full custom system bent to fit.

Caution: Do not let the technician hard mount the system to the chassis. This will transmit noise and vibration into the chassis and the entire car. Insist that he use standard rubber mounts. Use the most common hangers possible. By using standard parts as often as possible you will make life a lot easier for yourself when it comes time to replace a worn-out part, and they will wear out. Keep the pipes as high as possible so you are not dragging them over speed bumps or when the suspension compresses. You can anticipate this if you note that you have 4" of compression (for example) and 4" of clearance between the pipes and the road. You might make it without ever hitting something, or not.

Pipe Size—What size exhaust pipe (including a crossover) is correct for your application? Although the specifics of your engine will determine your choice, there are some basic rules of thumb. A 2-1/4" diameter collector and exhaust pipe will flow the proper amount of exhaust for engines making between 300 and 325 horsepower. A 2-1/2" pipe is good for 325 to 400 horsepower and 3" is good for 400 to 650 horsepower. Larger is not always better. If the pipe size is too large, the velocity drops off, scavenging from the cylinders drops off, and the cylinders don't get a clean charge of

The Super Turbo muffler from Dynomax Performance Exhaust features a 3" internal flow tube and patented flow directors, providing extraordinary exhaust flow for reduced backpressure and improved performance.

air and fuel. Your pipe diameter should be as large as the exhaust manifold or the collector diameter. Any larger is a waste of your money. This in general will be from 2" to 3", with 2-1/2" being best suited for most small-block street machines. A 2 1/2" diameter pipe is a good compromise in noise vs. performance.

Scavenging—When a pulse of exhaust comes rushing out of a cylinder, through the header and down the exhaust pipe, it leaves a vacuum behind it. This vacuum can help pull fresh air and gas into the cylinder if the valve overlap is long enough. As the pulse moves by the next exhaust port it can help pull the next pulse of exhaust from that cylinder. If the diameter of the pipe is too large the pulse will slow down and that effect will be lost. If the pipe is too small, it will be restrictive and not allow the exhaust to flow freely, and it will have a hard time getting out the pipe (at higher rpm).

Mufflers

There are a variety of opinions when it comes to mufflers. There are many performance variations on the market now designed to maximize flow. Walker Dynomax, Borla, and Flowmaster all make good products. As for location, some say that they should be as far away from the engine as possible. By doing this you maximize the amount of time the exhaust has to expand before it runs into the baffles in the mufflers.

The other school of thought says that the amount of difference (if any) probably won't matter on a street car, and the further away it is the faster it will rot out because the condensation that gathers in an exhaust system will sit longer in a muffler that is far away from the engine. The closer it is the faster it will heat up and dry out (if it ever gathers any water vapor).

Mufflers come in straight through, dual pass and triple pass designs. As the name implies, dual pass means the routing of the exhaust gases double back and make a second pass through the muffler and triple pass means it does it three times. At a minimum, use a muffler with the same size inlet

and exit as the exhaust pipe and locate it as far away from the engine as possible. Use the least restrictive mufflers you can use for that neat sound and low back pressure. If you need tailpipes use the same size pipe for them also. ■

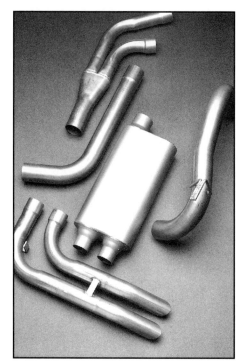

Flowmaster offers complete, street-legal exhaust systems for increased performance.

DRIVETRAIN TIPS

6

The drivetrain generally includes everything that lies between the engine and the drive wheels; the transmission, driveshaft, and differential. The engine you choose will dictate your options. There are plenty of OEM transmissions readily available in scrapyards, and an entire aftermarket devoted to the entire drivetrain.

TRANSMISSIONS

Transmissions come in all shapes, sizes and styles: 3, 4, 5 or 6 speed manual transmissions with top gear ratios of 1 to 1 and overdrive; and automatic transmissions with 3 or 4 speeds and top gear ratios of 1 to 1 or overdrive. If you use an overdrive transmission (automatic or standard) with a short rear end gear of 3.55 or 4.11 to 1 for example, you will have plenty of pull off the line and the ability to cruise quietly and comfortbly. By this I mean that once the transmission shifts into overdrive, the rpm drops to a reasonable level, generally between one and two thousand rpm.

Whichever transmission you choose, your most important concern should be whether or not the

The third generation Camaro was equipped with a variety of bulletproof transmission during the third generation run. Many are still available in scrapyards in excellent condition.

transmission is capable of handling the torque the motor will deliver.

Chevy

You may want to stay away from 1994 and newer electronic transmissions. The transmissions don't have speedometer gears, and the speed information is transmitted through wire to the speedometer gauge that is an integrated part of the gauge cluster. So you would need all the gauging that goes with the engine

and transmission, and if you are building a classic car, these gauges may not provide the look you want.

GM Automatics—Basically you have six automatic transmission options when it comes to GM: the lighter Turbo 350, Turbo 375 and Turbo 400. All are 3-speed transmissions. The Turbo 350 has a locking torque converter and a lower 1st gear ratio than the Turbo 375 and 400. The Turbo 375 is basically a Turbo 400 with a short Turbo 350-

The T-5s in the '85 Mustangs had significantly improved gearsets as well as a wider ratio. This gearbox remained essentially unchanged until 1989, when it was beefed up considerably for improved torque. It also came equipped with the venerable C-4 automatic.

style tailshaft that uses the smaller 350 size universal joint. The Turbo 400 and 375 have top gear ratios of 1:1, and neither have locking torque converters. The Turbo 400 has a long tailshaft and a large (heavy-duty) universal joint.

The 700R4 and 4L6OE, an electronic version of the 700R4, are 4-speed overdrive units. The heavier 4L80E is an electronic overdrive version of the Turbo 400 and the only apparent drawback to this transmission is that its shifting and torque converter lockup is controlled by the engine's ECU. Because it is electronically controlled, it must be used with the fuel-injected engine it was intended to be bolted to. In order to use this transmission behind a carbureted engine you would need a separate controller. Accel Corp. is developing such an electronic controller for the 4L80E. Their transmission controller handles the shifting and torque converter lockup chores. It is designed to enable real-time programmability of part throttle and wide open throttle (WOT), up- and downshifts, transmission line pressure and torque converter engagement. Its harness plugs directly into the 4L80E transmission connectors. This controller is still in development and has not been officially released yet.

The 700R4 does not require an ECU and therefore can be used with a carbureted engine. Unfortunately, the 700R4 has received a bad rap. Rumor has it that it will not stand up to any "real" horsepower; but in fact, it is regularly used in drag racing with the addition of some valve body kits and other aftermarket items that beef it up a bit. Don't rule it out without taking a closer look.

The only GM transmissions that are not universally recommended are the "metric" transmissions, and the Turbo 250 that was typically used behind 4 and V6 cylinder engines.

Manual—General Motors has offered a number of manual transmissions over the years worth considering. From 1954 through 1980, the Saginaw 3- and 4-speed transmissions were built for mild performance applications of less than 300 horsepower. From 1957–63, the Borg Warner 4-speed was used. This was replaced by the '63-'74 Muncie 4-speed, but in late 1970 through the early 1980s, the Borg Warner 4-speed returned.

In 1983, the Warner T5, 5-speed overdrive transmission was first offered in pick-up trucks and Camaros.

From about 1984 through 1987, the Corvette had a Doug Nash four-speed transmission with an electronic overdrive unit bolted to the rear. The 1984 overdrive units had a .68:1

overdrive and the 1985-1988 units had a .59:1 overdrive. The overdrive units could be engaged with 2nd, 3rd, and 4th, hence the 4 + 3 designation. Around 1989, GM introduced two 6-speed transmissions, the Borg Warner and the ZF. The Borg Warner 6-speed was available in the Camaro and Firebird; and the German-made ZF 6-speed was only available in the Corvette. All of these transmissions will interchange and can be used on any V8 and 4.3-liter V6 engine.

Note: The ZF 6-speed transmission had something called "Computer Aided Gear Selection" (CAGS). To achieve higher fuel mileage numbers around town, the computer caused the shifter to bypass second and third when upshifting from first to second. Instead of second, the computer only allowed fourth gear to be selected. Fifth and Sixth were also locked out. The ZF transmission is more expensive, and rumored not to be as robust as the Borg Warner 6-speed transmission, and therefore is not recommended. The GM 69.5mm 5-speed transmission is not considered worth investing in either because it was not intended for use with an engine that generates very much torque and is therefore considered unreliable.

The only other major point of concern with any of these transmissions is the differing lengths of the tailshafts. Logically though, the driveshaft will not be cut until the engine, transmission and rear end are in place, so this should not be an issue.

Ford

Automatics—Ford's C-4 and C-6 have been around for a number of years and have proven to be stout performers. The FAOD (Four speed Automatic Over Drive) is newer and was introduced in the mid eighties.

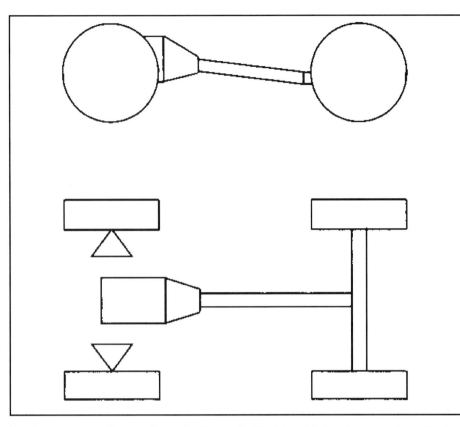

This is an example of a one plane drive line angle. The "slope" is in only one angle, vertical. This is a preferred situation.

These are all fine transmissions and will work well, even with modified engines.

The C-6, intended for "bigger" motors, can have its bellhousing replaced with a C-4 bellhousing and bolted to a small-block V8.

The FAOD can also be used with any of Ford's small-block V8 motors from the 289, 302 or 351W. You will need the flexplate from an '80-'93 Mustang for the 289 and 302. In order to use an FAOD on a 351, you should use the flexplate like those used on mid- to late-'80 Ford vans and trucks.

In the late eighties, the oiling system was redesigned to improve lubrication to the tailshaft.

The gear ratios seem to have been pretty standard with a first gear ratio of 2.40:1; second gear at 1.47:1; third gear 1.00:1; and fourth gear at 0.67:1. Third and fourth gear bypass the torque converter to eliminate converter slippage.

Note: You need to be careful when adjusting the transmission throttle pressure linkage. The pressure within the transmission is controlled by the throttle position, and if incorrectly adjusted you could burn the clutches in the transmission. A transmission shop or your Ford dealer should be capable of doing this. If your motor is carbureted, Total Performance in Clinton, MI offers a kit to connect and adjust linkage to the FAOD and shifter.

Total Performance also offers a number of kits for engine and transmission swaps and may have the parts you need to mate the engine and transmission of your choice.

Five-Speed Manual—These gearboxes have been available for a number of years in Mustangs (four-cylinder), Thunderbirds and 5.0-liter Mustangs. The gear ratios for the 3.8-liter Thunderbird five-speed gearbox are first gear at 3.75:1; second gear at 2.32:1; third gear at 1.43:1; fourth gear at 1.00:1; and fifth gear at.75:1. The 5.0-liter Mustang five-speed had a first gear ratio of 3.35:1; second gear 1.93:1; third gear, 1.29:1; fourth gear at 1.00:1; and fifth gear at .068:1.

In order to use a T-5 (5 speed) gearbox on a 289 or 302 older than 1979 and all 351 to current, you must change flywheels to part number 6375A302—(157 tooth) with a 10.5" diaphragm pressure plate.

Miscellaneous Transmission Tips

Remember, a radically modified engine may benefit from having its transmission massaged in order to deliver reliable service. Shift kits are available for all of the above transmissions and will boost their torque handling capabilities. Most are inexpensive and easy to install. Consult a reputable transmission shop first, before you buy any parts.

When it comes time to match an engine and transmission, you'd be well advised to contact Ford Motorsport or the Chevrolet Raceshop for details. These are the people that can tell you what pieces will work together.

DRIVESHAFT

If the car you are building requires that you to have your driveshaft shortened, then you'll have to take it to a shop to have it shortened. Driveshaft length, alignment and installation angles are critical to obtaining a vibration-free ride. What follows are some universal driveshaft tips to help you achieve satisfactory results.

Length

What may be obvious to one person may not be to another, so when measuring for the new driveshaft

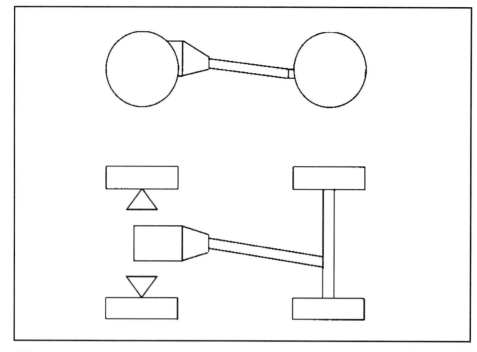

This is an example of a two plane drive line angle. In addition to a vertical slope, the driveline is offset horizontally. Because of this additional offset, this is not a preferred situation.

length, the chassis must be at its ride height and the engine/transmission and rear end aligned properly. Depending on the type of suspension your chassis has, the driveshaft may move in or out of the transmission as the suspension moves up and down. If the driveshaft is too long, it could be driven into the transmission and damage the tailshaft when the suspension compresses. If it is too short, it could fall out, which aside from the general embarassment, could be dangerous and cause severe damage to your car.

To position your driveshaft correctly, simply insert the slip joint into the transmission and align the shinny part or wear mark at the tailshaft seal. Measure the distance from the center of the front bearing cap to the center of the saddle on the rear end bearing saddle. That will be the length of your driveshaft from bearing center to bearing cap center.

Vibration

When checking your driveshaft for vibration, it is important to understand the difference between "run-out" and "oval." Run-out is when the tube is slightly bent from end to end, but is still round. A dial indicator will show run-out once per revolution. An oval-shaped driveshaft is one when the tube is not round, but oval in shape. A dial indicator will display an oval shaped tube twice per revolution. Even though a tube may be straight, the oval shape will make it seem bent. A driveshaft tube that is oval up to .010 run-out may be used. Anything beyond this limit the tube must be discarded.

Driveshaft Angles

When you install the engine, transmission, driveshaft and rear axle they must be examined for proper alignment. The rear axle pinion center line should be close to parallel with the center line of the crankshaft. Both universal joints should have about the same angle of operation. If misalignment is not kept to a minimum, this could cause a joint failure or create a vibration when the car is at high speed. Higher driveshaft

speeds require smaller universal joint operating angles.

There are two kinds of u-joint angles. The simpler, one-plane angle is found in most installations. It has all driveline slopes confined to one plane, usually the vertical plane. The other type of driveline angle is the compound angle in two planes. This is found in driveline designs where offset exists in both the vertical and horizontal planes.

High universal joint angles combined with high driveshaft rpm are the worst possible combination and will reduce the u-joint life. Too great and unequal u-joint angles can cause vibrations and contribute to u-joint, transmission and differential problems. Improper u-joint angles must be corrected. Ideally, the operating angles on each end of the driveshaft should be equal to and within 1 degree of each other. Universal joints (pairs) should have a combined maximum 3 degree operating angle and have at least 1/2 degree continuous operating angle.

Driveshaft rpm is the main factor though in determining maximum allowable operating angles. As a guide to maximum normal operating angles, refer to the chart on page 76.

When the transmission output shaft centerline and axle input shaft centerline are parallel, the maximum u-joint operating angle permissible is the length of the driveshaft divided by five. Example: A short 24" driveshaft would be limited to 4.8 degrees maximum operating angle, a 30" long driveshaft would be limited to 6 degrees.

When the transmission output shaft centerline and axle input shaft centerlines are not parallel, but intersect midway of the driveshaft, then the angles of each joint are equal. However, the joint angles will change during the up and down movement of

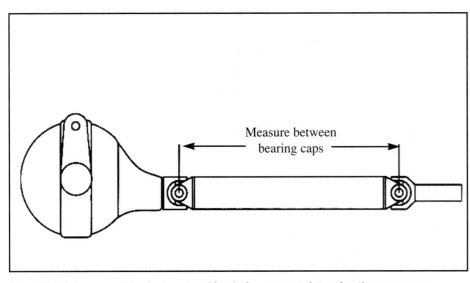

If you find that you need to shorten your driveshaft, you must determine the necessary distance between the bearing caps in order for the machine shop to cut it to the correct length. Always have the driveshaft rebalanced.

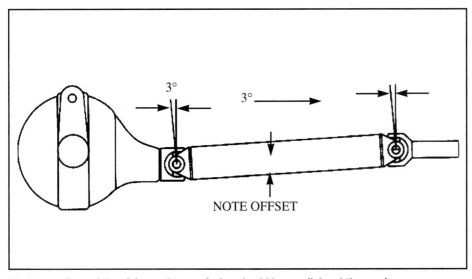

The center lines of the pinion and transmission should be parallel and the maximum recommended universal joint angle is 3°. Take your time when installing and adjusting the angle of your rear axle.

digital level. Simply place the level or inclinometer on the component to be measured. A display will show the angle and which way that angle slopes, or use a protractor to determine the angle.

All angles should be read within .25 degree and should be on a clean, flat surface. Always measure the slope of the drivetrain going from the front to the rear. A driveshaft slopes downward if it is lower at the rear than the front. A driveshaft slopes upward when it is higher at the rear than it is in front.

4. Check the driveshaft angle between the transmission and axle. Measure the angle on the tube at least 3" away from the circle welds or at least 1" away from any balance weights. Be sure to remove any scale or sound deadening compounds from the tube to obtain an accurate measurement. Record this angle on a work sheet as "driveshaft angle."

5. Check and record the angle of the transmission and pinion shaft. This reading can be taken on the yoke or a flat surface that is parallel or perpendicular to the yoke lug plane. Record your readings on a worksheet under "transmission and rear end angles."

6. To determine u-joint angles, simply find the difference in the slopes of the components.

If you need to rotate the rear end to adjust the pinion angle, wedges could be used on a leaf spring rear end and adjustable rod ends on a four-link located rear end. However, if you adjust the pinion angle, be sure to recheck the squareness of the axle to the chassis and the centering of the tires in the fender openings.

In the illustration above, note that

the axle. This is a more undesirable condition than parallel centerlines.

Checking Driveshaft Angles in the Vertical or Horizontal Plane

Use the following procedure to check driveshaft angles for proper u-joint operating angle. This procedure assumes that the car is complete or at least sitting at the finished ride height.

1. Inflate all tires to the pressure at which they are normally operated. Park the vehicle on a surface that is as

level as possible both from front to rear and from side to side. Do not attempt to level the vehicle by jacking up the front or rear axles.

2. Shift the transmission to neutral and block the front tires. Jack up a rear wheel. Rotate the wheel by hand until the output yoke on the transmission is vertical, and lower the jack. This simplifies measurement later. Check the driveshaft angle in a loaded and unloaded condition. Use the angle finder as described earlier in the book, a digital inclinometer or a

Driveshaft RPM	Maximum Operating Angle
5000	3.25 degrees
4500	3.67 degrees
4000	4.25 degrees
3500	5.0 degrees

the transmission and rear end are parallel in the horizontal plane and at 0 degrees. The driveshaft angle is about 3 degrees so each universal joint angle is only 1.5 degrees. If you look at the rpm vs. driveshaft angle chart above, you will note that example is OK for in excess of 5000 (shaft) rpm.

• When the slopes are in the same direction on the two connected components, subtract the smaller number from the larger to find the u-joint operating angle. Maximum angle for this example is driveshaft length divided by 5.

• When the slopes are in the opposite direction on two connected components, add these measurements to find the u-joint operating angles on your drawing to the rules for ideal operating angles mentioned above. Maximum angle for this example is the driveshaft length divided by 10.

Vibration Troubleshooting

Vibration in driveshaft is categorized as either being "transverse" or "torsional."

Transverse—Transverse vibration is the result of imbalance acting on the supporting shafts as the driveshaft rotates. When a part having an out-of-balance, or heavy side, is rotated, an unbalanced force is created that increases with the square of the speed. The faster the shaft turns, the greater the imbalance force acting on the shaft.

Each end of the shaft must be balanced individually, as each end is responsive to an out-of-balance condition. Transverse vibration caused by a driveshaft out of balance will usually emit sound waves that you can hear and mechanical shaking that you can feel. The driveshaft speed is determined by vehicle speed and the vibration is demonstrated best by road testing the vehicle, disengaging the engine, and feeling or listening for vibrations while coasting (with engine noises eliminated).

Torsional—Torsional vibration, although similar in effect, is an entirely different motion. The transverse vibration is a bending movement whereas torsional vibration is a twisting motion. The energy to produce torsional vibration can occur from the power impulses of the engine or from improper u-joint angles. This type of vibration is difficult to identify in road testing but certain characteristics do exist. It causes a noticeable sound disturbance and can occasionally transmit mechanical shaking.

Torsional vibrations can exist at one or more periods anyplace in the operation range and tend to be more severe at lower speeds. Changes in torque load (part to full throttle) usually affect the vibration. The non-uniform velocity obtained when a u-joint operates at an angle produces torsional vibration. It is practically impossible to maintain the desired joint angles throughout the operating range. Other vibration problems in a driveshaft could be caused by worn or damaged u-joints.

GEAR SELECTION

An engine produces torque and horsepower, and the gears in the transmission and rear end transmit those forces to the rear wheels. The ratio of one gear to another in your transmission and rear end multiply that power and determine the amount of work your engine can do.

Gears need to be chosen carefully, depending on the type of driving you'll do, the engine's torque and horsepower output, and the tire size.

If you plan on adding some larger tires and wheels for a little club track activity, your performance may suffer unless you change the gear ratio. Use the formula in the text to determine how the larger tires and wheels will affect your performance.

We could get overly technical here or keep it simple, and I like simple. In this case, the ratio is how many times one gear will turn compared to the gear it meshes with.

Let's cut right to the examples. If in first gear the input shaft turns 3.75 times for every one turn of the output shaft, the ratio of these gears is 3.75:1. If in top gear the input shaft turns 1 rev and the output shaft turns once, the gear ratio of these gears is 1:1.

That tells us that as the ratio numbers move further apart, 4:1 vs 2:1, the motor will spin faster to produce the same road speed. The closer those numbers are together, 2:1 vs 4:1, for example, the slower the motor will turn while cruising.

Carrying this line of thought further, it stands to reason that a car with a rear end gear ratio of 2 to 1 will be slower off the line, get better fuel mileage and be quieter when cruising than a car with a ratio of 4 to 1, which will accelerate faster, get poorer fuel mileage and be noiser when cruising.

So which rear end gears should you choose? This really depends on what parts are available for your

application. You can have it all—good acceleration, good fuel mileage, and low crusing rpm. If you were to select a rear end gearset of, say 3.55:1 and a transmission with an overdrive top gear of .62:1, then you will have a car that will accelerate very nicely and the overdrive will allow the motor to idle along while on the highway.

If the selection of gears for your rear end is limited however, the following might be of interest to you. Select a rear end gear ratio of 3.00:1 (or whatever "Highway" gear is available) and a transmission with a very short 1st gear and a top gear of 1:1. This will give you similar results as in the first example.

The specific gear ratios of these parts will ultimately depend on what is available and whether or not you can afford them. The amount of horsepower and torque your motor will produce and the type of driving you plan to do must be considered also. Remember, a motor such as a V6 will produce more torque than a 4-cylinder, but not as much as a V8, and will therefore be more tolerant of taller gears.

Oversize Tires

You may want to add some bigger street/strip tires, your performance may change considerably, and you'll be running around trying to determine why. Fortunately, if you know the diameters of both the new and old tires and the vehicle's existing final-drive ratio, you can calculate the effects the bigger tires will have ahead of time on your gear ratio. The source where you purchased the tires should have the diameter of the tire you are running. Or, you can simply apply a tape measure to one of the tires currently on your car and to one of those you're considering as replacements.

Section Height & Width

You may also be able to figure out the diameters of the tires based on their respective sizes. In the old days when 6.00x16 was the standard size on many popular cars, that was easy. The tire's section height—the distance between the edge of the rim and the face of the tread—and the section width—the distance between the sidewalls on either side—were about the same. In the case of a 6.00x16, the section height and width were both about 6.0 inches and the tire was mounted on a 16-inch wheel. To find the diameter, you simply multiplied the section height, 6.0 inches, by 2, giving you 12 inches, and added that to the wheel rim diameter, 16 inches, for an overall figure of 28 inches.

Aspect Ratio

Modern passenger car tires and light duty truck tires aren't sized quite so simply. In most cases, their section height and width are no longer alike. The height is usually much less than the width, and the relationship between the two—the aspect ratio—is an important part of their specs. The aspect ratio is the percentage the

The aspect ratio is the percentage section height is of the section width. To find the effective drive ratio, you need to divide the old tire diameter by the new tire diameter, and multiply that value by the aspect ratio.

section height is of the section width. Generally speaking, passenger car and light truck tires are now produced in metric sizes that indicate the section width in millimeters, the aspect ratio in percent and the wheel rim diameter in inches.

As a case in point, let's take a P235/75R15 tire. The "P" means it's a passenger tire; if it were a light truck unit, it would have the initials "LT" instead. Similarly, the "R" means it's a radial, while a "B" would indicate it's bias belted. The "235" is the section width in millimeters and the "75" is the aspect ratio, indicating that the section height is 75 percent of the section width. Finally, the "15" is the rim diameter in inches.

Metric Diameter—To find the diameter in inches of a metric size tire, you must first find the section height in inches. To do that, you convert the section width, 235 millimeters in our example, to inches by dividing it by 25.4, the number of millimeters in an inch. Then you convert the aspect ratio, 75, to a decimal figure by dividing it by 100. Multiply the quotients of these two calculations together to find the section height in inches. Double that

figure and add the wheel rim diameter, which is already given in inches, and the result will be the diameter of the tire in inches. Expressed as a formula, that would be:

2 x section width/25.4 x aspect ratio/100 + rim dia.

That can be simplified somewhat to:
Tire Diameter = 2 x section width x aspect ratio/2540 + rim dia.

Plug in the appropriate specs for a P235/75R15 tire:
Tire Diameter = 2 x 235 x 75/2540 + 15
Tire Diameter = 2 x 6.9 + 15

That would work out to a section height of 6.9 inches and an overall diameter of 28.88 inches which, of course, could be rounded up to 28.9 inches.

Effective Drive Ratio

To find what the effective overall drive ratio would be with a given increase in tire diameter, the formula is:
Effective Ratio = Old tire dia./new tire dia. x original ratio

Example—Suppose you have a set of 28.9-inch P235/75R1Ss on a Camaro with a 3.08 final-drive ratio and you want to replace them with 33-inch 33x12.50x15s. To find the effective drive ratio with the bigger tires, the figures would be:

Effective Ratio = 23 9 x 3.08
Effective Ratio = 0.8757576 x 3.08

With the bigger tires, the effective ratio is only 2.70! That's enough of a change to cause a noticeable loss in responsiveness.

Equivalent Drive Ratio

To find the final-drive ratio needed with the new tires to provide the equivalent of the vehicle's performance with the original tires, the formula is:

Equivalent Ratio = new tire diameter/old tire diameter x original ratio

Note that the positions of the tire diameters in this formula are reversed from their positions in the formula for effective ratio. In the case of the switch from 28.9-to 33 inch tires on a vehicle with a 3.08 final drive, the figures would be:

Equivalent Ratio = 33/28.9 x 3.08
Equivalent Ratio = 1.1418685 x 3.08

That works out to 3.51, so a set of final-drive gears in the 3.50-plus range would be needed to restore the lost responsiveness.

When adding larger tires and wheels, you must also be concerned with tire clearance. Checking for adequate tire and wheel clearance is discussed in the next chapter. ■

BODY TIPS

7

Quite often, car builders encounter quite a few problems when it comes to assembling and hanging the body on the chassis. With a little bit of knowledge and planning, the task can be made much easier. What follows are general tips, from paint to hanging doors, to make the body assembly stage of your project go much smoother.

WORKING WITH FIBERGLASS AND OTHER COMPOSITES

Most kit cars are composed of fiberglass body panels, so you will have to become familiar with working with the stuff. Fiberglass is often used as a generic term to describe materials composed of fiber reinforced plastic, or FRP's. The term Fiberglas™ is the registered trademark for the glass fibers produced by Owens Corning. FRP's can include glass fibers, Kevlar or carbon fiber materials. Each of these materials have different strength and load characteristics, and some of these are better suited for certain applications than others. HPBooks publishes an entire book on the subject, *Fiberglass and Composite Materials,* if you want to investigate

These ERA Cobra bodies are having flashing trimmed and holes cut. Note the white material inside the engine compartment. This is core mat which helps produce a stronger panel and reduces the likelihood of print-through.

further. For now, we'll confine our discussion to some basics when selecting and working with FRPs.

As with anything, if you use materials in the wrong way you are inviting disaster. In this case when we bond or fiberglass something in place, we expect it to stay put and not come apart. Which materials are better for your car, you ask? The more exotic materials, such as Kevlar and carbon fiber, as well as honeycomb type panels, do have their place if higher strength is required, such as in monocoque structures (a car with no chassis, like a unibody car for example).

All of these materials are good. It just depends on what the body is required to do and what loads it will be expected to carry. So, when you are evaluating different manufacturers and bodies, the fiber density is as important as the type of material used.

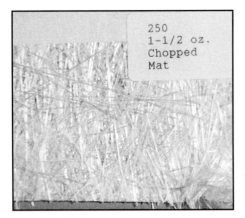

1-1/2 oz chopped mat commonly used as reinforcing. It is easily saturated but does not have the strength of fabrics. Chopped mat is good for rapid build-up.

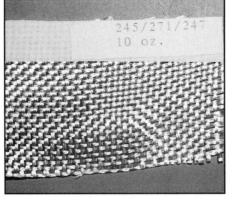

10 oz cloth is used for mold making and high strength fabrications.

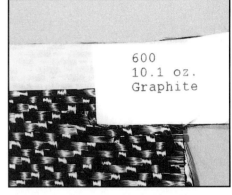

Graphite reinforcements offer the highest strength to weight ratio. Graphite also offers optimum stiffness and electrical conductivity. This is 5.7 oz cloth.

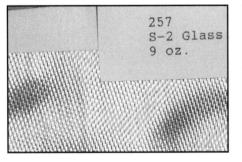

9 oz high tensile strength S-2 glass is very tightly woven and is typically used in high strength applications.

5 oz Kevlar has higher strength than fiberglass, provides good stiffness, high abrasion resistance and light weight.

Let's assume that you have a traditional kit with a full chassis that will fully support the engine, transmission, rear end and suspension. If there is a dashboard hoop or brace, then it will most likely support most of the mechanical parts under the dash. In this case the body and everything inside it are just along for the ride. No special or unusual loads, such as engine and suspension components, will be imposed as in a unibody or monocoque-style construction. The unibody or monocoque style car is designed to enclose and support the suspension, engine and transmission and other mechanical components without the aid of a (full) chassis. However, most kits have bodies that are bolted on to the chassis. They are typically composed of the following materials:

Resins

Polyester resin is usually the material of choice for most kit car body panels and is more than adequate for the job. Body panels made with polyester resin are both durable and economical. Epoxy resins, although stronger, don't justify their additional cost for most street/kit car applications.

Fibers

Chop refers to the technique of feeding straight glass fibers into a gun that looks like a paint spray gun. Inside the gun the fibers are chopped, mixed with resin and sprayed on the mold in one easy step. The random pattern is strong and the cheapest method of making a body, but usually weighs the most. If you look on the inside of a body panel made with chop it will have a random pattern

similar to wood panels made with wood chips.

Mat comes in sheets and a variety of weights and thicknesses. It has a similar pattern to chop. It does not offer the same strength characteristics of fabrics but it is cheaper, easier to lay-up and will conform to irregular shapes easily.

Cloth will have a woven pattern. Cloth comes in many weights, weaves and styles.

Woven roven has a woven pattern like the cloth but is much heavier. Woven roven is used where inexpensive, low resin, high impact, high strength reinforcement is required.

Hand lay-up refers to the procedure when fiberglass cloth is laid inside the mold and resin is applied to the cloth by hand until it is saturated. Hand-laid fiberglass will produce a more uniformly thick piece and is said to be stronger and can be done with mat, cloth or woven roving. Hand lay-up cloth could be used to reinforce parts of the body that might see higher loads such as door hinge and latch areas or if you needed to bond inner fender panels into your body.

Core mat, polyurethane foam sheet, vinyl foam sheet, end grain balsa or Nomex honeycomb is used to produce a stiffer, stronger and lighter panel by

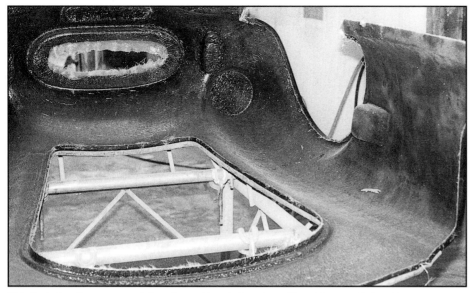

This body has been removed from its mold and placed on this table so additional internal panels such as the firewall and inner fender splash panels can be installed. Notice the supporting structure for this table. It is very important that the body be held rigid while it is green in order to produce a body that is true and square. Before this body is removed from the table, the excess cloth will be trimmed.

separating the layers of fiberglass. It is applied between the layers of cloth.

Core mat is said to minimize panel distortion and minimize print through where another panel is joined on the inside of the panel. You will sometimes see it used in hoods and trunks or in large flat panels.

Most car bodies and panels included in a typical kit are manufactured by the following process. The panels are made in a mold, which is generally turned upside down or on its side to provide easy access to the fiberglass technicians. The mold is cleaned of any material left from the previous body. Wax may be applied to the surface of the mold and mold release is sprayed over the entire surface that will have fiberglass and resin applied to it. The next step is the application of a gel coat that may be sandable or a gel coat with color pigment in it. (Gel coat is resin with a color pigment mixed into it that is sprayed into the mold and is the surface you see on the outside of the car. The next step is the application of the resin (most likely polyester) and reinforcing fibers.

Post Curing

Polyester resin can withstand a maximum service temperature of about 220° F before problems start to develop. The best thing you can do for your fiberglass body before painting it is to let it sit in the sun for a week. However, if the body was manufactured during the cooler months and is painted before summer, you should post cure it first. If you paint right away, you may experience problems the first time the car is exposed to summer heat, above 80° or so. The fillers and gel coat may shrink, or sanding scratches may print through. The last thing you should do prior to painting is to warm the body. A week in the hot sun, time in a paint booth oven or heat lamps systematically placed around the body will do the job. If your body was constructed using epoxy resin this step is a must to achieve its highest strength. If possible, cure the body in temperatures of 150° F, or at least above the hottest temperature the car will be exposed to.

The body should have a quality "surfacing primer" such as Duratec from Fiber Glass Developments, applied next. These surfacing primers are catalyzed polyester-based primers that have a high build capability to fill

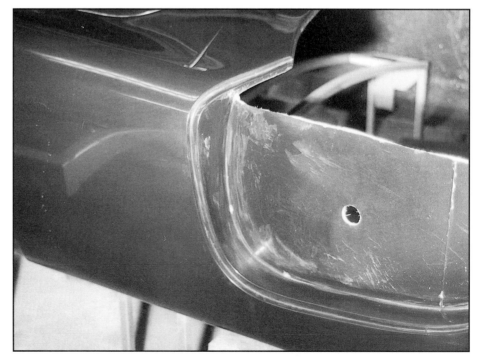

In this closeup of a Cobra body, you can see just how smooth the surface of the gel coat is. Some manufacturers offer bodies with such good surface finishes that painting is not required. Buffing with rubbing and polishing compound can shine the gel coat so it looks like paint.

FIBERGLASS TIPS

• Minimize your exposure to chemicals and the glass fibers. Make sure you have adequate ventilation. Applying baby powder to any exposed skin will keep fiberglass dust out of the pores of the skin.

• If you are unsure about your polyester resin being cured, take a rag soaked with Acetone and wipe it across the surface. If the rag shows a residue, the resin is not fully cured.

• To increase the pot life of your resin, mix small batches in large containers.

• Laminate your part in thin layers or sections. This technique can double your working time. How do you know if you are getting close to the pot life of your resin? Pour off a small amount and monitor it as you are mixing more resin and laying up more layers.

• When color matching a repair (Gel Coat), sand and polish a portion of the existing gel coat to remove the oxidation and faded layer. This is the color to match.

• If you purchase a large quantity of glass fabric, protect it by storing it in plastic in a cool dry place. Handle the fabric carefully to prevent soiling it with dirt or body oils.

• If you find that you do need to cut cured fiberglass, "carbide" saw blades will last a lot longer than regular blades.

• Polyester resins are typically catalyzed at 1%. At higher temperatures (on hot days), the increased temperature accelerates the curing. If this is a problem, reducing the ratio of catalyst to resin 1/2% will slow down the cure rate and extend the pot life. On cold days if the rate is too long, you can accelerate the cure rate by increasing the ratio to about 2%. Caution: Too much catalyst can cause excessive exothermic (overheating) and result in a weak part.

• If you are repairing fiberglass or adding a patch or panel, make sure the surface is wiped clean with acetone first to get rid of any residual mold release agent. Roughen the surface to provide a "bite" with sandpaper or disc grinder, then taper the edges of the patched area.

This Total Performance roadster body is awaiting painting. The entire body has been block sanded and any low spots were filled with polyester body filler. Notice the wood edge at the rear of the body; this will be very handy to attach the upholstery too.

small scratches and are capable of withstanding high heat from the sun. They will provide a uniform surface to apply the paint over.

Body Prep

Painting is another good place to spend a little extra to have it done professionally. Anybody can do a bad paint job, but it takes the right equipment and facilities to do a good paint job. To save some cost, you can prep the body yourself. Prepping, which involves mainly sanding, takes a fair amount of time, which is how you are often charged by the body shop. Fiberglass does not require any different method of preparation prior to painting other than block sanding. Because of waves and mold irregularities you should "block sand" your body before shipping it off to be painted. The process of block sanding means that you use a long sanding board (the longer the better, but use common sense here) to take out any high spots and show you where the low spots are. Sanding boards will help prevent dips and valleys in the big panels and will get rid of or show you where they currently are. Fill the low spots with filler and once cured, block sand again. Don't rush the curing process. Remember most fillers shrink as they cure, so let it completely cure before you start sanding. Use a catalyzed filler so that it will cure quickly and won't continue to shrink for days or weeks like solvent-based products.

Sanding Tips—Be careful when sanding with a grinder, because you could sand through a fender if you're not careful. Do not use the ball of your hand or your fingers to hold the sandpaper because you will leave depressions or valleys where your fingers pressed against the body. When you are sanding, don't go crazy with the coarse sandpaper. Remember

POWDER COATING

You may want to consider having some of your parts "powder coated" instead of painted. Powder coatings will not sag, run, or bubble and may be better than paint, when done correctly. Materials like glass, plastic and metals including castings can be powder coated. Powder coatings are comprised of dry resins and pigments and fall into two categories, thermoplastic and thermosetting. Thermoplastic coatings use vinyl, nylon and fluropolymer resins and are better suited for thicker, higher performance applications. Thermosetting coatings consist of epoxy, polyester and acrylic resins and are used in decorative and protection with thinner coating thickness applications. Epoxy resins typically do not have ultraviolet blockers and will "chalk" or oxidize and develop a white surface film but can be top coated with a clear coat with a UV blocker. The polyester resin is a better choice for things like roll bars or parts that will be exposed to the sun. Powder coating will fill surface irregularities better than paint and has exceptional toughness and impact and chip resistance. Parts can be assembled immediately without worrying about marring the finish. Powder coat can be lightly sanded with 1500 grit sandpaper and then buffed to a high luster. If your powder coater can not provide this service find someone else.

Note: If you are going to paint some of your parts yourself you need to make provisions for painting these parts. Either make arrangements to rent a paint booth, or a simple paint box and filter system can be constructed using a large cardboard box fitted with home HVAC filters.

Locating a fan in back of you so the fumes are blown through the filters will keep the fumes away from you and the fan motor out of the paint fumes. Warning: Protect yourself! Do not put an electric fan in the paint fume stream. Most solvent based paints are flammable and unless the electric motor is sealed, you might have an explosion. Do wear a respirator that is rated for the chemicals you are working with.

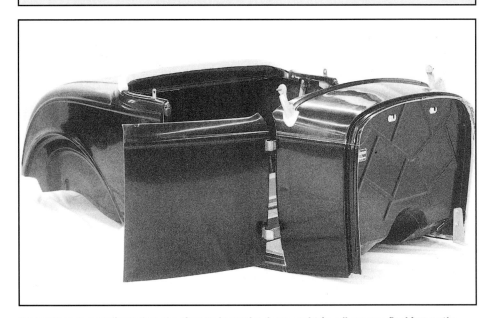

Wescott auto restyling takes the time to hang the doors and trim all excess flashing so the owner doesn't have too. The manufacturer has even installed the windshield posts and other brackets. You may not be so lucky, and will have to assemble much of the body yourself.

all those sanding scratches will have to be filled or sanded out by removing more material from the surface.

The effort and time you put into block sanding the body will pay off after it is painted. If done correctly you will be able to look down the side and not see any ripples or waves in the fiberglass. There is no reason why fiberglass can not look as good as steel!

From this point on, unless you have done bodywork before, it may be better to leave the remainder of the prep work and painting to a body shop or get professional help.

It is beyond the scope of this book to get into painting. HPBooks has several other bestselling books on the subject, listed at the back of this book. Let's move on to assembling the body.

BODY ASSEMBLY

When you first receive your car body, inspect it carefully. Look underneath and examine the corners for voids or air pockets in the fiberglass. Another concern is whether or not the body is strong enough where it counts, namely, in areas where it is bolted to the chassis or supporting mechanical components, such as suspension. In these areas, there should be extra thick reinforcements.

All mold seams should be in areas such as the peaks of fenders, etc., and not down the center of a hood, roof or door. Look for translucent, spotted or streaked gel coat. This condition could indicate poor quality equipment, materials or application methods.

When inspecting the new body, look for ripples or waves in the fiberglass—there shouldn't be any. If it is a warm day, look for what look like little (less than 3/32" dia.) bubbles or bumps on the upper

This Cobra body has been trimmed and is awaiting packaging and shipment to the new owner. Notice that the manufacturer has stored the body on the chassis while waiting. This will help ensure a body that is true and not twisted.

cured in about a month if stored in adequate temperature. If you are building the car in the winter, you may need to help cure the fiberglass. The easiest method is to use a heat lamp on the body. Every 30 minutes or so move the heat lamp to a new location and be sure to monitor the temperature. Don't allow the fiberglass to become any hotter than 150°.

Caution: Do not forget the lamp and burn the fiberglass! Keep track of the spots that you have cured, so you will be sure to cure the entire body.

Trial Fitting

You should trial-fit the body at least once before final installing it. During the trial-fit you need to look for areas where you will need to insulate, route ducting for ventilation, provide clearance for mechanical parts and trim or build up the fiberglass.

We will assume that the chassis has been fully assembled at this point with the suspension, wheels and brakes, radiator, engine and transmission, and the fuel and exhaust system. Aligning the body to the chassis will require you to make measurements from the ground and the chassis to the body. For this phase of construction (if you

surfaces of the fender creases. These indicate the possibility of voids under the gel coat, and are sometimes caused by incomplete working of the fiberglass/resin mixture into that area of the mold. If a body manufacturer is attempting to produce a large number of bodies, excessive catalyst is sometimes used to force the fiberglass to cure faster than it will normally. This condition is bad news, because when the car is all painted and sitting in the hot sun, the air trapped under the gel coat expands and causes little blisters to appear on the surface of the body. Sometimes shining a flashlight from behind will illuminate those pesky voids.

Look the body over carefully for any imperfections, damage, twists, dips or areas that will require attention.

Body Storage

Do not re-crate the body unless you have no other choice. Set it aside in a warm place so it will continue to cure. Normally, you would have to spend quite a bit of time preparing the chassis, so the body won't be needed

for awhile. Be sure that you take your time and carefully block the body so it is level and square. Support the ends so the door openings don't go out of "square." If you do not take these precautions, the body could develop a twist or bend, which might make it difficult to mount to the chassis or align the doors, hood and trunk lid.

When you receive your body, the fiberglass may still be "green" depending on when it was built. However, it should be completely

Occasionally you will need a third hand and no one will be available. A simple spring clamp can be your best friend as shown here. One clamp on each hood hinge holds them open, freeing your hands to align the hood and insert the bolts.

This Phaeton body has finished panels on the inside of the doors and steel bracing for the door hinges and door latches for added strength. This body even has a fresh air door on top of the cowl.

Attaching Fiberglass Panels

Your body may have arrived without the inner fender panels or firewall installed. If so, these need to be bonded into the body. Most of these panels will add strength and rigidity to the body, so they must be installed so that they will withstand the loads exerted on the bond line. For example, if your chassis does not have a windshield hoop, the firewall and floor, when bonded together, will reduce the amount of side to side and fore and aft movement at the windshield. You may also find that you need to install other pieces on your car. The bond of these pieces must be strong and permanent. If the pieces are large, you will need the ability to hold the pieces in place so they can be marked for trimming while you bond them in place. You can fabricate a number of simple brackets to do this. These brackets can be metal or fiberglass. Fiberglass tabs will allow you to bond them in place and grind them to shape if they are not quite right, then leave them there after the fitting is complete. I recommend fiberglass, but light gauge aluminum or tin tabs can also be used. Regardless of the tab material you choose, you can pop rivet, screw or bond these to the body or other panels in a way that will allow you to hold the panels in place while you trim them for a proper fit for your application. You may find that you need to provide clearance for engine or exhaust system heat shields. Once the panels fit correctly, prepare them for bonding. Roughen the surfaces with a grinder and then wash them with a solvent to remove any oils or mold release agents. You will need to lay enough bonding agent to the area between the panels so that it fills any voids between the panels. Hold the panel to the tabs with screws or pop rivets while the adhesive cures. Once cured you can remove the tabs and fiberglass the edges of the panel.

Note: Be sure you ask the manufacturer what bonding agent they used.

Body Mounting

The best source for mounting the body properly should be the instruction manual that should have come with the kit. In general, look for close quarters around the shifting mechanism, spark plugs, exhaust manifolds and pipes, suspension parts, chassis parts or any part that might require room for a heat shield, movement, removal, or service after the car is completed.

Warning: Be sure to wear a particle mask when you are cutting or grinding the fiberglass.

Mounting Points—In general, the

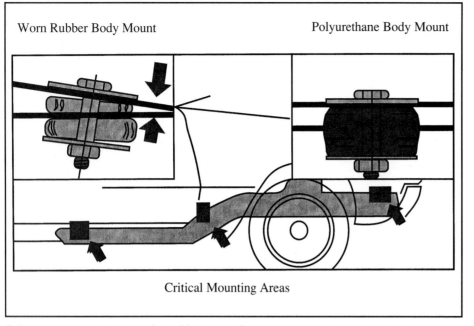

Worn Rubber Body Mount

Polyurethane Body Mount

Critical Mounting Areas

Rubber body mounts are a basic addition to any fiberglass bodied car, however in your installation you may find that the rubber OEM mounts are too soft and allow the body to move around. Polyurethane body insulators will not degrade over the years and may be more appropriate for your car.

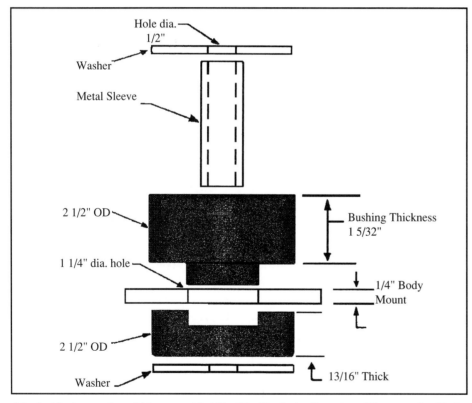

Hole dia. 1/2"

Washer

Metal Sleeve

2 1/2" OD

Bushing Thickness 1 5/32"

1 1/4" dia. hole

1/4" Body Mount

2 1/2" OD

13/16" Thick

Washer

A typical body mount would be assembled like this. The body sits on top of the upper bushing and the sleeve extends through the floor with the large washer and a bolt capturing the body.

a minimum you must secure the nose as far forward as possible. If you leave the nose inadequately supported, it will vibrate as the car proceeds through the wind and as the suspension transmits road irregularities into the rest of the car.

Locate the body side to side by measuring from the wheel openings to the brake drums or rotors, and fore and aft from the axle centers to the center of the fender opening. The accuracy of some of the bodies I have seen is not the greatest, so you may have to shift the body side to side or front to rear so the tires end up as close to the center of the fender as possible.

Attaching the Body

Once the body is located on the chassis and with all possible areas of contact checked and appropriate stiffening added, you can move to the next step, bolting the body down. In order for the finished car to ride quietly and not creak, crack, rattle, and squeak, you must isolate it from the chassis. If your kit does not have enough body mounts or does not already have any provisions for rubber body mounts, now is the time to install them. Twelve points (4 in the rear, 4 in the cockpit and 4 in the nose) should give the body enough support while providing enough points to align the body. If your body is bolted directly to the chassis using long bolts that pass straight through the floor and the chassis, simple isolators can be made from 3/4" and 1/8" hard sheet rubber, some large diameter washers (sometimes referred to as fender washers) and bolts long enough to pass straight through all of that. You can purchase rubber body mounts from your parts store or car dealer. Polyurethane body mounts can be purchased from aftermarket manufacturers that specialize in the

body mounting points should be as far outboard as possible and not on large flat horizontal surfaces that don't have any reinforcement (like the middle of the floor). Choose locations near a

vertical section of the firewall, door jams, and rear bulkhead. The front and rear of the trunk floor are also suitable for securing the rear section. Don't neglect the nose of the body. At

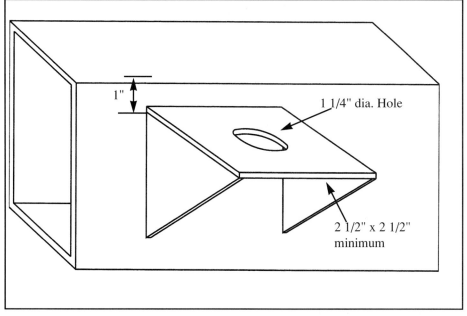

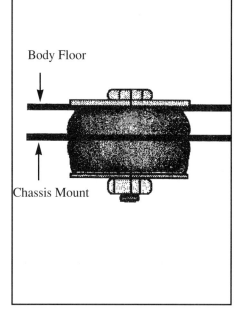

Here is an example of a simple body mount that can be fabricated from 1/8" steel and welded to the side of the chassis. Two important considerations are that one, the mount is positioned high enough (less than the thickness of the bushing) to prevent the body from contacting the chassis and two, that the mount is large enough to support the bushing itself.

This is how the rubber or polyurethane bushing would look when everything is tightened.

restoration of older cars.

An alternative to bolting through the chassis is to fabricate a simple three-sided perch similar to production mounts that can be welded or bolted to the side of the chassis that could use any of the previously mentioned rubber insulators.

Remember: You are trying to isolate the body from the chassis, so drill the hole in the body oversize. Use a thin piece of rubber under the upper large flat washer to isolate the bolt and washer from the body. The thicker rubber mount will sit directly below the body. This will allow the body to float on rubber above the chassis.

Now is the time to tighten the body bolts and secure the body. With the body located, you need to establish reference lines or points on each side of the body. You can clamp something straight along the side of the body from the front to rear along any body lines or creases. A string stretched between two jackstands would also work. It might be helpful to have the doors hung in the openings at this

point, so be sure that the body line at the front of the door lines up with the fender. Using the body mounts, tighten or shim each point until the body lines are straight and the body is square to the chassis. Don't reference the shop floor unless you are certain the floor is flat and the chassis is parallel with it.

Correcting a Poor Fitting Part

Okay, so what happens if the body doesn't line up, now what? All is not lost. As with anything else, in order to make a correction you must know what is wrong, right? The solution could be as simple as making a compromise in aligning the body or as major as slicing a fender and moving it forward or back in the opening. If you are going to make the correction yourself then the key here is to just take your time and approach it systematically.

Hinges—Poor fitting panels can usually be attributed to one of two things. Either the problem lies with the hinges or the panel itself. In order

to make adjustments to doors, hoods and trunks so they do not strike the body, you need to understand how hinges work. Look at any hinge from the end of its rotational axis. As you move it, you notice that it all rotates around the hinge pin. The hinge pin is the center of the arc or rotational axis. Examine the illustration of the trunk lid on page 100, and you will notice a few things. As you lift the trunk lid, it also rotates around the hinge pins and rises out of its recess as it moves forward. At first it rises more than it moves forward and then gradually, the ratio changes until it nears the end of its travel, when it moves forward more than it rises. This is no accident, the leading edge of the lid travels in an arc that is the distance from the hinge pivot. In order for the lid to clear the body, it must rise to clear the body before it moves forward. If that arc is too short, the leading edge will strike the body. How do you correct this? As you examine the lid, opening and hinges you may see that the hinge pin (or pivot) is not far enough away

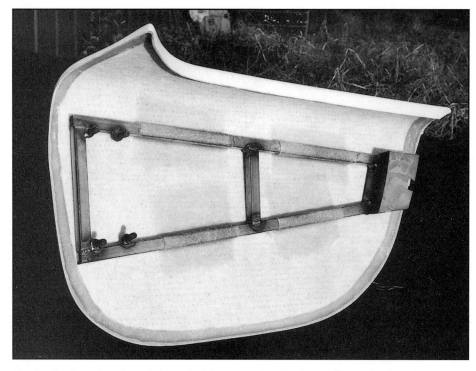

Bracing for doors is extremely important to ensure that the doors will remain aligned and work as they should. In this design, the door skin does not carry any load except for its own weight. The core mat in the door skin will prevent print through where the skin is bonded to the brace.

Doors Do Not Fit

If your door appears to be too long to fit in the opening, examine the location of the hinges. If they are not far enough forward it will force the door to the rear. Compare both doors and the openings. Are they the same? If the hinge pocket is not the same, then consider changing the location to match the door that works. This will probably involve cutting fiberglass and relocating the bolt surface of that hinge pocket.

Shaky Doors

Doors and their support structures are sometimes not strong enough to prevent flexing. When a door is fabricated entirely of fiberglass without any steel or composite bracing for the hinges or latches, that door will not stay in alignment for long. The door will flex and be difficult to get aligned. If the door doesn't have any internal bracing you may be better off to start at the beginning, so to speak. The door must have some sort of internal bracing. If

from the panel leading edge of the lid. If you have any adjustment, try to slide the lid away from the hinges. If you don't have any more adjustment, then you can relocate the hinges further away from the lid. This may require you to do some fabrication work, but it will be worth it because the lid will open smoothly and not chip the paint as it hits the body. Sometimes the edge of a trunk lid or hood will be lower than the center (the panel may be crowned in the center) and only the edges hit the body. Your solution here is to rework the corners by raising them. This will require two things. You must build up outside corners so they are even with the body and remove fiberglass from the underside of the lid corners so they then clear the edge of the body.

DOORS

Doors are often difficult to hang, and can be the most frustrating part of the build process and have been a

nightmare for quite a few novice car builders. The bulk of the problems can be traced to the same two general areas, hinges or panels.

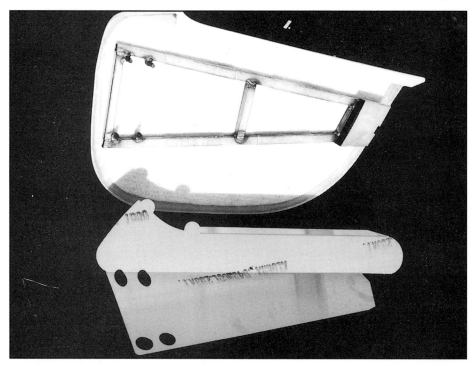

Once this door is trimmed, mounted and aligned, the aluminum skin is attached to provide a surface that can be polished or covered with a fabric. The brace offers some protection from side impact.

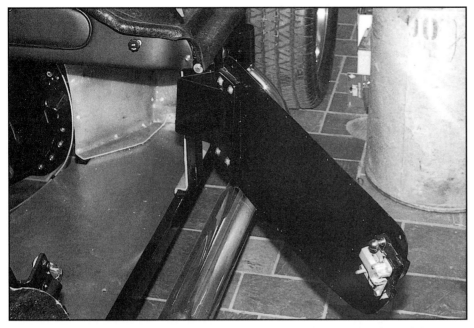

This manufacturer approaches door rigidity differently. This car uses a large piece of sheet metal to locate the door latch mechanism and offer protection from anything penetrating from the outside.

not, the door will flex and bounce around as the car moves over irregular surfaces.

As you are working with the doors, make sure that the door hinges and hinge mounting points are supported well enough so the back of the door doesn't move up and down. You should not be able to flex the door up or down! If it does flex, you will have trouble with the doors staying in alignment. The strikers will collide, causing them to not open or close smoothly and quietly. Your problem may be in the strength of the door, door hinge mounting area or both. A simple solution that works well is to fabricate a steel (or aluminum) brace for the door. Simply put, this is a brace or bracket inside the door. The hinges should be attached to a cowl brace of some sort that secures the front of the door hinges to the chassis or cowl area and keeps the hinges from moving around at that point.

Take your time, don't get discouraged and most of all, don't give up. For the more advanced (and adventurous) builder, braces could be made from a sandwich of composite cores. These can actually be stronger for their weight, and they will help the body maintain the same rate of expansion and contraction consistently.

Door (Internal) Bracing

The first thing you must do is design the brace on paper. It could be triangular in shape tying the two hinges and latch together. You may find it easier to remove the door from the car, design the brace and then modify the door to fit the brace. With the hinges and striker on the body, measure from the mounting surfaces of the hinges to the latch (or where the inside of the door will be). Your brace will sandwich the door between the hinge and the brace and extend to the rear and locate the door latch (or striker) so add shims to compensate for the door. If the latch is through-bolted (the bolts go directly through and out the other side) then you can sandwich the latch between the brace and the door skin. If the latch cannot be sandwiched then design the brace so that it secures to the rear of the door above and below the latch. You

want this assembly to open, close and latch smoothly. Spend as much time as is necessary on this step, if you don't get this right the doors will always be a problem.

Warped Door

If the door does not fit squarely in the opening or it has a warp and three of the four corners are flush with the body, then the door will need to be cut apart and reassembled to fit the opening.

To correct a warped door you will need to dismantle the door and separate its pieces. Using a saw, cut along the bond line where the skin attaches to the inner part of the door. Mount the inner part of the door with hinges and latch (and brace if necessary) in place on the car and adjust it so that it opens, closes and latches correctly.

Reassemble the Door

With the inner part of the door closed and latched, hold the skin in the proper alignment with the body lines. You may find that one or two corners are high or stick out. If you find that your door is perfect except that one corner sticks out from the body or is sunken compared to the surrounding body, think about slitting the door inner panel and taking out a wedge that is as wide as the corner is mismatched. Close the door (latched) and hold the corner flush with the body. Be creative here, use a piece of wood or pipe long enough to fit between the door corner and something immovable. Bond the pieces together with 1/16" milled glass fibers and resin.

Take the time to trim the inner door so the skin fits flush with the body. The last item to correct is the gap between the door and body. Build up or trim the door skin so you have 1/8" to 1/4" around the outside (your

Internal bracing is very important with fiberglass bodies to prevent the panels from flexing, bending or breaking. This cowl brace will be installed after the body is aligned on the chassis. Bolts will pass through the brace, floor and chassis, tying everything together.

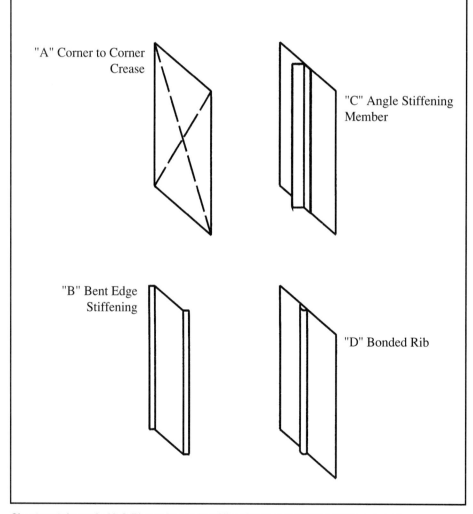

"A" Corner to Corner Crease

"C" Angle Stiffening Member

"B" Bent Edge Stiffening

"D" Bonded Rib

Sheet metal panels (A & B) can be made stiffer simply by putting a slight crease from corner to corner or by bending the edges in the same or opposite directions. Fiberglass panels will require attaching by adhesive or fasteners, and stiffening members such as angle or a half round.

clearance requirements will depend on how the doors swing), and be consistent. The smaller the gap the nicer the car will look.

Caution: Don't makes the gap so small that the door rubs on the body after it is painted as it is opened or closed. When you are satisfied with the fit of the door skin and the inner door you can reconstruct the door. Using a few (4 to 6) tabs attach the skin to the inner door. These tabs can be fiberglass or light gauge metal that is screwed or pop-riveted in place. Once secure you can open and close the door to verify its smooth operation. You need to look for any point of rubbing and make sure that you have enough clearance for your door panel and weatherstripping. Clay can be used to check for clearances. By placing a wad of clay in the area to be checked and closing the door, the clay is compressed to reflect the size of the space. Cut the clay in half and measure the thickness.

FRONT END

For our purposes, the front end concerns the area of the car from the firewall forward as pertaining to the body, not the chassis or suspension. Here are some strengthening, alignment and assembly tips that you will find helpful.

Reducing Cowl Shake & Flex

It has been my experience that one of the weakest areas in a fiberglass body can be found in bracket design and component mounting. This is especially prevalent with brackets for steering columns and windshield frames. Door latches and hinges probably come in a close second. Convertibles and roadsters are more prone to cowl and steering wheel shake because these bodies lack the

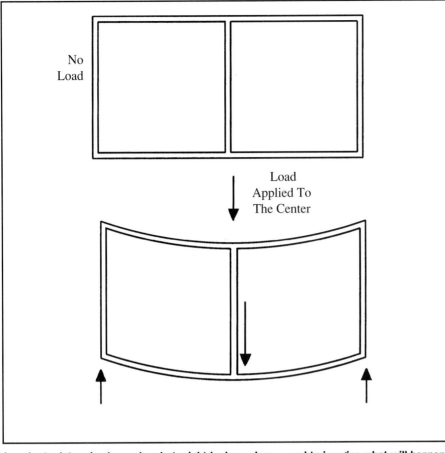

No Load

Load Applied To The Center

In order to determine how a bracket might be braced, you need to imagine what will happen as a load is distributed through that brace. This simple frame has its edges supported and a load is applied to the center; notice how the horizontal members bow downward.

structural stiffness provided by a roof.

Cowl shake (side-to-side and fore-and-aft movement), and steering wheel shake, can sometimes be traced to the same source, a weakness in the support of the firewall and cowl area. Fore-and-aft movement seems to indicate a weakness or flexing in the chassis, side-to-side seems to indicate a weakness in the firewall area (in the direction of movement). Hoops or cowl braces should extend across the car from door to door and tie the windshield frame, door hinges and steering column together to the body and maybe even the chassis. This brace, if properly designed, can also provide support to reduce the fore-and-aft movement.

Inspection

Start by determining where the movement is taking place. A video camera can be helpful. Check to make sure if any of the brace or brackets in place are bending or flexing, or if the legs of the brace are pointing in the wrong direction. The legs need to brace against the movement. Is the point where the bracket mounts to fiberglass bending or buckling?

If the brace is flexing, note how it flexes as the load is applied. Check to see if the brace can be modified to make it stiffer. This may be as simple as bending one side at a right angle or adding a piece of tubing to make a triangle.

If the body is flexing where the brace is mounted, check to see if that part of the body can be made stiffer. The mounting point may be able to be strengthened by increasing its thickness or by adding a rib.

Adding Strength Panels— Remember, when you bolt your body

down, corners are strong, flat panels are weak and easily bent. If you must use a large flat surface, such as the floor, you need to reinforce it to direct the load to the vertical panels. If your

91

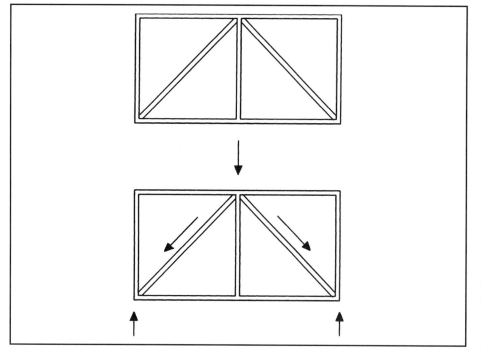

If braces are extended from the center down to the points where the bracket is supported, notice how the load is then directed into the supporting member.

floor (or any other panel) is too weak to support its intended load, all is not lost. You could increase its strength by adding a core of end grain balsa, polyurethane foam sheet, vinyl foam sheet or Nomex honeycomb to stiffen the panel. Balsa wood is one of the better choices because the edges can be easily tapered for a smooth transition, and they will conform to irregular surfaces easier.

Roughen the side of the panel where the sheet will be added. Apply a coat of resin with a filler such as "milled glass" to the roughened surface, lay the balsa sheet and apply resin and mat over the sheet. Mat is the better material for the first sheet because it will conform to the irregular surface better than cloth. Cloth can then be added over the mat to build up necessary thickness.

If the existing panel is made from a chop gun, one layer of mat followed by two layers of (approximately) 7.5 oz cloth should do the job. If it is hand laid, the thickness of the new fiberglass should equal that of the existing panel.

Strengthening Ribs or Channels—
An alternative to that might be adding a stiffening channel or rib to the flat panel. You can buy lengths of fiberglass angle or channel that could be epoxied in place and glassed over, or if you only need a small stiffening rib, one can be made using a cardboard tube slit lengthwise as a mold. With the shape on a flat surface, cover it with plastic food wrap or thin sheet poly. Mix up some resin and use fiberglass mat to build the thickness to at least 1/8". After it has cured, it can be bonded in place using the same resin and cloth. Be sure to grind both bond surfaces smooth and wash any oil, grease or mold release from the bond line.

Caution: You need to ensure that you have at least two inches between any exhaust parts and the body so you can install heat shields between the heat source and the fiberglass to prevent transferring heat to the interior and burning the fiberglass (see section on insulation and shielding).

Firewalls

Some people may argue that a fiberglass firewall, if correctly designed, would be strong enough. I agree, but that requires more creative engineering than most smaller manufacturers are capable of.

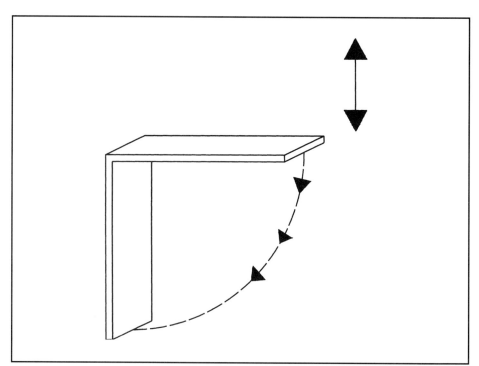

A simple right angle bracket is incapable of supporting much of a load in the vertical direction. Depending on its width it could support a minimal horizontal load. As a downward load is applied the bracket would merely bend near the bend.

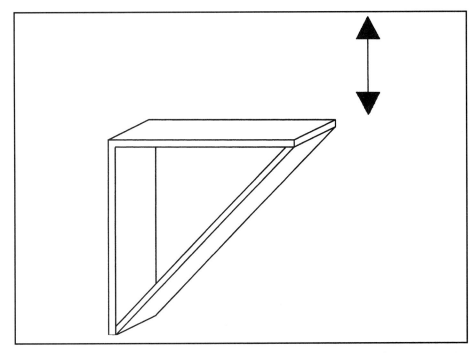

If a simple brace is extended from the outermost point downward, any load is then redirected to the supporting structure.

This oil cooler is mounted to the lower radiator shroud. The majority of the load associated with the mounting of this oil cooler is carried by the shroud and a simple strap is all that is necessary to provide any additional rigidity for the oil cooler mount.

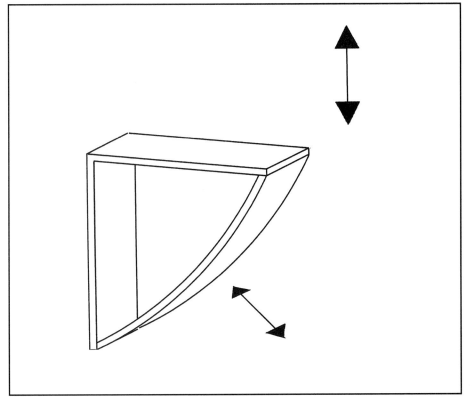

The failure mode for this simple bracket would then most likely be the brace buckling either in or out. If that leg were bent in an angle, buckling would be far less likely.

How can you tell if your firewall bracing needs help? Look under the dashboard area, and check to see if there is a network of bracing that ties to the chassis. If you see mostly a flat fiberglass panel without ridges or bracing, then you may need to beef up the mounting system.

Regardless of what you see, the only way to know for sure is to test it!

Mount your steering column on its mounting brackets as instructed by the manufacturer's instructions; do not leave any pieces off. Temporarily mount a steering wheel on the column so you will have something to grasp. Find something to sit on behind the steering that approximates the correct seating position. Grasp the steering wheel as you might when you are driving and push the steering wheel up and down and side to side. If the mounting system flexes and the steering wheel moves, then you need to examine the support system a little closer.

Does the mounting system spread the load out to the body in such a manner that it resists movement up and down or to the sides? Does it cause another part of the body to bend or flex?

Steering Column Brace

Sometimes a manufacturer will use a production car pedal bracket that is bolted through the firewall. These hold the master cylinder and steering column, in addition to the pedal

93

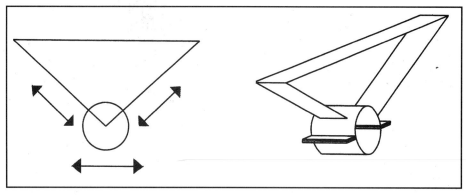

Here is an example of a simple steering column support bracket. By triangulating from each side to the body or cowl brace, any side loading is resisted. The support collar can be split to capture the column or flat bolt surface can be welded in place.

This steering column brace is fabricated from panel tubing instead of sheet metal, while not pretty, it is strong. If you need to fabricate your own, this design may give you some ideas.

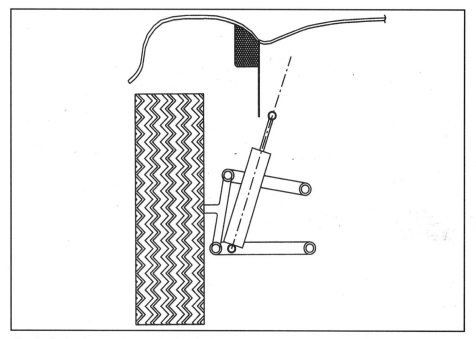

Simple air ducting can be attached or fabricated in the upper inside of the front fenders. Before you do any permanent fabrication, make a temporary duct from cardboard and turn the wheels to make sure the tire will not interfere with the location of the duct.

assembly. By itself, this is not strong enough to prevent the steering column from floating around. If your mounting system is like this, take the time to tie the column support into the cowl brace. If your body doesn't have a cowl brace, fabricate one! Run the brace or hoop across the car from door opening to door opening and extending down to the floor to support the column and resist any side movement. You may find that you need to gusset the corners of your hoop to minimize flexing.

Ignoring this might result in a car whose steering wheel will move side to side and up and down as you apply pressure to it as you might when you are parking, or shake around when you go over a bump. The cost in labor and materials will be small and the car will have a more secure feeling.

Design Concept—Triangulate if you can. Align the legs of the bracket so that they are in line with the load. This way the legs are under tension or compression, not bending. If you can not triangulate, add gussets to minimize flexing.

Examine the illustration showing a simple triangulated steering column brace. If the steering wheel is forced up or down, the two angled legs of the brace are pushed evenly (in compression) or pulled evenly (in tension) and prevent movement in those directions. If the wheel is forced to the side, one leg is put under compression and the other is put in tension, again, preventing the steering column from moving. Also note the ends of the legs are tied together to prevent them from spreading apart or moving towards each other. Anchoring each leg will produce the same effect.

Engine Air Intake

Let's spend a moment considering the air your engine will consume, its

The first step in sealing the hood scoop to the carburetor was to transfer the carburetor center to the inside of the hood. A reference mark was made midway across the cowl to measure forward to the air cleaner stud.

A yardstick was laid from fender to fender over the center of the carburetor and marks were made on the fenders at the point where the yardstick crossed it.

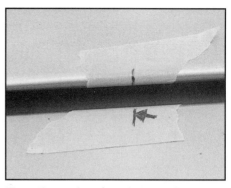

These three points were then transferred to the inside of the hood. These three points intersect directly above the center of the carburetor. This point is important to make sure the scoop floor is centered around the air cleaner.

filtering and routing. Dust particles are abrasive and will cause accelerated internal wear of your engine, so do not run your engine for extended periods without an air cleaner. The amount of horsepower and torque your engine will produce is affected by the amount of air and fuel it can ingest. Your choice of air cleaner should therefore not be taken lightly, and nor should your grille area or hood scoop, if any. How big should your air cleaner be? As a place to start, you should use the largest air cleaner that will fit under the hood of your car. Consider using an air cleaner at least as large as the factory unit and if you have enough room above the carburetor or throttle body, consider installing a taller filter element. The larger the air cleaner element, the more surface area available for filtering and the less resistive.

Grille Opening—The grille opening is a high pressure area and a good location for the air intake. The inlet and ducting should be at least the same size as the bore of your carburetor or throttle body, at least 4" in diameter. The inlet and ducting don't have to be round but its opening should have the same number of square inches. The ducting should be as smooth as possible with smooth turns; ribbed (wire reinforced) ducting will be turbulent and not flow as

much air as a smooth pipe or duct will.

Hood & Hood Scoop

As you are fitting the hood the items you want to look for are: Does the hinged end of the hood strike the body as it swings through its arc? If so can you shift the hood away from the hinges toward the latch enough to clear? If not the next area to look at is whether or not the pivot point of the hinge can be moved further away from the hood. This will increase the radius and allow the hood to rise out of the recess more before it moves.

If your car's hood has a scoop, you might consider using it to feed fresh cool air to the engine. Remember, the cooler the intake charge of air and gas, the denser the mixture, and the more efficient the engine is.

This is not a difficult job but does require a bit of patience. For this discussion we will assume that your hood is fitted to the body and works correctly. We will also assume that the engine is fed fuel by a carburetor or throttle body injection system sitting in the center of a conventional intake manifold and you will be using a factory style air cleaner housing. The filter element will be your choice of a factory style paper or one of the high flow reusable styles that fit within the confines of the factory air cleaner

housing. Take advantage of the situation and put in a taller air cleaner element if you can. You will only be limited by the distance between the carburetor flange and the inside of the hood. Leave about 1/2" for clearance. The air cleaner snorkel will be discarded and the upper half of the air cleaner housing will need to be modified. Tuned Port Induction systems typically will take their air from the front of the car and will benefit from having a duct to a scoop or into the grille area ahead of the radiator.

Note: When the engine is first started on a cold morning, ice can form on the throttle plates if the atmospheric conditions are correct, i.e., air temperature, dew point, etc. This could prevent the engine from idling until the throttle plates heat sufficiently to melt the ice. If you live in an area where carburetor heat is necessary, then you may want to consider directing warm air into the finished scoop by using the valve from the factory air cleaner snorkel. The valve (sometimes referred to as an air motor) could control a flapper that would seal the scoop opening. The duct would feed warm air into the scoop and air cleaner, and once the motor warms up the vacuum motor would then open the scoop and allow

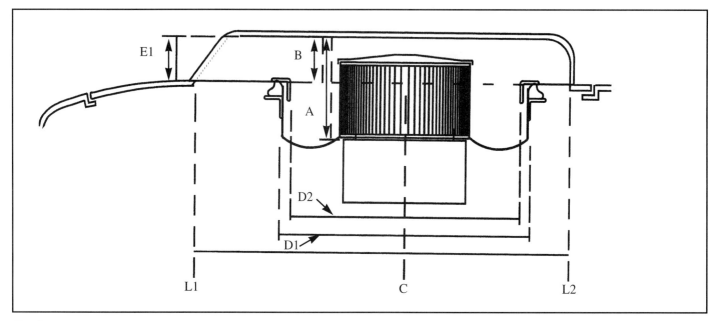

Here is an example of sealing a hood scoop to a carburetor or throttle body. A little sheet aluminum, a factory air cleaner housing and a Saturday afternoon are about all you need. The dimensions are the measurements you'll need to make.

Cardboard was used to make a mockup of the scoop floor. Once satisfied that the air cleaner would clear the mockup, the shape was transferred to aluminum and mounted to the inside of the hood using the carburetor center as reference.

cool outside air to enter.

Making a Plenum—In order to make a functioning sealed hood scoop, you must create a box or plenum by making a "floor" for the hood scoop that will seal to the air cleaner base. Cardboard works well for making a template. You can cut and trim it with scissors, bend it and add to it using glue (hot) or masking tape until you have the shape that will

work best for you. Before you can start any fabrication, though, you need to understand what you have for clearance between the inside of the hood and the carburetor. You need to know the exact center of the carburetor and its location relative to the hood scoop opening. For example, you must know its location, left to right, front to back and distance from below the hood. To fabricate your

scoop floor, you will need sheet cardboard, light gauge metal, masking tape, a fine point marker, a straightedge long enough to bridge the engine compartment, a tape measure or yard stick, and an air cleaner of some sort. You will need to attach a rubber gasket to the edge of the air cleaner to seal against the scoop floor. Extruded aluminum wheelwell trim is a good choice because it is easily bent and provides a suitable location for the sealing gasket.

Measurements—First you will need to know the following measurements:

A = vertical distance between the air cleaner flange (top of the carburetor) and the inside of the hood.

B = the vertical distance between the inside of the hood and the scoop floor (this is determined by the height of the scoop inlet at the front of the hood).

C = the center point (or center line) of the carburetor.

D1 = the diameter of the air cleaner base.

D2 = the diameter of the opening of the scoop floor, (this is smaller than D1).

E1 = the height of the scoop inlet at

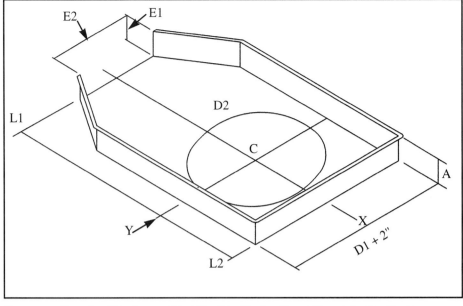

Your scoop floor should look something like this. The length, width and depth will vary depending on your hood. Note the location of the necessary measurements.

the front of the hood.

E2 = the width of the scoop inlet at the front of the hood.

L1 = the distance from the center of the carburetor forward to the opening in the hood.

L2 = the distance from the center of the carburetor rearward to the end of the scoop or where the scoop floor will end.

X and Y = the two lines that you made on the fenders and cowl of the car to locate the center of the carburetor. X will be the fore-and-aft line while Y the left-to-right line.

Next, you need to locate "C," the center of the carburetor, from the front to back and left to right. This can be done by laying the yardstick or any other straightedge from fender to fender, across the body so it passes over the air cleaner mounting stud. Do the same from the front of the engine compartment to the firewall. This will be the center from where all your measurements are derived from. Put a piece of masking tape on each fender and mark next to the straightedge. These marks will be X and Y, your forward and aft and left and right reference line.

Caution: Before you make your marks on the masking tape, measure from a fixed point, such as the firewall, forward to your straightedge and make sure your "X" and "Y" lines are square to the body and 90 degrees to each other. Close the hood and transfer the "X" and "Y" marks to hood. Open the hood and draw a (light) line across the inside of the hood. Where the two lines intersect will be "C," the center of the carburetor. These lines will be used to align your cardboard template to the hood for trial-fitting before transferring it to the final material.

In order to determine "A," the distance between the carburetor flange and the hood, put something long enough on the carburetor flange to hold the hood open. This can be cardboard, plastic or metal. The important thing is that it is strong enough to support the weight of the hood and long enough to prevent the hood from closing. Gently close the hood until it touches this object and then measure the distance that the hood is held open. Knowing the length of the object, subtract the distance that the hood is held open.

This will tell you "A," the approximate distance from the top of the carburetor flange to the inside of the hood. Next, determine "D1," the diameter of the air cleaner housing; "L1," the distance "C" is from the front of the scoop; and "L2," the distance rearward form "C" to the end of the scoop.

Make a Template—Once you have these measurements, you can design your scoop on paper. This will allow you to have an idea what it will look like before you start. Start with the "X" and "Y" lines, remembering that almost every other measurement starts or relates to "C," the point where "X" and "Y" cross, so they must be square to each other. Transfer all the measurements to the cardboard using your design and be sure to extend the X and Y lines all the way out to the edge of the template. Fold, trim and glue until the template will fit against the inside contour of the hood and the left-to-right and forward-to-back lines align with those on the hood.

The scoop floor must extend from the hood scoop opening "B" and "E" to the rear of the hood and could make a transition in height. Remember, we are using a factory air cleaner housing to mate the carburetor to the scoop, so the scoop floor must be at least as wide as the air cleaner base to seal against "D1" plus 2" for a sealing gasket. At a minimum, the scoop must extend beyond the center of the air cleaner stud 1/2 of "D1" plus 1", so the air cleaner base will have adequate sealing surface to the rear. You will need to cut hole "D2" into the scoop floor. This should be slightly smaller than the diameter of the air cleaner base. You will need a piece of aluminum extrusion to fit into "D2" and extend down into the air cleaner base. This will add strength to the scoop floor without blocking the path of the incoming air.

A factory air cleaner was modified to fit up into the scoop floor. The top half of the air cleaner housing was reduced in diameter to the size of the air cleaner element. The lower half of the air cleaner housing was lowered and a gasket mounting surface was added to press against the scoop floor.

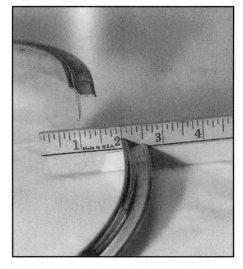

This is a sample of the aluminum extrusion used as a gasket surface for the air cleaner and reinforcing for the air cleaner hole in the scoop floor.

The modified air cleaner housing and high performance K&N air cleaner element will protrude into the scoop as the hood is lowered. By using a factory air cleaner housing, you are assured that the carburetor and transmission linkage are sure to clear.

The same extrusion will work well on the outside of the air cleaner housing to stiffen it if it has to be cut down and/or provide a place to bond the rubber air cleaner to the scoop floor seal.

The height of the sides of the scoop floor at "D2" will be determined by "A," the distance from the air cleaner mounting surface on the carburetor minus the height of the air cleaner base. If the scoop floor slopes up from the scoop opening, that's bad. We don't want the space to be small enough to be restrictive. Trim the height of the air cleaner base sides if you have to so the floor is level or slopes down. The greater the amount of air cleaner element exposed the better. The side of the air cleaner base should be tall enough to attach the aluminum extrusion so a seal can be installed.

Note: If the scoop floor is large and floppy, you can stiffen it by creasing it slightly in a criss-cross pattern from corner to corner before you cut "D2." This is easily done by laying the metal on a flat surface and locating a metal straightedge from corner to corner across the large floppy area. Bend it enough to crease the surface. Be careful not to bend it too far, because it could throw off your other measurements.

Fiberglass Option—You are not forced to use metal for your scoop. You could very easily use this design and information to make a fiberglass scoop floor. Simply transfer all these measurements to a block of urethane foam and make a plug. Follow all the procedures, including trial fitting. If all is satisfactory, coat the plug with wax and lay up the fiberglass and when done, bond to the inside of the hood.

Securing Scoop Floor—Once the scoop is made, you need to secure the floor of the scoop to the inside of the hood. If the scoop floor is to be removable, consider using two strips of heavier aluminum or fiberglass, one on each side of the scoop. These should be drilled and tapped to accept screws to hold the scoop floor to the hood.

Attach the strips to the scoop floor.

The air cleaner element is now sealed to the hood and in the high pressure fresh air stream. The air that cooled the radiator is now forced to exit under the car and not be drawn into the carburetor.

This scoop is close enough to the front of the car so it will benefit from being in the high pressure area and receive an ample supply of cool air.

Mix up some epoxy (not polyester) adhesive, add a thickener if the surface is not smooth, roughen and wash the surface and apply the epoxy to the hood and strips. Hold the scoop floor securely against the inside of the hood. You could use small self-tapping screws and temporarily screw the strips to the hood until the epoxy cures, then remove the screws and fill the holes or clamps.

After the adhesive cures you can remove the screws and remove the scoop floor for any further work such as additional epoxy to fill any voids between the hood and the strips.

If your manufacturer has not provided a smooth finished surface inside the hood, now is a good time to take care of that detail; just apply body filler and sand smooth. If you don't do this, every time you open the hood and look through the hole into the scoop you will see that rough surface and regret not haven taken the time to smooth that surface. The scoop floor can be engine turned (tiny swirl pattern), polished to a mirror finish, powder coated or painted.

Modifying Air Cleaner Housing— The air cleaner top needs to have its diameter trimmed so that it is only large enough to cover and secure the air cleaner element. This will allow the air to freely enter the element when it protrudes into the scoop plenum. Tin snips will work for this. Finish the edge with a file. The air cleaner base will need all holes that may have once been used plugged or covered. You may need to cut down the side of the base and reduce its height so it is just below the floor of the scoop (about 1/2"). The height will be determined by "A" minus "B" and will depend on your situation. Form and attach an "L" shaped aluminum extrusion near the top of the air cleaner base. Remember, this must be high enough to allow the rubber seal to touch the scoop floor.

As a final step, check for interference with the distributor cap and wires, any hoses or linkages.

HOOD/TRUNK GAS SPRINGS

After you have mounted the hood and trunk to your body, you will need a method of holding them in the open position. Some manufacturers will supply ratcheting slide mechanisms similar to those on MGB's. If you

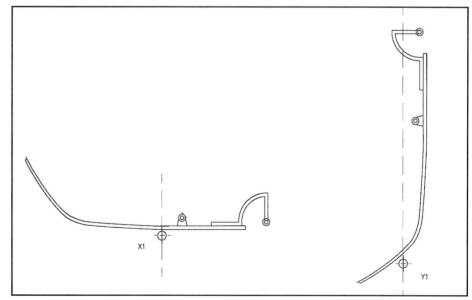

In order to find the center of gravity of you hood or trunk, you need to balance it in both the x & y planes.

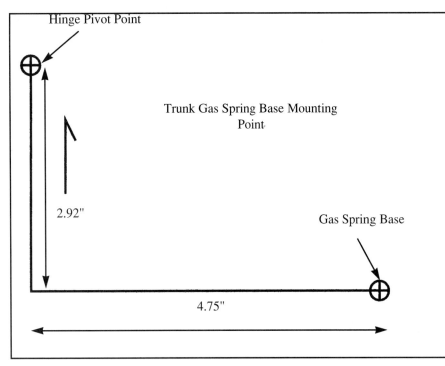

Hinge Pivot Point

Trunk Gas Spring Base Mounting Point

2.92"

Gas Spring Base

4.75"

This is a sample location for the mounting point for the base of the gas spring. The gas spring manufacturer will calculate the location based on the information supplied on the work sheet. The hinge pivot point is aligned with the hood hinge pivot and then you locate the ball mount for the gas spring.

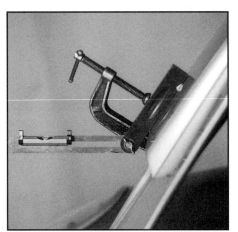

The gas spring manufacturer needs to know the maximum opening angle of the hood or trunk in order to specify the location for the mounting points. Using the angle finder and string bubble, set the level so the bubble is centered. Using a protractor, determine if there is any angle between the two parts of the angle finder. Make a note of this angle.

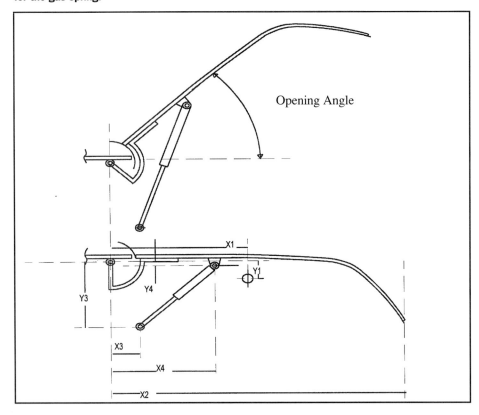

Opening Angle

X1

Y1

Y4

Y3

X3

X4

X2

These are the points that need to be measured in order for the gas spring manufacturer to calculate the correct gas spring size, pressure, and mounting locations. Take your time and double check your measurements. Any error will effect the gas spring performance.

Open the hood to its maximum angle and reset the angle finder so the string bubble is level. Using the protractor again, determine the new angle of the angle finder. Subtract the smaller from the larger angle and this will be the total opening angle.

fit into. Electric openers work well and use a mechanism that resembles a window crank mechanism. These are mounted to the body with a link that extends to the hood. Other variations include gas springs, motorized "Worm Screw" mechanisms and torsion bars to name a few. Torsion bars have been used on production cars for years and have proven to be reliable. Usually there are two that extend across the body from each side; one end of the torsion bar is anchored to the body and the other to the hood lid.

Counterbalancing your trunk and

don't already have something or would like to consider an alternative you could use a prop rod that is nothing more than a solid piece of round stock mounted to the body or hood and a socket for the other end to

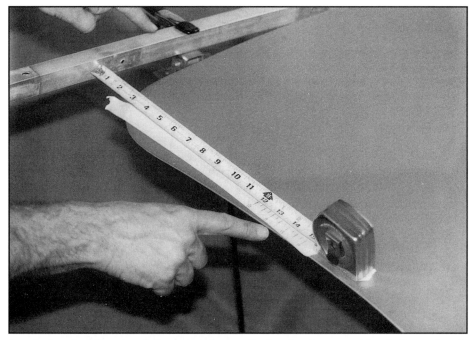

In order to select the correct gas springs for your trunk or hood, you must locate the center of gravity. This should be measured from the hinge pivot. Apply masking tape over the approximate mid point of the deck lid and mark it from the hinge pivot.

Balance the trunk or hood on a dowel or broom stick and note the distance from the hinge pivot point. This is the center of balance.

hood is one of those items that will make using it more enjoyable (and safer). These small touches add to the quality of your car and show that thought and attention to detail went into its construction and will add value to the car should you decide to sell it.

For this example we will consider installing gas springs. If you examine almost any production car you will notice that a number of them use gas springs to counterbalance the trunks, hatches, and some hoods. They are compact, relatively inexpensive, easy to install, and a lot nicer than a prop rod or the ratcheting mechanical prop that may have come with your kit. Most models can withstand temperatures of 212° F to -40° so underhood use should be no problem.

Gas springs can be installed so that the lid will rise automatically, meaning that when you pull the hood release (in the case of a hood), the hood will rise to its open position. Or, the installation can require you to lift the lid a few degrees before it rises. A word of caution though: If your hood is hinged at the rear, you must have a safety latch to prevent the hood from rising up if something happens while you are driving down the road. For front hinged hoods, this is not as critical, but it should be considered as well.

You have two ways of selecting and installing gas springs. One is to look for a car with a hood or trunk of approximately the same size and weight as yours and use those mounting points and springs. There is a downside to this approach though. Gas springs intended for use on steel lids have a stronger spring, typically about 150 lbs. For a fiberglass lid, that amount of pressure may cause the lid to bend without some sort of stiffening brace. Gas springs for fiberglass lids typically will have spring rates about one third that, or about 50 lbs.

The other more exact method involves making some calculations and installing the gas spring that is intended for the work load. Expect to use one gas spring on each side of the panel unless the hood/trunk has

enough torsion stiffness to resist twisting.

The worksheet on page 102 will help you determine the information for your specific application.

Locating the Center of Gravity

The first step is to locate the center of gravity of the hood or trunk lid. To find it, you must measure horizontally and vertically from the hinge pivot. The easiest way to do this requires removing the panel(s) from the car and doing the following:

Hoods—Because the hood is usually flat it only needs to be checked in one way (horizontally). To do this, place something round, like a broom handle or dowel, across a pair of sawhorses or chairs. Balance the hood (with hinges attached if possible) across the dowel. Measure the distance from the dowel to the pivot point of the hinge; that will be Y1, and in the case of a flat panel, X1 also.

Trunk Lids—Trunk lids are generally curved from front to rear and therefore require you to check their balance in two planes in order to find the center of balance. Finding Y1 and X1 is a little different, however. Using the same broomstick handle and sawhorse arrangement, turn the

Gas Spring Worksheet

Use the following worksheet to determine the information specific to your application. This information is the same for a hood or trunk lid.

	Hood	Trunk	

• Y1 and X1 determine a panel's center of gravity. Remove the panel and measure and balance accurately; guessing will not necessarily get you the results you expect.

Y1 = _____   _____ Inches (MM)

X1 = _____   _____ Inches (MM)

• X2 is the panel overall length from the hinge pivot.

X2 = _____   _____ Inches (MM)

• Opening angle is the difference between the closed position and the full open position.

Opening Angle = _____   _____ Degrees

• Weight of hood or trunk lid at (X2) the furthest point

Weight = _____   _____ Lbs. (N)

2. Based on the above information, the gas spring manufacturer will specify the correct gas springs and the correct mounting locations.

Hood PN _____   Trunk PN _____

• X3 and Y3 are the gas spring to body mounting location.

Y3 = _____   _____ Inches (MM)

X3 = _____   _____ Inches (MM)

• Y4 and X4 are the gas spring to hood or trunk mounting location.

Y4 = _____   _____ Inches (MM)

X4 = _____   _____ Inches (MM)

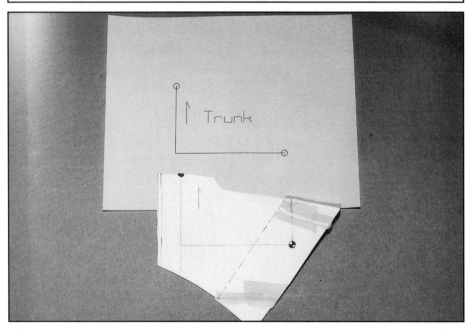

After supplying all the necessary information, the gas spring manufacturer will supply you with the proper gas springs and the proper location of the mounting points. Those points are then transferred to a piece of cardboard and a template is made to fit.

trunk lid upside-down and balance it as you did for the hood, this will be X1. Turn the lid so that it has the hinges pointing straight up toward the ceiling and balance on the rear of the lid, Y1.

Note: Wrapping a piece of rubber around the stick will help prevent the lid from slipping off as you are trying to balance the hood and (especially) the trunk. Along with the rubber, you may need to use something like vise grips or C clamps on the edge of the lid to prevent it from slipping.

Installation

Because the gas springs are always under pressure, you must make sure the mounting points are strong enough to handle the load. Your fiberglass hood or trunk could also bend if not reinforced with additional fiberglass, steel or aluminum at those mounting points. There is a very good chance you will have to redesign the mounts, because the body will flex and move as you try to close the lid. Just watch where the fiberglass is flexing and modify your design to stiffen those areas.

Caution: The gas spring cylinder is under approximately 2,400 pounds of pressure when they are open and higher when they are closed. Do not attempt to bend the mount on the cylinder end. If you crack the weld, you could have a missile on your hands.

• Do not bend the piston rod end to align it with its mount. Even if you are successful and don't distort the gas spring, when you close the hood /trunk, any misalignment will increase and the gas spring ends will still be out of alignment again.

• Install your gas springs on ball joints instead of pins. This will allow the gas spring to move as necessary if the mounts are not in alignment and

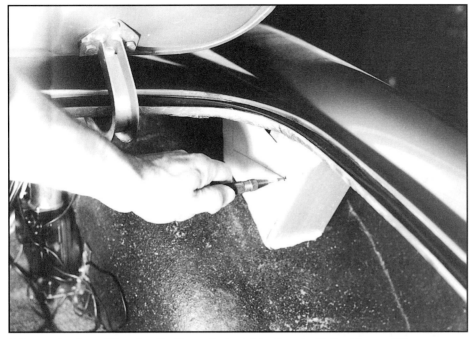

This template is positioned so the hinge pivot point is aligned with the hinge and the gas spring base mount point is transferred to a suitable bracket.

The gas spring ball mounts can be threaded into any existing brace or bracket or finished brackets can be ordered with the gas springs.

This deck lid uses two gas springs that are installed in such a manner that the trunk "auto rises" as soon as the trunk is lifted beyond two inches. This is a nice feature if you have both hands full of goodies from the auto parts store or packages from shopping with your wife.

This gas spring has had its ends bent so they will align with their mounts. Do not do this! Gas springs can have as much as 2,400 psi. If you snap an end off you could have a rocket in your hands. Even though this gas spring had its ends bent to align with the mounts, when the lid is closed the ends will be out of alignment again. Use ball mounts!

prevent any twisting.

• The gas spring should be installed with the piston rod facing down, this will allow the oil to keep the seal and shaft lubricated.

• Protect the piston rod from water, dirt or paint, etc.

• Using the X3 and Y3 dimensions supplied by the manufacturer, locate the gas spring to the body. Be very careful about this step because this location determines the opening leverage. If the gas spring is not located properly, the spring may not stay open or you could damage the gas spring if it bottoms out when you are closing it. Attach the base at X1 and Y1 (manufacturer's recommendations) and open the lid to its maximum opening angle, swing the gas spring up to the lid. Hold the upper mount to the lid and mark it for attachment.

BODY INSULATION

A very large part of what makes a production car comfortable is its acoustical and thermal insulation. Think about how nice and relaxing it is to ride in an expensive (and quiet)

Here is a novel approach to raising a hood, trunk or pickup truck bed cover. This owner uses hydraulic cylinders mounted and aluminum flat stock as lever arms.

Thermo Tec "Cool It" mat is intended to insulate floors and firewalls from heat and noise. This resin bonded silica blanket can also be used indoors and on the inside of hoods. The foil reflects the heat and the silica absorbs the heat and noise.

car. When you first planned out what you wanted this car to be, I don't think hot and noisy was on the list, unless you're building a sports car and want a racing exhaust note to add a few extra "audible horsepower."

While on the highway, all you want to hear are the tunes on your radio. You certainly don't want to toast your toes because of the heat coming through the firewall and floor either. The noise and heat generated by the motor can be oppressive if allowed to conduct through the floor and firewall unimpeded. Remember, excessive heat and noise can cause fatigue and will have a dramatic impact on the comfort of both the driver and passenger.

Excessive heat in the engine compartment can cause lubricants to deteriorate quickly. If you are using an automatic transmission, the routing and protection of the cooling lines must be carefully considered with regard to heat. Remember, one line will be carrying hot fluid from the transmission to the transmission cooler and the other will carry cooled fluid back.

And, don't forget your brake and gas lines must also be protected from the heat. If you boil the gas in your fuel lines, you could create vapor lock, and I guarantee it will be at the most inopportune time. Thermal protection must also be provided for the parts of the fiberglass body that are within close proximity of exhaust pipes.

Let's not forget how easily excessive and unwanted noise can ruin a nice ride too. A little insulation in the right places and your ride will be much more pleasant, just as you imagined it would be.

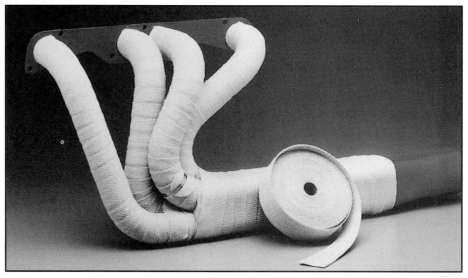

Exhaust insulating wrap will help retain most of the exhaust heat so the exhaust gases will be less dense and flow faster. Higher velocity equals increased scavenging.

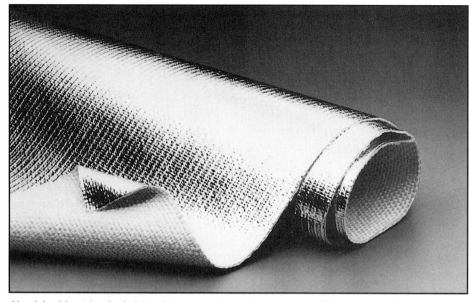

Aluminized heat barrier is intended as an exhaust header or manifold wrap. Retaining heat in the exhaust generates increased engine efficiency. Keeping more heat in the exhaust will lower the engine compartment temperature.

Heat Insulation

Let's start with the heat where it is being generated. As the exhaust gases leave the cylinder through the exhaust valve, it is still expanding and cooling. If we can keep most of the heat in the engine and the exhaust system, we can improve the efficiency of the engine.

By using insulation or wrapping at least your headers/manifolds the exhaust temperatures remain high because you reduce the loss or transfer of the heat through the exhaust pipes. By keeping more heat in the exhaust, you maximize exhaust scavenging. Also, along with lower engine compartment temperatures, if you happen to be running catalytic converters, they will light off quicker and prolong the life of the exhaust system.

Now let's talk about what you can do for the body. The more heat you keep away from the body and its parts the better. If you are planning on installing an air conditioner, this will help reduce the amount of heat that the air conditioner has to deal with. Air conditioners are "sized" for a particular "heat load." That means that they have the capacity to remove only a certain amount of heat from the air. If you have a lot of heat radiating into the passenger compartment, this heat load will be added to all the other heat coming through the glass and body, and the A/C may not be able to remove that much heat. In cooler weather, the opposite occurs. As the car moves down the road and air rushes over the windshield, doors, windows and under the floor, heat is absorbed and removed from the passenger compartment. Insulating the firewall under the transmission tunnel, floor and even inside the doors will minimize the amount of heat loss.

Magically, the car is easier to heat, cool, and is quieter.

Proper Insulation Location

At a minimum you should insulate the transmission tunnel, firewall and the underside of the floor using insulating mat material intended for exterior use. In the areas of more intense heat, metal heat shields may be required. Attached these to the body or the source of the heat in addition to the insulation attached to the body.

Thermal Insulating Materials

Exhaust wrap is composed of silica based fabric. It is intended to wrap headers and the exhaust pipes. It will lower the temperature under the hood, because more heat is kept in the exhaust system.

Aluminized heat barrier is made up of woven silica with a flexible aluminized finish and is used on the body to reflect heat.

Thermo Shield is a fabric-based high silica material with a metallic reflective finish. It is in sheet form and is intended to wrap around hoses, tubing and wiring bundles.

Mat is intended to insulate fire walls, floors, above transmissions, hoods and doors. It is composed of

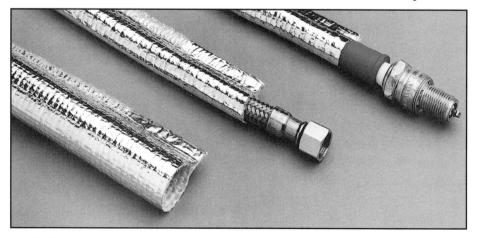

Existing hoses and wiring harnesses can be protected from radiant heat with Thermo Sleeve, an adhesive backed thermal laminate.

Thin aluminum polyurethane HVAC insulation works well to shield and reflect heat from the foot panels. Notice that aluminum strips are used to hold the shield in place.

resin-bonded silica blanket insulation, sandwiched between a Mylar facing and a foil facing. The foil reflects the heat and the silica dissipates the heat that isn't reflected and acts as a sound barrier also. These materials can be held in place with mechanical fasteners or adhesives.

Thermo-Sleeve is basically Thermo Shield in a sleeve form and is intended to protect tubing and wires in high heat areas.

Metal Heat Shields—These are easy to fabricate from flat aluminum or steel (galvanized or stainless) sheet for floors and tubing for pipes. If you are trying to make a shield to reflect exhaust heat, simple, inexpensive exhaust pipe of a larger diameter works well. The choice of material isn't as important as its design and how it is attached.

There must be an air space between the heat source, the shield and the material it is protecting. The idea behind the shield is that as the heat is radiated, it is reflected away from the object being protected. The shield is cooled because as air flows around all the sides of the shield, heat is given up to the air and is prevented from radiating to the object being protected. The spacing between the body and the shield must be large enough to allow unrestricted airflow. At least three quarters of an inch is necessary.

A very simple and effective shield can be fabricated from inexpensive exhaust tubing. The tube is cut lengthwise, then cut to the length necessary with the exception of leaving a tab on each end. These tabs are bent to provide an offset and mounting point.

These simple heat shields can be very functional and if you coat them with "Spray Cold Galvanizing" or one of the ceramic exhaust coatings available, they will last a very long time.

Don't overlook other items in the engine compartment, like your starter motor or battery that may need shielding from the heat.

Noise & Vibration

As you operate your car, you will be exposed to a variety of noises and vibrations. The sounds you will hear are a combination of noises produced by items like your engine, i.e., the fan blades, the valvetrain, camshaft gears and chain, and exhaust note. Other noises will come from things like the tires rolling along the road and wind as it flows over the car's body.

Different parts of the body will vibrate at different times due to the natural harmonics of that component. Dealing with them all will require different methods, so you need to work with them one at a time.

When it comes to controlling the noise that you will be exposed to from your car, you need to think about a couple of things.

Identify the Source—In order to treat the noise problem, you have to identify the source of the noise and then its path. Of course, the best way to deal with noise is to eliminate it at the source. In the case of a vibration in the steering column when you drive over expansion joints, a rubber

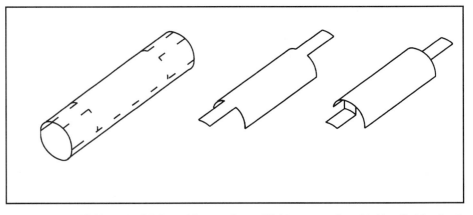

A simple heat shield can be fabricated from a piece of light gauge exhaust tubing that is about 1" larger than the pipes you are shielding. Cut the tubing as the dashed lines indicate, bend the tabs, and clamp in place with worm style hose clamps of the appropriate size.

You can determine the approximate maximum width of your tires and wheels by holding a piece of cardboard against the drum or rotor as shown and measure as shown. In this case the distance is approximately 4 1/2 inches. If you need to put more rubber on the road, you can determine if a wheel with negative offset will fit by measuring in from the edge of the cardboard. Adding the two together gives you an approximate width.

steel, much like you would spray undercoat on firewalls, floors and on the inside of your door skin. It can also be rolled or brushed on. Because of this method of application, it will cover more of the panel more easily and get into nooks and crannies. It is water-based and is fully cured in about 48 hours, delivering its maximum dampening ability. It can then be painted with almost any paint. This material is temperature tolerant and is a thermal insulator also. Noise Killer has been used on catalytic converter heat shields to stop the harmonic vibration that sometimes causes heat shields to buzz. Admittedly, it is a little expensive, but the ease of use allows you to insulate your cockpit in a very short amount of time.

TIRE & WHEEL CLEARANCE

What size tire will fit within the wheelwells of your car body? If the manufacturer hasn't, can't, or won't supply that information, all is not lost. The following information will help you determine what will fit. Determining tire diameter, and deciphering the sidewall markings, is covered on page 78 in Chapter 6. Review this information before reading on.

Tires

You can get a rough idea of what diameter tire will fit by measuring the fender opening and subtracting about 4 inches. For example if the fender opening measures 30" across, subtract 4" (2" each side) for clearance. This results in a tire diameter of about 26". You will only be able to get a more precise measurement after the body is mounted on the chassis.

Axle Center—First, locate the center of the axle, a large "framer's

insulator between the steering box and the steering column will isolate the steering wheel from most of the vibrations. In the case of exhaust noise you could eliminate it by shutting the engine off but then that's not why you are building the car, so you need to deal with the noise. With the exhaust, check first to make sure the pipe is not touching the chassis or body, or that it is mounted with rubber mounts. If it isn't touching the body, or is mounted with rubber mounts, then adding resonators, additional mufflers or re-routing the exhaust pipes and tip so the exhaust exits to the rear of the car will reduce the exhaust noise. With side pipes, pointing the exhaust tips down will improve the noise level somewhat.

Insulate the Path—Next, you need to insulate the path the noise is taking from the source to your ear. Insulation on the floor will absorb the noise and a barrier will prevent the noise from

entering the space. Most of the noise will probably enter through the floor, the firewall or the entire body may vibrate. Insulation mounted inside the cockpit will help block and absorb the noise plus the mass of the insulation will tend to dampen any vibrations and reduce reverberation noise that may occur.

You have a few options for insulating the firewall and floor. Insulations available include resin bonded silica blanket with Mylar and foil facings; asphalt-based sheets and nylon-based sheets. These need to be cut and fit in order to conform to the contours of the surface.

Noise Killer—There is another material on the market called "Noise Killer." This material is a "Viscoelastic Coating" that is marketed as a dampening material for use primarily in the automotive stereo market. It is a liquid that can be sprayed directly to fiberglass and

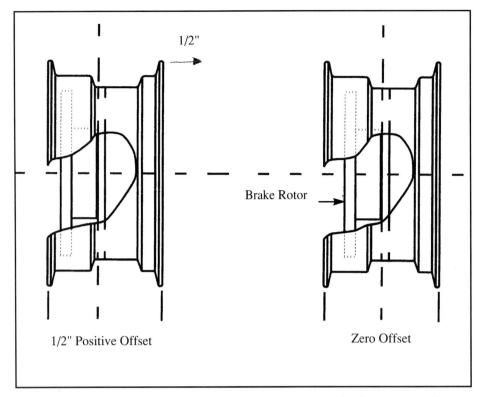

1/2"

Brake Rotor

1/2" Positive Offset

Zero Offset

Wheel offset refers to the location of the bolt surface. A wheel with 0 offset has 50% of its width on each side of the bolt surface. A wheel with 1/2" positive offset has an additional 1/2" to the outside.

square" will help. The square will allow your measurements to be relative and "square" to the axle. Place one edge of the square on the drum (or disc) bolt surface and measure from the edge that sticks out to the fender edge (you are looking for the closest point). Don't forget to factor in the distance from the edge of the square to the center of the axle.

Let's assume that you found the distance to be 15" at the closest point. This means your tire diameter will be about 30" minus the necessary clearance. You need to subtract room for tire clearance. For our example, let's use 2" on each side. This results in a tire diameter of 26", (i.e., 30" − 4"). Half of this is the radius, or 13" as measured from the center of the rotor or drum.

Tire Width—In order to see how wide a tire you can fit in the fender, you need to measure from the bolt surface of your drums or rotors to the nearest object inside the fender at that

13" radius. Holding the square against the bolt surface as the rim would sit, rotate the drum. Measure to the nearest point inside the fender and note the smallest distance. Multiply that by 2 and that is the approximate width tire you can fit under the fender if you use a rim with "0" offset. Let's say that you found that the minimum dimension was 3.5". Multiply that by 2 and you see that you could put a 7" wide tire in the fender. This gives you a place to start. You could even go to the tire store with this information.

Knowing the diameter and width of your theoretical tire gives you a point to start from. Add in a wheel (rim) diameter and an aspect ratio for the tires' sidewall and you will know the maximum tire size that will fit your car's body.

Wheels

What kind of offset do you want or can you put under your fenders? Start with a wheel with the offset that is

recommended for the donor car. Measure the clearance from that tire/rim to the fender, this will show you how much room you have.

Note: Center line and offset are terms that refer to your rims. This is the location of the bolt surface that contacts your rim or disc. On a rim with "0" offset, this line is in the center of the width of the wheel. Some manufacturers offer rims with positive or negative offsets from the center line. A rim with a positive offset will move the tire out away from the axle, and a negative offset will move the tire in the fender.

Caution: Be careful when you get into really big tires and close quarters. Try to maintain 1/2" clearance between the fender and tire side wall. The offset could cause the tire to hit the suspension when you turn the tires all the way left or right or if the suspension is fully compressed as might happen if you go over a dip in the road.

You may require large amounts of rubber on the rear, and a rim with "0" offset will not allow a wide enough tire because the tire will hit the fender. A rim with a negative offset may do the job for you. However, in the front you must be careful which offset you use. The steering axis may project through the center of the contact patch. If you draw a line from the upper ball joint through the lower ball joint and tire to the pavement, that is the steering axis. If you move the center of the tire in or out too much by using a negative or positive offset rim, you may find that the car doesn't like to go straight, especially if you hit a puddle. Also, the tire may contact the inside of the fender or a suspension member if the offset is too much. ■

ROLL BARS

8

oll bars can satisfy two needs. First and foremost is the safety issue, and then there is that certain look that a roll bar adds to a car. As a safety device, a roll bar is intended to protect the driver and any passenger from being crushed should the vehicle flip over. A full roll cage will offer maximum protection, but is generally a bit much for a street car. A roll bar crossbrace also adds a place to anchor a shoulder harness or upper anchor for a three-point seat belt assembly.

From a performance standpoint, a simple roll bar may improve your car's traction and performance and a full cage will greatly reduce chassis flex. If your car happens to be a roadster or you think you might like to race it (drag race, club road race, or any organized sanctioned event) you may want to consider installing a roll bar. The sanctioning body will have specific guidelines regarding its installation.

Note: Don't ever be tempted to use exhaust tubing for a roll bar. The material type, diameter, and thickness will be specified by the sanctioning body. If you can't find a ready-made, race-ready roll bar for your custom street rod or kit car, then any race

Roll bars can be the single hoop design just behind the driver or full width to offer protection for passengers also.

chassis shop can bend a bar up for you. If you can't find a chassis shop, then roll bar companies that manufacture kits for OEM or other applications may be able to do a custom piece for you. Just make sure you check the requirements of the sanctioning body you plan to race under (SCCA, NHRA, IMSA, or whatever). It is your responsibility to make sure that the bar is manufactured to the specifications of

that sanctioning body. Furthermore, even though a roll bar or cage material type and size is approved, it is only as good as the installation. The installation of a roll bar must be done in a manner approved by that sanctioning body.

That being said, the installation of most roll bars is a relatively simple procedure, but will require the fitting and welding of some of the tubes. It's all really quite simple though. You

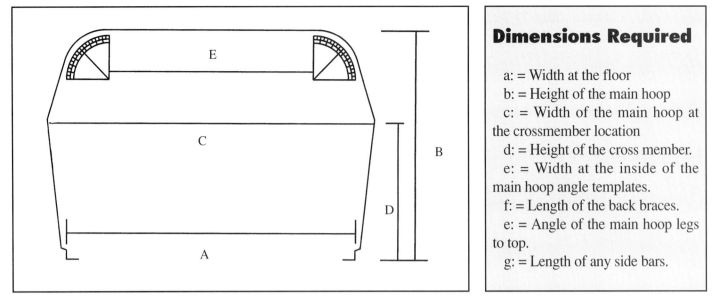

Dimensions Required

a: = Width at the floor

b: = Height of the main hoop

c: = Width of the main hoop at the crossmember location

d: = Height of the cross member.

e: = Width at the inside of the main hoop angle templates.

f: = Length of the back braces.

e: = Angle of the main hoop legs to top.

g: = Length of any side bars.

These are locations that must be accurately measured in order for the roll bar manufacturer to bend the tubing accurately.

If your car has a folding roof, you need to start by making a template to ensure the roof will clear as it is folded. Some sanctioning bodies require the roll bar to be higher than the helmet. The NHRA requires a minimum of 3" above the helmet.

could install it yourself or hire a welder to take care of all or part of the fitting and welding.

SINGLE HOOP ROLL BARS

Roll bars come in a variety of styles ranging from a single hoop to full roll cages welded into the chassis, which offer greater protection.

If your car is a street-driven roadster that will occasionally be autocrossed or driven enthusiastically, a simple hoop that has two legs attached to the floor behind the seat will provide some added protection. This hoop could be located just behind the driver, or extend the width of the car and offer protection to the passenger as well. The bar should have 1 or 2 braces that run to the front and/or 2 braces to the rear. In order for the roll bar to be effective, it should attach solidly to the frame, and not be mounted to the body. Do not attach the roll bar to a fiberglass floor unless it has been reinforced to take the load it could be subjected to.

Measuring for a Custom Bar

If your car requires a custom roll bar, you take accurate measurements and give the correct dimensions to the manufacturer. The roll bar we had made in this example was for a roadster. It is a simple full width, 4-point bar, comprised of a main hoop with two rear-facing braces.

Template—Start by making a cardboard template. The cardboard must be thick enough to be glued together and stand freely. The template should stand behind the front seat, and as close to the roof as possible. This will allow the roof mechanism to function properly and place the top of the main hoop high enough over your head to be effective. Position it near the rear of the door window at about the same angle as the rear of the door or its glass. The bar should be installed within 6 inches of the rear of the driver's head or helmet. The braces need to extend to points on the chassis as far enough away from the main hoop as possible. The further away, the stronger the assembly will be. The other end of the brace should join the main hoop as high as possible; NHRA dictates these braces be welded within 5" of the top of the hoop. This will provide the greatest amount of support in the event of a roll over.

Once you are happy with the template, you can transfer the dimensions to paper for the chassis shop or roll bar manufacturer. It is very important that all of the dimensions are taken and recorded accurately. These dimensions will be used to bend the roll bar, so take your time and measure twice.

Main Hoop—Remember, the main hoop should be located so that the forward edge of the main hoop is no more than 6 inches from the back of your head. Measure from the floor to the roof to determine the height of the main hoop. For appearance, you will want the vertical portions of the main hoop to be aligned with the door pillar, window seam or rear of the window glass. The roll bar should be centered from side to side between the door jams so the roof mechanism will clear when folding or extending the roof. It goes without saying that the car will look funny if it is off center too. Measure the maximum width of the bar at the floor.

Seat Crossmember—This is the part of the roll bar that spans the width of the car/main hoop at about shoulder height and is used to secure your shoulder harness. This point should not be above the driver's shoulder or more than 4 inches below them. Measure the maximum width at this height. Record the width and the

This roll bar kit from S&W race cars was bent using their guidelines to fit a particular car. The main hoop will require a little trimming, while the cross bar and rear braces, which are cut to length and notched, may require minor trimming.

distance from the floor.

Note: If the shoulder harness attaches lower than your shoulder and you have retractors, the constant tension could become uncomfortable on a long journey.

Rear Braces—The rear braces and side bars tie the main hoop and chassis together and can add stiffness to the car. The rear braces connect the main hoop to the rear frame rails, somewhere near the shock mounts. They should be installed so that they are parallel to each other and located directly over the frame rails.

Floor Plates—Your roll bar is going to be only as strong as the point where it is secured to the car body or chassis. Floor plates are intended to mount the roll bar to the floor. The roll bar is generally welded to the plates and the plates bolted or welded to the floor. A bolt-in assembly may be preferable to a welded-in roll bar. An alternative to welding the bar to the plates of the chassis might be to weld pins or sockets to the plates, and then bolt the roll bar to the pins or sockets. Bolting the floor plates to a fiberglass floor may not be strong

If the roll bar is going to be attached directly to the chassis, holes will need to be cut in the floor for the main hoop to pass through. For this car, fiberglass covers will be made to cover the holes. Exhaust tubing or plastic pipe that is about 1/2" larger than the main hoop will be cut on an angle to match and used as a mold. These covers will be fiberglassed in place and covered with carpeting.

enough to support the weight of the car.

INSTALLATION TIPS

Tools needed:
• Common hand tools

• Jackstands

• Floor jack

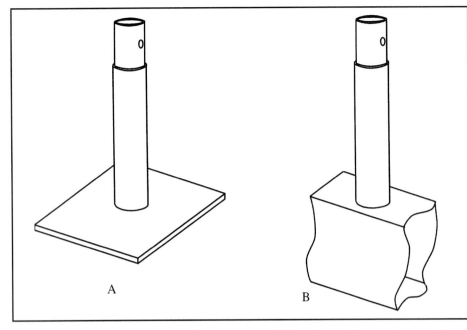

Roll bars can be secured to the chassis in a number of different ways. Here are two socket and pin alternatives. "A" is a plate with the mounting pin welded to it. The plate is then bolted or welded in place. "B" is a pin that is welded directly to the chassis. Different sanctioning bodies require different mounting methods.

After trimming the height of the main hood trial fit the cross bar. If the cross bar is even a little long, it will force the legs of the main hoop apart. Trim the cross bar as necessary.

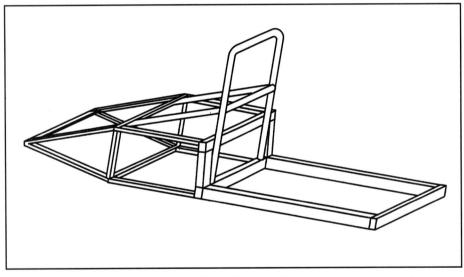

This example of a four-point roll bar would be NHRA legal if the two rear braces joined the main hoop within 5" of the top. Shoulder belt anchors should tie in at the cross bar level.

Consider the following:

• You will need to remove any upholstery or other flammable material from the interior. Protect any wires or switches likely to be cut when positioning the roll bar tubes or burned during welding.

• It may not be necessary to raise the car but it must be level. Be sure that the doors open and close properly and securely, check the gap between all the panels to make sure that everything is straight.

• As with every other part you have ordered, inspect it first. Check the main hoop and any other bent part for flatness; it is not impossible for them to have been damaged in shipping. Trial-fit the main hoop while the seats are in place. If you are using floor plates, double check the locations to be sure they will not create a problem.

• If you are using floor plates, fit the plate to the floor. The plates may need to be contoured to fit. Heat and a hammer may be required to form them for a good accurate fit.

• Trim the ends of the main hoop to fit

• Measuring tools: 16' tape measure, carpenter's square, level, felt tip pen or soap stone.

• Cutting tools: bench grinder, hand grinder, belt sander, oxyacetylene torches, tubing notcher, power hacksaw.

• MIG Welder (recommended). TIG welder is not necessary for this kind of work.

Note: An arc welder is fine but will not leave a nice clean weld without additional work.

During the installation of the roll bar, it is critical that the car is sitting or supported evenly and not twisted or drooping in any way. If your car/chassis is not sitting even (twisted), and you are installing a full roll cage this condition could remain. The resulting condition may create chassis tuning and handling problems.

Double check all of the notched ends of the roll bar pieces for a close fit. The closer the fit the less filling the welder will have to do, and the nicer the welding job will look.

This roll bar also serves as anchor points for a three point seat belt system. The location of these anchors shouldn't be any higher than the shoulder of the occupant or lower than 4" below the shoulder.

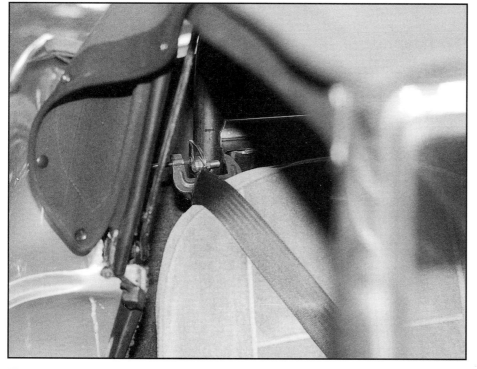

These tabs needed to be angled in so the roof mechanism will clear when folded or raised. If the shoulder belt is too low, it will apply pressure to the neck of the wearer so take your time when setting this height.

with the floor plates and tack-weld the main hoop to the floor plates.

• If the main hoop will be secured with pins or sockets welded to the chassis, cut holes in the floor material to locate the bottom of the main hoop and sockets on the frame rails.

• Simple sockets can be made by ordering extra main hoop material and a smaller size pipe that will slide (snugly) inside the main hoop. The smaller pipe is welded to the hoop. The pin is slid into the socket and a hole is drilled through both. The length of the socket must be long enough so the bolt can be passed through the socket and pin at a point where you can get wrenches on the hardware.

• Fit and install the rear braces. These connect the main hoop to the rear part of the frame. Carefully trim and notch the braces so they fit snugly against the main hoop.

• Install the seat crossmember, again trimming and notching as necessary. Tack-weld the brace in place.

• Any other braces should be fitted and tack-welded in place. Check all your notches for fit. Your pieces should fit tightly together with no more than 1/8" gap. If everything looks good, remove the roll bar and finish weld all the joints.

Warning: The hoop will move around during the welding process as the pieces heat up and could require tweaking after welding in order to fit properly. Don't assume, check this before having your roll bar coated.

Special considerations should be given to things like any area where the roll bar fits through the body or bulkhead. A piece of exhaust pipe could be cut to fit the contour of the floor and allow the pipe to pass through. The bar could be sealed to the pipe with a rubber door gasket to keep any water or cold air out.

If the bar is a bolt-in installation, now would be the time to have a finish applied or a cover fabricated for it. ■

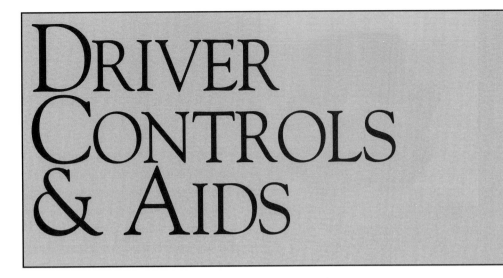

DRIVER CONTROLS & AIDS

9

T he placement of these controls will have an immediate and direct impact on how safe and comfortable the car will be to drive. I recommend that you install them in the following order because all of these parts need to be located relative to each other as well as the driver. I suggest you start with the pedal assembly because it is generally more difficult to relocate and the steering column is generally hung from it. If your steering column must be positioned separately from the pedal assembly, use common sense and locate it where appropriate.

PEDAL ASSEMBLY

The pedal assembly must not be too far from the seat. It can't be so far away that you are forced to straighten your leg out when you push hard on the pedal as you would in a panic situation. This is because once your leg straightens past a certain point, you can't generate as much pressure as when it is bent at a slight angle. The proper seating position will allow you to raise your foot from the gas and touch the pedal without having to bring your knee to your chest, yet be close enough to have your leg bent

Gauge choice is sometimes subjective, sometimes not. Make sure you go with the right set for the type of car. This street rod has a custom gauge panel, with a neat, clean, easily readable display.

slightly.

Armed with a tape measure and pad of paper, go to the car that you normally drive. Position the seat as it is when you drive, and make note of the distances of things like the seat from the steering wheel (vertical and horizontal). The angle of the steering wheel, the distances from the gas and brake pedals to the seat and the steering wheel, etc. These dimensions didn't just happen, the manufacturer of that car spent a lot of time and

money figuring out where these items should be placed. I realize that the car you normally drive may not have the same seating posture that your new car will have. You may sit lower in the car you are building, for example. You may have to make some concessions, but those measurements will give you a place to start. The following information and the measurements you take from your car should allow you to locate these components correctly.

Notice that these pedals are all at about the same height and close enough to each other so the driver can easily move from one pedal to another without getting caught between them. The gas pedal is curved so the driver's foot will never be forced to be at an uncomfortable angle.

Gas and Brake Pedals

Generally the manufacturer of your car's body will have provided pedal mounting instructions for either a factory pedal assembly or an aftermarket pedal assembly. The mounting location will either be indicated in the form of written instructions with dimensions and reference points or dimples on the firewall where you drill the mounting holes. Before you do any drilling, read the information we have provided and the measurements you took from your car. Position any templates you may have from a donor car, make any minor location adjustments required, measure twice, drill and bolt them in place.

Pedal Locations—The gas, clutch, and brake pedals should be at approximately the same height from the floor because you will generally use the ball of your foot to apply pressure to all of these pedals. The brake and clutch pedals should be approximately the same distance from the seat. The brake pedal will be higher or closer to the seat than the gas pedal when no pressure is being applied to either pedal. The brake and clutch pedal should be centered in front of the driver and not off-center. If your car has an automatic transmission, the centerline of the brake pedal should be the same as the driver's centerline.

Is the pedal location really important? I was once contacted by the owner of a '57 Thunderbird kit. The customer complained that the car didn't have any brakes. The foot box in some of those early kits wasn't deep enough to locate the pedal assemblies far enough away from the driver, and as a result the driver assumed the primate position while driving the car with is knees on either side of the steering wheel. In an attempt to correct this situation, the builder had lowered the brake pedal. Unfortunately, he moved it too far away without realizing it. The result was that the driver's leg was straight before he applied enough pressure to stop the car. The fix was to move the brake pedal assembly closer (horizontally) to the seat and steering wheel. The proper location was determined by measuring his production car, and using those measurements to relocate it. Once you have these numbers you can sit down and decide if you want to move them slightly one way or another to fit your particular body size and proportions.

Gas Pedal Operation—The gas pedal must be positioned so you don't get your foot hung up underneath the brake pedal when you try to step on the brake. The driver should always be able to rest his or her heal on the floor while operating the throttle.

The gas pedal return spring needs to be strong enough to support the weight of your foot but not so heavy that you have to press hard to move it. Move the throttle through its entire range of operation, verify that the throttle plates are opening completely when you press the gas pedal to the floor.

I suggest that you consider installing a gas pedal stop if it doesn't already exist. If your pedal has more travel than the carburetor, you could stress or bend the linkage or throttle shaft if you stomp on the gas. This can be as simple as a tab attached to the pedal assembly or a bolt threaded through the floor that can be adjusted to fine tune the amount of pedal travel.

SEATS

The seats (base and back) should be securely mounted and not wiggle around as your weight is shifted. The seat should be mounted square to and in line with the steering wheel and pedals. Your shoulders should be parallel to the steering wheel. The seat back must be reclined enough to allow a stress-free posture.

Your seats and the position they are

The minimum clearance between the seat and the rim of the steering wheel should be about 12". This street rod has a tilt wheel to make getting in and out easier, a nice touch.

mounted in should allow you to drive comfortably all day long. If they are mis-aligned in any way, they can cause fatigue quickly. When you mount your seats, sit in the seat for a while, and note how it feels after ten or fifteen minutes.

The seat base should be pitched up in front slightly to support the upper legs, otherwise, you will always have the feeling that you are falling out of the seat. Your legs should be comfortably supported behind the knee. Too much angle of the seat bottom can press on the nerve behind your knee and become painful. Too little can give you the feeling that you are going to slide off the seat.

The height of the seat off the floor must be high enough so that the driver's vision is not blocked. Are you going to be high enough to see over the hood, or so high that your head will hit the roof? If you can find a car with a similar shape, sit in it and note where your shoulders are in relation to the top of the door, etc.

STEERING COLUMN

I will assume that at this point you have the steering box installed and secured, and that the engine exhaust manifolds are in place. As you install the steering column, make sure that the steering column support system is capable of holding the column rigidly and without any shaking. (See page 93 for possible solutions should your column mount be inadequate.) Now is the time to correct any weaknesses in the support brackets. The steering column must be well supported at the steering wheel end to prevent the wheel from moving all over the place as you are trying to control the car.

Seat/Steering Wheel Clearance

The minimum clearance between the seat and the rim of the steering wheel should be about 12". The seat should have about 8" of travel to accommodate average-sized drivers.

When you assemble your steering

shaft assembly do not leave out the rubber or plastic insulator disk between the column and steering box. This is there for a reason. It isolates the steering wheel and the driver from vibrations that are generated from the wheels and suspension. If you don't use the insulator the car will be tiring (and sometimes painful) to drive.

If you find any part of the steering shaft comes too close to the engine or exhaust system, or the universals are at too great an angle, consider rotating the steering box a little. Don't forget to consider a heat shield for the steering universals either.

GM Steering Columns

Did you realize that directional cancellation switches in the steering wheel are not all the same? They are designed to match particular ratio steering boxes. Slower steering boxes (on larger, heavier cars) take more turns from lock to lock, so a "slower" switch assembly allows the wheel to be turned more without canceling the directional. Smaller cars have faster steering boxes, and the steering wheel doesn't have to be turned as far so they have switch assemblies that cancel sooner. If you find your directionals cancel with the slightest turn of the wheel, or require the wheel to be turned a lot in order to cancel the directionals, you can correct this. These switches are interchangeable and are available from the GM dealer. This is also a part that is interchangeable over a broad number of years.

Did you know that the end of the GM steering column shaft will fit inside the very end of a Ford steering shaft? So if you really like a GM steering column and you have a Ford steering rack, you have another option.

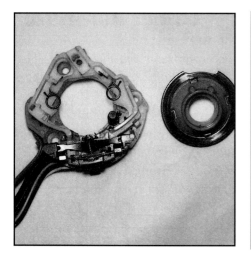

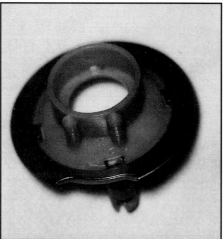

This is a General Motors directional switch and cam. When the left or right directional is activated, one of the two little round springs is moved closer toward the center. As the steering wheel is turned, one of the two bumps located near the top of the cam comes in contact with the round spring and pushes it out and cancels the directional. Notice the single pin below the right spring; this pin is part of the horn circuit and rides on the ring around the outside of the cam.

In this closeup of the directional cam you can get a better look at the two bumps that cancel the directionals. Larger cars have these bumps further apart and smaller cars with faster steering panels have them closer together. The metal ring around the outside is the horn contact that mates with a pin from the directional switch assembly.

Make sure the gearshift falls easily to hand, without reaching forward. You should be able to row through all gears without much movement.

SWITCHES

Can you reach all the switches without leaning forward out of the seat and taking your eyes off the road, especially the radio? What about in the dark? If you can't comfortably see and operate all switches, knobs and controls, consider moving them.

GEAR SHIFT

Sitting in a relaxed position, does your hand fall onto the shifter naturally? When you shift through the gears do you have to lean forward, or do you feel like you are reaching? Does your arm clear everything? If you have to use a short lever, will it require too much effort because of the reduced leverage? These are questions you should ask yourself when you are selecting and installing your shift lever. To be comfortable and safe, you should not have to reach or lean forward while shifting to the point where your back loses contact with the seat.

GAUGE LAYOUT

Of course, some cars demand a certain style gauge and others allow you the freedom to select from a variety of styles and sizes. Remember you have options here also. Spend your money wisely. Don't cut corners and try to save money on cheap inexpensive gauges. Examine and compare the major companies like VDO, Stewart Warner, and Smiths, for example.

Think about the location of the gauges as you plan the layout. With the steering wheel straight ahead can you see the important gauges, should you consider another steering wheel that is larger, smaller or has different spokes? Swapping gauge locations may make sense. Is it better to see the fuel or amp gauge easily and have to look around the steering wheel to see the fuel or oil pressure gauge? I would rather see the oil and fuel gauges.

Use a connector on the dash wiring between the dash and the body. This will allow you to pre-wire the dash and install it as a unit. If you ever have to remove the dash for service

you will appreciate having done this. Wiring for gauges is covered in the next chapter.

REAR VIEW MIRRORS

Rear view mirrors that have mounts bonded to the fiberglass can be a real pain to re-secure sometimes. Your local auto parts store carries an adhesive that will work or you can use silicone sealant. After cleaning both surfaces with a solvent like alcohol, apply a thin layer on the mount, and then hold it firmly against the fiberglass, rotating it around until you can see that there are no air pockets left and the layer is as thin as possible. Scrape off the excess silicone and tape or clamp it firmly for about eight hours. I have never had one fall off.

WINDSHIELD WIPERS AND WASHERS

A number of kits utilize the wiper assembly from the Pinto or Mustang II. These units can deliver acceptable

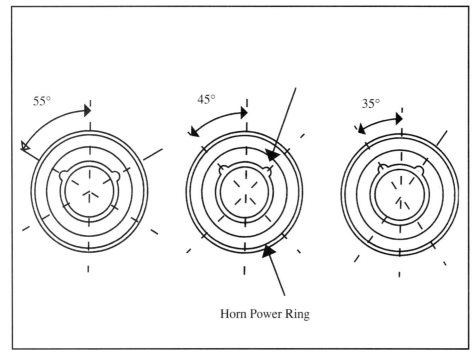

Here is an example of three different directional cancellation switches. The further apart (angle) the bumps are the greater (more) the steering wheel will have to be turned in order for the directional to be canceled. Larger (heavier) cars would have slower steering boxes and require more turns to cancel the directional and a smaller car (mid-size) with a faster steering box would require fewer turns.

55° 45° 35°

Horn Power Ring

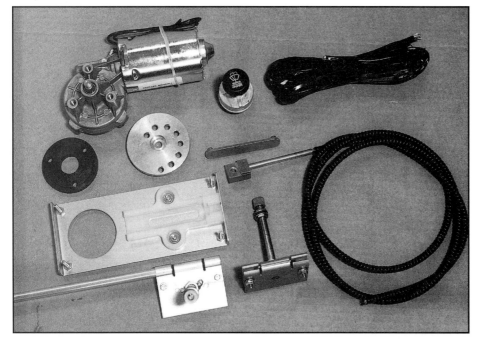

When transplanting windshield wiper systems from a donor car to a hot rod or reproduction, installation problems sometimes occur. Wiper motor mounts may need modifying, or the spacing between the wiper arm transmissions may need to be altered which requires you to cut and weld the rigid arms, just to name a few. Specialty Power Windows offers complete cable driven windshield wiper systems with all the features of an OEM type system and at a reasonable price.

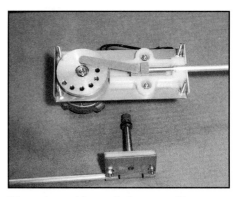

The motor and transmission assembly are compact and easy to mount. The tubing that leads from the motor to the wiper arm transmissions can easily be bent and routed around all the other parts under the dash. The motor could even be mounted behind a kick panel if you need to. The tubing is then cut to fit between the motor and wiper arm transmissions.

applications. The Specialty Power Windows unit offers a lot of flexibility with its design. Electrically, the MGB units are positive ground and must be insulated from the rest of the electrical system. The Specialty units are negative ground and don't require any special electrical consideration.

Windshield Wiper Arms

Regardless which system you use, any installation still requires similar considerations. The wiper arm shafts should be installed through the cowl so that they are 90° to the windshield in both axis, horizontally and vertically. Wiper arms should have about 30 ounces of pressure on the glass. If not, helper springs can be purchased at some parts stores.

Wiper Arm Chatter—If you find that the wiper arms chatter or jump as they move across the glass, it is most likely due to worn parts or a loose motor mount. Check every joint in the linkage assembly, including where it connects to the motor. Check the mount to make sure that the motor doesn't move as pressure is applied to the arms. A good way to check for an inadequate motor mount or worn linkage is to have someone move a wiper arm with their hand while you

service if located accurately, securely and the parts are in good condition. One aftermarket wiper system of interest is the Specialty Power Windows unit that is similar to the Lucas Windshield wiper assemblies from an MGB. Both are cable driven and easily adaptable to a variety of

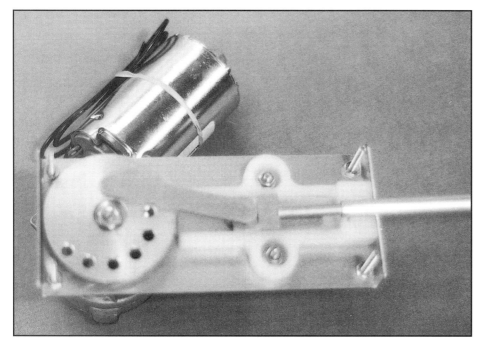

One chronic problem with fiberglass body cars is the fitting of all those donor parts so they don't interfere with other donor parts. The Specialty Power Windows wiper motor can be rotated to any angle to get the best fit under a crowded dash board. No more being limited to where you mount the motor because the parts won't fit anywhere else.

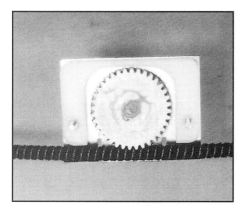

After the wiper motor and wiper arm transmission are mounted and the tubing is bent and installed, the drive cable is slid through the tubing and meshed with the gear on the end of each wiper arm shaft.

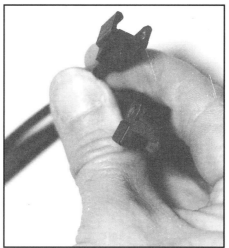

Chrysler has supplied us with what could be the best windshield washer nozzles. These washer nozzles clip to the windshield wiper arm and deliver water in front of the wiper blade as it sweeps across the windshield. A small hole drilled next to the wiper arm shaft allows tubing to be routed from the washer pump to each nozzle.

watch the mechanism for movement. Any movement or slop will result in a wiper assembly that is noisy or chatters.

Wiper Motor

The motor must be mounted so that it will not move or deflect if a load is applied to the wiper arms. The motor should be mounted with rubber insulators to reduce noise generated by the wiper motor and its gearbox.

Washers

Many different types of windshield washer assemblies are available. Some pumps are separate and some aftermarket and production systems combine the pump and reservoir in one assembly. Reservoirs are available in rigid plastic, flexible bags or even a custom stainless or aluminum reservoir. Enthusiast magazines will list a number of suppliers for these products. If you can find a bottle from a production auto, all the better. The advantage to using a production washer is that the parts are readily available at any parts store.

Nozzles are available with aftermarket wiper/washer kits, separate from British parts suppliers, or from your donor vehicle. You can even make your own from tubing. For example: select a soft tubing with a diameter that your flexible tubing will slip over. Form the tubing so that it will pass between your hood and the cowl. Solder or epoxy a tab to bolt through and pinch the discharge end down and pass a very small drill through it. If you scour the junkyard you may find a nozzle that works better for you.

My favorite style is from the Chrysler Corp. (Dodge, Plymouth, etc.). These are made of plastic and clip to the wiper arm. You bore a hole through the cowl near the wiper arm shaft for the vinyl tubing to pass through. The hole should be located so that when the arm is parked it is covered. The vinyl tubing connects the pump to the nozzles. As the arm sweeps the water jet wets the glass in front of the wiper blade. The only potential problem I have seen with them is that the Chrysler wiper arms are little wider than the older wiper arms. A little ingenuity can correct this problem. A simple "C" clip can be fabricated from hose clamp spring steel that will snap over the arm and nozzle from the side. ■

ELECTRICAL 10

Perhaps one of the most intimidating jobs you will ever have to contend with in any automotive project will involve the wiring—lots and lots of wiring—that runs through a car from end to end. The best advice we can offer is to take your time, be organized and keep the wiring neat. This will go a long way to keep you out of trouble during the wiring process by making it easier to trace the wires. This will also be helpful when you need to add or modify the harness when you want to add that other little do-dad in the future. I also recommend that you purchase and read HPBooks' *Automotive Electrical Handbook.*

ELECTRICAL SYSTEM COMPONENTS

Battery

The battery is the heart of your car's electrical system. If you treat it with respect it should serve you well and last a long time. Current technology lead acid batteries should last at least five years. New batteries being developed, such as gel cells and dry cells, promise to pack more power into smaller more efficient packages.

There are two basic ratings of

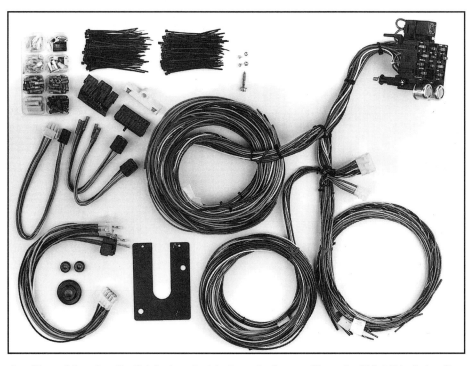

As with anything else, the finished product is dependent on quality parts. This kit includes the fuse panel, connectors, grommets and mounting brackets/hardware. Most of the better wiring houses can provide all the necessary parts for a quality wiring system.

power that need to be considered: power to crank the engine, and how far the car can be driven on battery power if the charging system stops functioning.

Cranking Power

The specification of cranking power is usually expressed in "cold cranking amps" (CCA). A rating of 500 CCA is a powerful battery. Anything in the

650 CCA range is a very powerful battery, and those with a rating near 350 CCA are approaching the minimum. There is no such thing as "too much of a good thing" when talking about battery power. Starters last longer and work better with a strong battery, and a high rating battery is less affected by radical temperature changes. The official definition of cold cranking rating is

This fuse panel has the nice features of a directional and four way flasher, plastic fuses and a terminal strip for connecting the wires from your harness.

the number of amperes a battery can deliver for 30 seconds at 0 degrees F and still maintain a voltage of 1.2 volts per cell or higher. If your battery is rated in watts, 3,000 watts of power at 0 degrees is a comparable rating.

Reserve Capacity—This is the second basic rating and concerns how far you can drive on the stored electricity in the battery, if for some reason your car's charging system ceases to function. This reserve capacity is defined as the number of minutes a fully charged battery, at 80 degrees F, can be discharged at a 25 amp rate and still maintain a voltage of 1.75 volts per cell or higher. Incidentally, 25 amps is a general but realistic figure when considering total power usage by the ignition system, headlights and possibly a defroster fan or the windshield wipers. The reserve capacity is rated in minutes and

generally speaking, 100 minutes is a strong battery, whereas 120 minutes is a very strong battery and 80 minutes is on the small side.

Amp Hour Rating—This rating is another method of measuring a battery's ability to deliver small amounts of current for long periods of time. Using this method, a battery with an amp hour rating of 100 or more is of average strength. Amp hour rating is defined as a unit of measure obtained by multiplying current flow in amperes by the time in hours during which the current flows.

Alternator

Alternators can be divided into two categories: those with internal voltage regulators and those without. If you must have an alternator with a built-in regulator, be aware that you may have to install a warning light on the

dashboard, a special resistor wire or a diode in the exciter wire to provide the proper amount of current to turn on the alternator. The diode prevents the power from flowing backward to the ignition. This will prevent you from shutting the engine off. If you have a problem with your alternator "turning on" look at this area also. A symptom of this will be that the amp gauge will not show "charge" when you first start the car, but if you race the engine a little, the amp gauge will suddenly jump to the charge side when it turns on. This could also be the result of a cheap alternator with inexpensive parts.

Voltage Regulator

The job of the voltage regulator is to regulate the amount of voltage that the alternator sends into the wiring system of the car and battery. This keeps the system at a "regulated" voltage regardless of the load placed on the alternator. Remember that each of the different circuits of a car will use a certain amount of electricity. The alternator is generally sized in capacity to provide enough current to meet that expected demand. If you add more electrically operated goodies and exceed the alternator's capacity, you could deplete the battery if you tried to use everything at once. Voltage regulators are designed to permit the charging system to produce more charging voltage during cold weather than during warm weather.

A word of caution regarding the wire that feeds power from the battery to the ignition switch: resistance in this wire will cause a substantial voltage drop. Since the voltage regulator uses this circuit to sense how much to charge the battery, it is important that the voltage difference at the battery and the ignition switch be kept to a minimum, so be sure to use a 10 gauge wire for the power

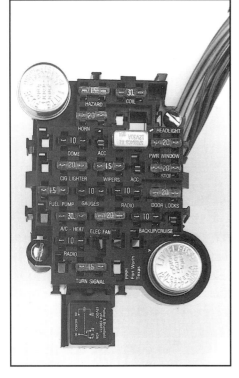

This fuse panel offers approximately 20 fused circuits as well as having both the flashers and a relay. This style fuse panel has the wires terminated behind the fuse panel.

This fuse panel offers approximately 10 fused circuits as well as the directional and four-way flashers.

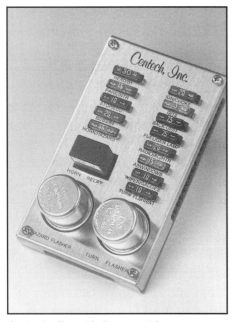

Centech offers this fuse panel for a more custom look. Aside from its technical merits it offers a high tech, highly organized look.

feed from the battery to the ignition switch.

Circuit Protection

This is a must to prevent system overload and possibly electrical fires. Circuit protection can be in the form of fusible links, fuses or circuit breakers.

Fusible Links—A fusible link is a special wire made from an alloy that has a lower melting point than regular copper wire does. It is also insulated with a special insulation that will not burn if the link melts. The fusible link is generally installed at a connection that leads to the battery and is designed to melt in the case of a short or overload in the wiring system. The fusible link is intended to protect main feed wires and will not melt if there is a brief short or overload but will melt if the short persists. It is important to select the correct size and length fusible link and it is not a simple thing to calculate; this is best left up to someone like the harness maker to determine. A fusible link is generally two (2) sizes smaller than the wire it is connected to. Requesting one in your harness could save your car from an electrical fire.

Fuse Panel—I have only a few suggestions on fuse boxes. You will see many different styles advertised. Some will even have the old style glass fuses. I urge you to select a fuse box that uses the colored plastic bayonet type ATC or ATO fuses. If you can find one with circuit breakers for the headlights, all the better. Some aftermarket wiring harness and electrical system parts suppliers such as Ron Francis Wire Works, Painless Wiring, Centech Wiring and Cole Hersee offer headlight switches with internal circuit breakers.

Circuit Breakers—As with everything else, circuit breaker designs have improved over the years and should not be dismissed as a fad. Circuit breakers are available in the same bayonet style as the plastic ATC and ATO fuses. Adapters are available to retrofit glass type fuse holders with circuit breakers. Circuit breakers come in most of the popular sizes, 3,

This is the circuit board inside the Centech fuse panel. Note that it takes a departure from the norm because it is small enough to fit within a recess or custom panel. Notice the terminal strips for terminating the harness. This type of terminal eliminates the need to add connectors to the wires. This could eliminate a potential problem area.

4, 5, 6, 7.5, 10, 12.5, 15, 20, 25, and 30 amp ratings. Circuit breakers are available in:

• Type I—automatic reset type
• Type II—will remain open until the short has been corrected. The power must be removed before the circuit breaker will reset
• Type III—manual reset.

The manual reset types have a tab that pops up, making detection simple by feel or sight. Automatic reset types may be better for certain applications. As the name implies, the "auto reset" breakers will do just that: reset after they cool down. They will continue to cycle until the problem is corrected (within reason). This sort of breaker might be appropriate for something like the headlights or other critical circuits.

Some breaker boxes are much more sophisticated with relays and indicator lights to alert you if a fuse fails. The

Hi-tech style is nice and sometimes makes a lot of sense.

Fuse Box Location

Where should you mount it? Choose carefully. Consider how it will be mounted and how easily you will be able to get to it. I suggest that you consider the center console if your car has one, or the glovebox. These locations allow you to see the fuse box without getting out of the car or getting on your back. Instead you can replace a fuse while you are sitting in your seat. This is especially important in bad weather. Instead of laying on your back with your legs hanging out the door you can do it in the safety and protection of your seat. Besides, fuse boxes installed under the dash are never at the correct angle and you never have enough lighting.

A third possible location you might consider is under the hood, with a removable splash resistant cover. If you have the option of choosing

which side to mount on, consider the passenger side of the car. In the event of a problem on the road, you can check the fuse box on the shoulder side, where it is safer. The point I want to stress is this: If a fuse blows while you are on the road, you need the ability to replace it quickly and safely.

The likelihood of this happening will be greatly reduced if: you use quality parts; the electrical system is designed by someone that understands electrical systems; and you use good workmanship when assembling the system.

Relays

Relays could be considered switches. Instead of having a lever that is moved to close the contacts of the switch, an electric coil closes the switch. Typically, a small capacity switch controls the power to a coil which in turn closes the relay. How do you know if you need a relay? For this discussion we will assume that a circuit is made up of a power supply (battery), a switch between the power supply and a load (lights or a cooling fan). Switches are rated to conduct a certain amount of current, ten (10) amps for example. The lights (or fan) require a certain amount of current to operate correctly. If the load requires more current than the switch is rated for, the switch will fail after a while. Headlight switches are designed and rated to conduct enough current for the average headlight systems, but if you install additional lights or use high current lights you may exceed the switch's rating. Oh, it may work for a while but the contacts in the switch will burn and corrode after a while and become a problem. Examine the current load for all the components you want to put on that circuit carefully. A relay may be the answer to this type of situation. The

This is an example of standard ring style crimp connectors. Not only are they sized for different gauge wires but for different size studs to be mounted on.

nice thing about using a relay is that your switch, no matter how small, only conducts a small amount of current and should last for many years.

WIRING CONCEPTS

Faulty or sloppy wiring in your car can surface later on in the form of lights that don't work, fuses that blow, or worse. By remembering a few tips, you can minimize these potential problems.

Depending on which principle you subscribe to, current flows through or on the surface of wire. For our discussions, I will not make a distinction. It is not important to us. Let's just think of copper wire as the conduit through which electricity runs.

Confused about electricity? Try thinking of it this way. Electrical wire is like a garden hose, electricity is like water and the volume of water is like the current. The larger the hose (wire gauge) the more water (current, which is measured in amps) will pass through the hose. Everything electrical on the car will need water (12 volts) but differ in the amount

(current) they need to work properly. Some components need lots of water and others not so much. Headlights, stereo amplifiers and motors sometimes need lots of current (measured in amps) and things like your radio and power antenna need less. Small things like parking, courtesy, brake and taillight bulbs generally need the smallest amount. As you select your components, you need to realize this and make note of the current (amp) requirements. Record these items and the power requirements in your owner's manual for reference. The current requirements will dictate the size of the wire and fuses they need for adequate current and protection.

Wire Size

Electrical wire is measured in gauges, usually eight through eighteen in passenger cars. The lower the gauge number, the heavier the wire, and the greater the current capacity of the wire. Windshield wipers, radiator cooling fan, and headlights are examples of components that need heavier gauge wire. Things like the starting and charging systems in your car draw a large amount of power. Imagine the power necessary to turn the crankshaft on a cold morning! For this reason, the wiring found in the charging system requires at least eight or ten gauge and the cable from the battery to the starter is usually a minimum of 2 or 4 gauge. The same is true for the ground cable from the battery to the engine.

Warning: Stranded wire is intended to be flexible and solid is not. Do not use solid conductor wire. It is not flexible, and if forced to flex repeatedly, it will break. Also, remember that the gauge measurement for wire is not the same as that used to measure sheet metal. See the wire gauge chart in the tables

section for a more in-depth explanation.

Remember, when you build a car yourself, it never seems to be complete. You will always be tinkering, adding this and that. You might add gauges, lights, or something else. If you purchased a complete wiring system and add any wires to it, it is better to err on the side of larger gauge wire to ensure that you will have an electrical system that will not melt down. Pay attention to the color of the insulation. If you are extending a wire, use the same color insulation; if you are running a new feed try not to use the same color as an existing wire. If you have run out of color options you need to tag it on both ends so it can be traced.

Solderless or Crimp Connectors

Perhaps the best way to make sure all connections are secure is to use solderless connectors wherever connections must be made. Solderless connectors are easy to use, and as the name implies, require no solder. As a matter of fact, the manufacturer cautions against using solder on solderless connectors. Solderless connectors are generally insulated with color-coded insulators, so they can be used on the correct gauge wire. Red is the smallest and is used for 18 or smaller gauge wire, blue is used for 14 - 16 gauge, yellow for 12 and 10 gauge.

All types of crimp connectors are also available in both insulated and un-insulated varieties. The simple metal, un-insulated type can be used in any instance where a short circuit is not a potential danger, such as when grounding a wire to a bolt on your chassis. Insulated connectors that have plastic non-conductive coatings over the metal are used on power wires and any wire where it is

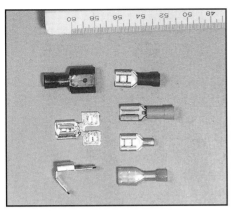

Connections that are likely to be separated for routine maintenance or part removal might be better made with spade style connectors.

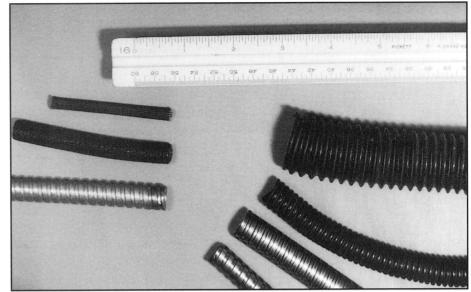

These are samples of some of the shielding options available to protect the wiring harness from heat, chafing, and electrical interference. Shielding is available in plastic, galvanized steel, stainless steel, and the older cotton cloths.

important that the wire not touch another wire or ground source. Insulated connectors are especially handy for joining power wires and for use on dash instruments where many wire connections are close together. Some connectors already have heat shrink insulation installed on them.

Your buddies may tell you that you can crimp a connector with a pair of pliers, well, yes you can, and you could also use a rock. However, the quality of the connection cannot be guaranteed. One day you could find yourself stuck on the side of a road with the wire waving in the breeze somewhere under the car. Good wire strippers and crimpers will make the job quicker, easier and minimize the likelihood of a bad connection.

Solderless Connectors—These are inexpensive and used for specific wiring purposes. For example, the ring connector is round with a hole in the center so it can be slipped over a small bolt; this is especially handy for connecting a ground wire to a ground bolt or screw, or when wiring to threaded terminals on gauges.

Quick Disconnects—These are useful for wires that may have to be disconnected at intervals. This precludes the need to cut the wires since they can simply be pulled apart at the connectors.

Butt Connectors—These are perhaps one of the most useful connectors. A butt connector is a cylindrical device that is used to join two wire ends together. All you have to do is strip both ends, slip them into the opposite ends of the butt connector, and crimp the connector ends. The two wires are now securely joined to complete the connection.

Forked Type Connectors—The most common connectors used in cars today seems to be the forked type. This type has two prongs that slip under the screw or the bolt you are connecting to. The forked connector has an obvious advantage over the ring-type connectors, in that you do not have to remove the nut or bolt to add the connector.

Ring Type Connectors—The ring connectors are less likely to fall off if the nut loosens up or you forget to tighten it. If speed of replacement is more important than the likelihood of the connection coming loose, then fork type connectors are the natural choice.

Tab or Receptacle Connectors—The Male/Female connector, also called the tab/receptacle connector, is

common in many factory cars where the component is one likely to need replacement in the future, such as a headlight or other lights. The male/female connector is disassembled simply by pulling it apart with your hands.

Shrink Tubing—Insulating tubing comes in various colors and diameters and slides over an electrical connection and insulates it from electrical shorting and contamination from outside elements. It is available both with a sealing adhesive inside or dry.

You select a size (diameter and length) that will slide easily over an existing connection. Once in place, it is then shrunk around the connection using a suitable heat source. This can come from a heat gun (preferred), solder iron or by carefully waving a flame over it. The resulting cover is tough and will protect as well as, if not better than, the original insulation.

Tie Wraps—Tie wraps are nylon strips that are used to bundle wires. The tie wrap is looped around the wires and fed back into a slot in its head. These are available in different sizes and colors. The only downside

WIRING TOOLS

Combination strippers and cutters are generally large and bulky and prevent you from working in tight quarters. At a minimum, you need a separate set of wire cutters and wire strippers. Large and small cutters would actually be better. Separate crimpers and strippers are also mandatory for working with solderless connectors and come in a variety of sizes, styles and costs.

Soldering—A soldering iron and solder will be useful for splicing wires or soldering those really big un-crimpable lugs to those really big wires.

Caution: Be careful of the flux you use on any solder connections. DO NOT use plumber's solder or any solder that contains an activated acid core or aggressive flux. Go to an electronics store and buy solder that contains a mildly activated rosin core flux. This is the type of flux used on wiring and electronics.

The surfaces that are being soldered must be clean in order for the solder to wet and flow over the surface. The flux is caustic and cleans the surface while it is being heated, preparing it for the solder by removing any oxidation or mild corrosion from the surface. Oil, grease or heavy corrosion must be removed by another method like a wire brush. If your surfaces are not clean, the solder will not wet the surface and you will chase the solder ball around and overheat the solder and wires and burn the flux, resulting in a connection that may have high electrical resistance and be mechanically weak. The more aggressive fluxes will work but they can be so aggressive that they continue to work and can corrode the wire to the point that it turns green and breaks in two.

Strippers—Strippers, regardless of the style, must have holes for each gauge wire so that you do not cut or nick the conductors. The deeper a wire is cut, the less flexing it will take before it breaks.

Automatic Strippers—Special "automatic" strippers are available that make stripping insulation from any wire a cinch. These are the best type of strippers available. The wire is stripped automatically as the handles are squeezed together. The stripper has a die for each different gauge wire and a flat clamp to grip the wire's insulation. These holes allow you to easily strip wires of different gauges without damaging the wire. After inserting the wire into the proper size hole, you press the handles together. The clamp contacts the insulation, the cutting dies cut into the insulation, and as you press harder, the dies are pulled to the side, away from the clamping side and the insulation is pulled off the end of the wire.

Solderless Lug Crimpers— Generally these will be a combination tool with 2 or 3 sections on the nose for crimping the various sizes of lugs, and behind the pivot will be a wire cutting section and then a section for stripping the different gauges of wire. Cheap crimpers stick, bend and bind and in general are made of poorer quality metal. Spend the extra money and get a good quality set.

Volt Ohm Meter—A volt ohm meter will allow you to measure voltages from hundreds of volts down to a fraction of a volt. You can also measure resistance within a circuit or determine if you have a complete circuit (called continuity). A digital VOM is better but not necessary.

Test Light—These can be purchased or a simple parking or tail light bulb can make a wonderful tester. Take a spare light socket and solder wires to the socket's ground and power points. Use black for the ground and red for the power side. Attach alligator clips to the wire ends and you are ready. Be sure to insulate both alligator clips to prevent shorting in tight quarters. By clipping the black wire to a ground and probing around with the red lead you can find any terminal that has power. You can also use it to check switch or circuit operation in the same way. Add a 9-volt battery and you can test circuits without external power.

Buzz Box—A buzz box is also a simple tool that can be used in the same way as the test light. These can be constructed using any under dashboard buzzer from any car and wired the same way. Some buzzers will change tone depending on the amount of voltage it is connected to. By installing a battery (9 volt) in series with the power lead a buzz box can check circuits for continuity without having the car's battery in place.

to a tie wrap that I am aware of is that the non-reusable style is generally the only kind offered in automotive stores. Tie wraps are available in permanent and reusable styles. Reusable tie wraps are preferable while you are in the assembly stage when you are continually adding and moving wires around. If your auto parts house doesn't carry them, your local electrical supply store will have both kinds.

Connectors can make your wiring clean, safe, and simple. If the harness has not had its connectors installed at the factory then the manufacturer will most likely supply the connector for your components; very few manufacturers will require you to supply your own connectors, unless it is an unusual installation. These will most likely be "Crimp On" connectors. Be careful when you are stripping the insulation. If you cut or nick the wire strands then you create a point where the wire diameter is reduced; this can create a "high resistance" point in the wire and it could overheat if more current is drawn than the wire diameter can safely deliver. You should leave extra wire (a service loop) so that the component can be removed if it is likely to need replacing. Don't they all?

Installing Connectors

Installing a solderless or crimp connector onto a wire is very simple. Strip the insulation from the wire, leaving only enough exposed conductor to fit into the part of the metal part crimp. Insert the stripped wire end into the connector until the wire's insulation passes just inside the plastic insulator of the connector. When the connector is crimped it grips the conductor and the insulation. This one step makes the electrical connection and grips the insulation that provides a strain relief, taking

any stress off the conductors. **Caution:** You don't want any strands of wire sticking out of the connector, it must all be inside. DO NOT trim any strands from the wire to make it fit in the metal part of the connector. Make sure you have the right connector for the wire gauge. If you trim strands from the wire, you reduce its current carrying capacity. DO NOT expand the connector so a larger wire will fit inside the connector either! The connector is designed to be compressed a certain amount and if not allowed to do so, the connector may not crimp tight enough to hold the wire and prevent it from pulling out.

Place the crimper over the plastic insulation and squeeze tightly to compress the connector's metal shank snugly onto the wire. If you have done this properly, the plastic should still be intact and the connector will be installed permanently on the wire. That's all there is to it! Use insulated connectors on everything. Grounds are the only place where you can use an un-insulated connector. An un-insulated connector used on the battery side of a circuit is asking for a possible short circuit.

Splicing Wires

If you must extend or repair a piece of wire, this can be done in a couple of ways. Strip both wires back about 1/2" and tin the end of the conductor using a solder iron and solder. Then, wrap it around something round to form a small hook at each end.

Tinning is the process where you apply solder to the stripped end of a wire before you attach it to its final location. Do not cause the solder to wick up under the insulation of the wire. If this happens, the wire is no longer flexible at that point.

Repeat this to the other wire that will be attached and hook one wire

over the other. Remember to slide the shrink tubing over one of the wires before you join them! While keeping slight tension apply solder to the connection. After the joint has cooled, slide shrink tubing over the joint and heat it so it shrinks down tight. Another method is to fan the strands of both wires out, then bring the two wires together so that the strands slip between each other. Press and twist the strands from one wire against the wire you are splicing to. Holding the strands of the first wire against the strands of the second wire, twist the second set of strands around the first wire. Solder and cover with shrink tubing or electrical tape. A butt crimp connector is another method of joining wires together. Strip the insulation from the ends of the wires to be connected together, insert the end into the butt connector, and crimp the connector as you would with any crimp connector.

Scotch-Lok Connectors—The easiest method of splicing or tapping into an existing wire without any cutting or stripping is by using something called a Scotch-Lok connector. These are those little plastic things that allow you to connect a new wire (like power for the radio or antenna to an existing power feed). These are usually found in installation kits for radios and other electrical goodies for your car. It fits over the existing wire, and the (new) wire being joined is simply slipped into an opening end of the connector alongside the existing wire. After you close the connector like a book, you squeeze the connector with a pair of pliers and a metal blade inside is driven through the insulation of both wires to make the connection. A plastic flap on the connector is then snapped down to cover the metal blade to insulate the connection. I have mixed feelings about these

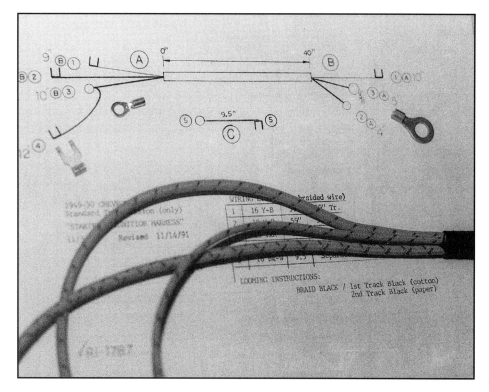

If for some reason you can not find the wiring harness that meets your requirements, a custom harness can be constructed. Rhode Island Wiring, for example, will construct a custom wiring harness based on information supplied by you. They must know things like the distances from point to point, and the current that will flow through those wires.

because if any of the conductors gets cut, the current carrying capacity could be reduced, but they are quick and simple.

WIRING HARNESS

You have at least two options here. First, if the manufacturer of your car has a harness available, you could buy that. The manufacturer's harness will most likely be designed to fit your car, but it may be wired for use with a carbureted or fuel injected engine. That is not to say that they will not be able to have one modified for your application. Second, if you look in any hot rod magazine, you will notice a number of companies that will sell complete custom wiring harnesses that have provisions for fuel injection and electric chokes, so it could be used in either application.

Personally, I think the most practical thing is to purchase the harness from the manufacturer. The rationale for this recommendation is based on the fact that the manufacturers have designed the harness to fit that car. They know what components are required and where they will be located within the car. Therefore the harness should fit within the confines of the body without any problems. So unless you change any of the components to another manufacturer, the factory harness should work just fine. However, if you do decide to use non-standard components, such as a fuel injected engine or something else, the custom harness might be the better option. Custom wiring houses also offer partial (stand alone) harnesses just for the installation of fuel injected motors and lock up torque converters.

If none of these options satisfy your specific wiring needs, then you will have to try to locate a custom wiring house that will create a harness for you based on the parts you are using.

Rhode Island Wiring is one wiring house that will create a custom wiring harness for you based on the (electrical) parts in your car and their location. If you provide them with a drawing with the wire lengths, the components to be used and the electrical schematics for those components, they will make a one off

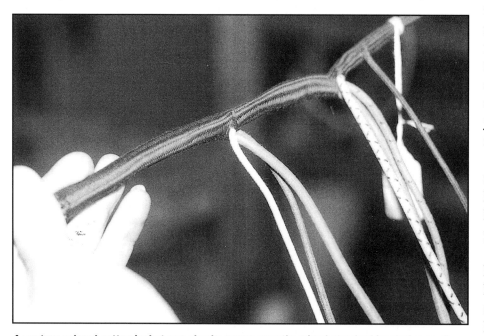

A custom colored cotton jacket can also be woven over the wires' standard insulation to give you a unique look. Once the harness is completed, it is fed through the jacketing machine and a jacket is woven over the entire harness. This will keep all the wires together to keep them neat and protected. Most of the better custom wire companies such as Ron Francis and Centech label their wire every few inches to help you identify each circuit/wire, even in the center of a harness.

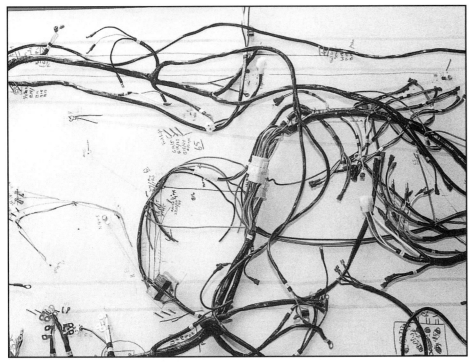

After you have determined that all your parts have arrived, lay the wiring harness out and become familiar with where each part goes. Adding paper tags to each group of wires could help minimize any confusion as you install the harness in the body.

harness for your particular car.

Contracting someone locally may be another option as long as it is someone experienced in automotive wiring design and fabrication, not just a local gas station or garage technician. Insist on talking with previous customers. Unfortunately in this day and age it is more difficult to take people at their word.

Warning: Regardless of whose harness you choose to use, check the harness out very carefully when you get it. Examine the connections to ensure that they are all tight. If you have the least bit of reservation, check it against the wiring diagram for the harness using a test light or buzz box. If the harness supplier refuses to include a diagram with the harness, I would really think twice about buying it. There are plenty of reputable suppliers out there.

Examine the ends of the wires between the harness wrapping and the connectors for exposed copper or cut insulation. Don't accept junk!

Installation

Now for the fun part, installing the harness. At this point you should have already installed all the mechanical components, such as the steering column, wiper motor, etc. Installing the wiring harness may at first seem like an impossible task, but take heart, thousands of car builders have done it and to my knowledge all have

survived. As with anything else, take the time to examine all the parts and literature.

If the harness ends have not had the connectors installed yet, don't! Lay the harness out on the floor next to the body, review the wiring diagram and become comfortable with it. Note how it is supposed to be routed, and study all labels and wires. Do they correspond with the mechanical components you have installed in your car? Is there enough wire to reach those locations? Are there holes in the firewall for the harness to pass through or do you need to make them? Will you reuse a factory OEM style firewall connector? The object of this exercise is to make sure you know how the harness is supposed to fit in the body (which part of the harness is for the engine compartment, the dash board, and the rear of the car), then you simply lay it in place.

Seal the Firewall

Fiberglass firewalls are generally quite thick. It is not uncommon for them to be about 3/8" thick or thicker. You will need to pass wires and hoses through the firewall and you are often left wondering how to seal them.

Equally important is the quality of the installation. Even the best components can be ruined if care isn't taken during installation. Notice that these components are mounted away from each other and other components. They can be replaced or connections made easily.

Once the harness is routed through the body and temporarily secured, only then should you cut the wires and add connectors. This type of connector is typical of one used on fuel injection systems.

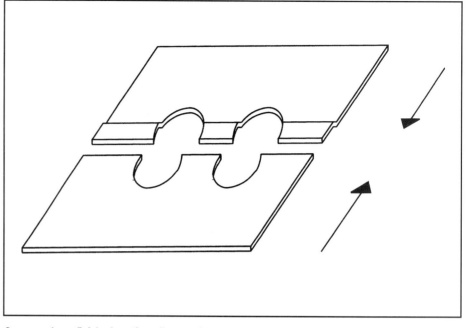

Once you have finished routing all your wiring harnesses and any other items, you are faced with the problem of sealing the resulting hole. A simple bulkhead can be made from two sheets of light gauge metal (steel or aluminum for example). The size and shape will be dictated by your application.

Standard grommets are usually included in the kits but those are usually intended for use on thinner metal panels, usually less than 1/8" thick. In order to seal the grommet and harness or hose to the firewall, you need to be pretty creative or hide the resulting mess.

Well, all is not lost. If you face a similar situation and don't know how you are going to make it watertight and not be an embarrassment, don't worry.

You can make a simple two-piece plate with as many holes as you need. The idea is that the two pieces of the plate slide together and capture a standard grommet for each harness or hose. One half of the plate will cover one side of the hole and the other plate covers the other side. The plates should overlap each other about one half an inch and overlap the edge of the firewall about the same. Where the two plates overlap you will drill holes for the grommets. Screw the two plates together and drill (using a hole saw) as many holes as needed

through the overlap. The holes should be sized to accept rubber grommets that will fit tightly around the hose or harness.

After you have finished routing all the harnesses or hoses through the firewall, install one half of the plate. Slit the grommet(s) so they can be put around the harness or hose and slide the plates together so the grommets are captured. Be sure to apply a bead of sealant to the firewall, between the plates and around the grommets as necessary. The sealant can be smoothed if you spray some glass cleaner or other soapy solution on the sealant before it dries and smooth it with your finger.

With this method, you can seal the firewall so that it can be opened and modified or replaced if you ever need to add components or replace hoses.

Temporarily Secure Harness— Secure the harness temporarily with reusable tie wraps, garbage bag twist ties or light gauge soft wire. You must tie up the harness to prevent it from being damaged or shifting around

while it is being installed. Don't use non-reusable tie wraps just yet, because you will be cutting them soon anyway. You can replace the temporary ties with tie wraps later. Also, you must not install any connectors or cut any wires until the mechanical components are in place and the wires are routed to the part. If you don't wait, you may end up having to lengthen and re-terminate the wires in order to reach the component.

Grounding

While installing the harness, remember that to work correctly, all your electrical components must have a good ground in addition to having a connection to the + (positive) side of the battery. Fiberglass is a wonderful insulator. That means it does not conduct electricity and most of your electrical components will be mounted to non-conductive fiberglass body parts. If a particular component fails to work or acts funny, look at the ground path. Does your ground have a

This is an example of just a couple of the ground strap sizes available for grounding things like the battery and engine to the chassis.

This Cobra uses standard glass fuse. Notice how neatly the components and wiring are installed.

good connection, or is the wire loose in the connector, broken or too thin? A good rule of thumb is to err on the side of too big. For the gauges, you might consider running a wire that will connect all the cases or ground lugs together, which will help reduce the likelihood of your gauges acting strangely when lights and other items are turned on and off. Wire all the ground wires to a central grounding point. The firewall hoop is usually a good location for the dashboard or interior electrical components, then ground the hoop to the chassis with at least a 10 gauge wire.

Remember: Install all your grounding bolts so that they will be accessible from under the dash while you are on your back.

Engine Grounding—This is very important also. Most hard starting or slow cranking problems can be traced to poor grounding. A poor ground will reduce the voltage available to the starter.

After the harness is routed and the connections made, secure that wiring harness to prevent it from becoming

damaged. Replace all those temporary wire ties or twist ties with harness clips and be sure that there is enough extra wire (called a service loop) so that the wires will not be pulled straight and put tension on the connectors at any time.

Note: Be sure not to tighten the tie wraps so tight that they cut the insulation.

GAUGES

VDO Electric Gauges

During normal VDO gauge operation (with everything working properly), when you turn the key on you should see the following:

• The pressure gauge should point to 0.
• The fuel gauge should indicate the amount of fuel in the tank.

The style and placement of your gauges can change the look and attitude of your car. This car has a contemporary look and feel of sophistication.

The gauges in this Ferrari give it a period look, almost as if it were the late 1950's.

• The temperature gauge should point to the temperature of the water.

All (electric) gauge pointers should go full left with the key off. If not proceed to the next section.

Test #1—With the key on, remove the sender wire from the sender. The pointer on the fuel and pressure gauges should go to the maximum right-hand position. The pointer on the temperature gauge should go to the maximum left hand position.

If this does not happen, the gauge or power supply should be examined closely.

Test: #2—With the key on, ground the sender wire to the engine chassis. The pointer on the fuel and pressure gauges should go to the maximum left-hand position. The pointer on the temperature gauge should to the maximum right-hand position.

If this does not happen then the senders require a closer inspection.

Troubleshooting—If you have a problem with a gauge try the following. If an electrical gauge is suspected to be faulty, the following tests can be performed on VDO gauges and senders. The first and most often overlooked test is to determine that not only do you have power at the gauge but that it is a good 12 volts. Low voltage can cause problems just like no voltage. You also need to check the sender still has a good ground. So get your volt meter, a digital meter is preferable but the older (analog, with a needle) style will do. With the key in the on position, probe the power or + side of the gauge. If all is well there, check the sender body to ground at the battery. If that has not found the problems then proceed to the next section.

Note: Never connect an OHM meter or a meter set to read resistance to a hot terminal. You will damage the meter.

Sender Troubleshooting—The sender resistance will change as the pressure or temperature changes. If this does not happen, verify that the sender is grounded properly. The next step is to test or replace the sender.

Temperature sender, cold = 700 ohms; hot (250 degrees) = 222 ohms.

Pressure sender, engine off = 10 ohms; engine running, 40 psi. = 105 ohms, 60 psi. = 152 ohms.

Fuel sender, tank empty = 10 ohms; full = 180 ohms.

Note: If the gauge operates in reverse, the float arm has been installed in reverse.

Stewart Warner Electric Gauges

Any Stewart Warner electric gauge can be tested as follows:

Test #1—Remove the wire that connects the gauge to the sender and ground it. When you apply power to the Pos. side of the gauge, the needle should read full scale. If the needle does not move, check the sender as follows.

Sender unit testing, 240 OHM systems:

Fuel Sender (in tank) check:
Full Tank = Should be about 33 (20 to 50) OHMS
1/2 Tank = Should be 103 (80 to 120) OHMS
Empty Tank = Should be 240 (220 to 260) OHMS

Temperature senders can be checked with either a battery-powered test light or a multimeter. Start by removing the wire from the sender, with a meter set on resistance check from the sender terminal to ground. If the engine is at temperature, the sender should read less than 3 OHMS, if you are using a test light, the light should light. When the engine is cold, the multimeter should indicate an open circuit and the test light will not light.

Oil Pressure Senders

Zero pressure will show less than 3

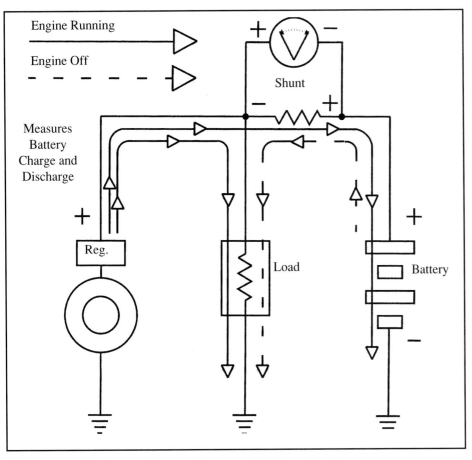

This is an example of a correct amp meter connection. The meter will measure battery charge and discharge.

OHMS, and the test light will light. With the engine running, the multimeter will indicate greater than 3 OHMS and the test light will not light.

Sender Installation

Most electrical senders, oil or water temperature and pressure, have a tapered pipe thread and are self-sealing. They do not require a thread sealant! In order to function correctly, the senders must have a good electrical connection to the gauge and ground. If not the gauge will give false readings. Remember, as the temperature or pressure changes, the resistance to ground changes. This change allows more current to pass throughout the gauge and the needle moves accordingly. Do not use any sealing tap or pipe sealing compound on the threads, it can prevent the sender from having a good ground. If you must use a sealant put it on the last upper thread of the sender, that way the lower threads will have good metal to metal contact. Do not use tee or angle adapters on temperature senders; this will keep the sender tip from being immersed in the fluid flow.

Fuel Gauge Needle Jump

Swing arm gas tank sender units are prone to bobbing around as the car travels over irregularities in the road or turns and the fuel sloshes from side to side. If this is a problem for you, VDO has a tubular gas tank sender that is not as susceptible to this problem. The only problem is that your gauge must be matched (resistance and polarity) to it and not all of the VDO gauges will work with

it. This sender happens to be a marine unit and must be ordered by its length (from 14" to 36"), or tank depth. It has a standard negative ground and a range of about 10 ohms when the tank is empty to about 180 - 200 ohms when the tank is full. This is the same as most swing arm VDO fuel gauges.

If you have electric gauges other than VDO or Stewart Warner and you don't have senders, all is not lost here either. VDO has universal senders for temperature as well as pressure. Cole Hersee Co. also supplies gauge senders and may have one that will work with your gauge.

Electric magnetic gauges will show an instant reading while thermomagnetic gauges will take approximately 30 seconds to obtain a full reading.

Ammeters

These come in two types, remote shunt and standard. The standard ammeter would be used normally when the gauge is located close (normal) to the engine and the gauge (heavy) of the wire will not pose any problems. If you need to locate the gauge at a great distance or using heavy gauge wire is a problem, then a "shunt ammeter" may be a better selection. Simply put, the shunt ammeter allows a shunt to be placed close to the engine and lighter gauge wires run to the ammeter. When installed correctly, the ammeter will indicate charge, and discharge. An improperly installed ammeter will either show improper polarity or charge only.

GENERAL ELECTRICAL SYSTEM TROUBLESHOOTING

As you proceed with the installation process you may find that not everything works the first time. If a

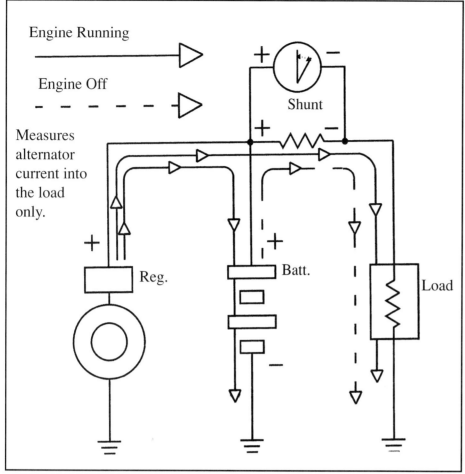

Engine Running

Engine Off

Measures alternator current into the load only.

Shunt

Reg.

Batt.

Load

This example will measure alternator current into the load only. The polarity will be reversed.

component does not work, all is not lost. First, be systematic about dealing with the problems. Before you do anything else, re-read the installation instructions. I wish I had a dollar for every time I found that I had made a mistake. After that, check for power and a good ground. Using a meter, a test light, buzz box or probe, check to see if the wire that is supposed to carry the power is getting a full 12 volts and make sure that you have a good ground without any resistance. This is where the digital VOM will come in handy. These meters are more precise than the analog (with the pointer that sweeps across the gauge face) types. Set the meter to a scale that will read at least 12 volts DC and connect the black or ground lead to a good chassis (or battery) ground. Using the Red or Positive probe check the positive contact (the one that is

supposed to carry the current). If all looks OK then temporarily bring power and a ground to the unit using heavier gauge jumpers. If the unit still does not work then I would suspect that the unit is faulty.

Light Troubleshooting

If your lights are dim, look for unusual things to happen, such as two lights going on when only one should, or anything else bizarre. If yes, suspect a bad ground. Of all the electrical problems I have experienced most were traced to a bad ground.

Flashers

Not all flashers are created equal! Flashers are designed for different loads. The number of light bulbs and their wattage determine the load on the flasher. Directional flashers flash

because the current passing through heats up a bi-metallic strip which then makes and breaks contact. The heavier the load the faster it will flash. If you are not happy with the rate that your directionals flash, you can try using a lighter or heavier duty unit.

Start Up Troubleshooting

It is inevitable that at some point you will try to start your engine for the first time. This is a very exciting moment for some people and a cause of dread for others. The majority of engines will fire right off but every once in a while you get one that remains silent. If you are one of those in the minority, no problem. Just use the same methodical approach you used in all the other phases of the assembly of your car. Note: More often than not, the problem will be something very obvious that you over looked. As humiliating as it is, the best method for troubleshooting is when someone else asks you questions, like, did you check this or how about checking that. Start by checking the obvious, is it getting gas and ignition? Gas is easy, look in the carburetor or throttle body. Port injection is a little more difficult; you can check the pump by disconnecting the supply or the return gas line and check for fuel flow. Warning: Be careful, fuel injected engines use high volume and pressure pumps. If fuel checks out okay, look at the ignition. Ignition system function can be tested by removing the secondary coil wire from the distributor cap and suspending it about 1/4" from the engine block. Have someone operate the ignition switch for you, and while the engine is cranking, a strong, blue spark should arc from the coil wire to the block. If it doesn't, check for the required voltages at everything that needs electricity.

There is no substitute for good quality parts. This tweeter, midrange and woofer speakers are a matched set and will perform well together. Stereo systems are definitely an area where you get what you pay for.

Example—Voltage to the coil should be observed while the ignition switch is in both the "start" and the "run" position. Some ignition switches use a separate route (contacts) to supply power to the coil in the "start" position. If adequate voltage is measured at the battery side of the primary ignition coil terminals but you can not detect any spark during cranking, check to ensure that the distributor is triggering properly.

If a voltmeter is connected to the distributor side of the ignition coil's primary terminals, it should read zero voltage when the points are closed with the ignition "on." Leaving the voltmeter connected to the distributor side of the ignition coil terminals, the meter should read voltage when the points are open. Without changing the voltmeter connections, the voltmeter should show a pulsing during cranking. If readings at the distributor side of the primary ignition coil terminals do not check out, but you are sure that voltage to the battery terminal of the coil is okay, then you have a malfunctioning distributor.

If everything checks out fine with the fuel and ignition system but your car backfires when you attempt to start the engine, chances are there's a problem with the timing or firing order. It is a good idea to recheck the fire order. Open the distributor, and check the rotation by cranking the engine. Make sure that the engine is rotated to number one cylinder, top dead center and that the rotor is pointing to the number one spark plug wire, then loosen the distributor clamp and turn the housing so the points just close and the coil discharges. The timing should be close enough to get you started.

STEREO SYSTEMS

Whether your car is a gentlemanly neo-classic like an Auburn or stompin' pavement-pounding Cobra, you'll want good tunes to cruise with. Hence, the stereo system must make loud and clear sounds, right?

No two stereo systems will be the same. The components you choose for your system will depend on the type of car, the way you drive it and the type of music you listen to. A roadster, or a car with sidepipes, lacks adequate sound insulation and will

What makes a good stereo?

When it comes to picking a radio, CD or cassette player, knowing what the following means can help you choose the proper equipment.

RMS or Continuous Power: The more power you have, the higher the volume and clearer the sound.

Peak Power: Refers to the maximum power the amplifiers can produce for a short period of time. (This is not a good measurement of an amp's ability, ignore this spec.)

FM Mono Sensitivity: This refers to how well the radio will pick up weak stations. Smaller number is good. Frequency Response indicates the range of sounds the stereo can reproduce. Greater is good.

Signal to Noise Ratio: Indicates how well the unit eliminates background noise. Higher is good.

Wow & Flutter: Indicates the stability of the cassette player's speed. The lower is better.

FM Stereo Separation: Indicates how well the stereo creates the stereo effect. Higher is the better.

Dolby Noise Reduction: As the name implies, reduces or eliminates tape hiss.

require a stereo with different output.

Purchasing a complete package system from a manufacturer such as Tweeter, Etc. or Crutchfield is one way to go. These systems are designed to work well with each other, and there is often some savings as well. Purchasing your pieces separately will give you the greater flexibility in design but will also cost you more money.

This is a passive crossover network. It is installed between the amplifier and the speakers. It filters and separates the frequencies it receives that have already been amplified. The speakers then receive only the frequencies that they were designed to reproduce. When a speaker receives only those frequencies that it was designed to handle, it will reproduce those sounds more clearly.

Selecting a System

Choose your radio, amplifier (if any), speakers, and any other components such as crossover circuits, etc., with consideration to how well they will work together as a system. If you choose your components with disregard for the other components, there is a very good chance that you will be disappointed with the system's performance.

• Decide where they will be mounted
• Determine the power and wiring requirements
• Route your wires
• Mount all the components
• Make your connections

Stereo Unit

You may want a plain radio or a combination radio and cassette player or CD player, or both. For this discussion we will limit the types of players to the single-disc indash CD players with AM/FM radio, or multiple-disc changer that fit in an out-of-the-way place such as your trunk or under the passenger seat.

Multiple-disc changers are great for long trips. These units have a magazine that can be loaded with an assortment of your favorite CDs and played consecutively. CD changes can be controlled with some cassette decks that have a changer controller built in. This will allow you to have both cassette and CD player (just in case you have a huge library of tapes you refuse to part with).

Some models of CD changers can plug directly into a factory car stereo so you don't have to remove your factory system to enjoy great CD sound.

Before you chose a radio, you should take a little time to investigate the difference between an okay car stereo and a great one.

If your system is going to be composed of separate components then you should understand the specifications associated with them. First you must choose a radio (main unit). Items you will need to consider will include: power, (RMS & PEAK Power); FM mono sensitivity; frequency response; signal to noise ratio; wow and flutter; and FM stereo separation. These are the factors that differentiate good systems from great ones.

AMPS & SPEAKERS

Power Amplifier

Why should you add a power amp to your system? Maybe you like your music loud or maybe you need just a little more volume to hear things clearly over road noise or side pipes. But even in a quiet vehicle, with your tunes at low volume, a good amp makes a big difference. You'll hear deeper bass, a wider dynamic range between loud and soft passages in your music, and less distortion. Low-power stereos can produce a distorted signal if turned up. The signal becomes erratic and distorted. This sort of signal can cause even the best speakers to overheat. A power amp is the best way to drive your car stereo's speakers. They amplify the signal from your head unit to your speakers. It produces much cleaner power than the tiny amp that's crammed inside your head unit. A good amplifier will deliver a clean, full sound that cuts above the road noise. Amps come in different configurations including 2 channel, 4 channel, 5 channel, 6 channel and so on.

If you choose to install an amplifier a large one is not necessary, but it should be larger than the power capacity (watts) of the speakers. Contrary to popular belief, your speakers should not have a greater capacity than the amplifier. Speakers with smaller (wattage) capacity than the amp will help prevent the speakers from a melt down. If you happen to loan your car to one of your children and they turn the volume up all the way and the amp doesn't have enough power, then the speakers will begin to overheat. If this condition is allowed to last, the glue that bonds the speaker together could melt or the coil within the speaker could warp. Once this happens, as the saying goes, your speakers are toast.

Mounting—Car amps may be mounted out of sight—under the passenger's seat or in the trunk are the locations that seem to be the most favorite. Both keep the amp hidden from view. Regardless of the location you choose, don't forget to allow air flow over the cooling fins.

Wiring—For amplifiers up to 100 watts (50 watts RMS x 2 channels or 25 watts x 4 channels) you should use a minimum 12 gauge wire and a 20 amp fuse or circuit breaker for protection. For an amplifier of up to 200 watts (100 watts x 2 or 50 x 4) you need a minimum of 10 gauge wire and protected by a 30 amp fuse or circuit breaker. For amplifiers up to 350 watts (175 x 2 or 87 x 4), 8 gauge wire and protected with a 50 amp fuse or circuit breaker.

Passive Crossover—Crossovers allow you to drive multiple speakers with a single amplifier. Crossovers are installed between the amplifier and the speakers to split the amplified signal into different frequency bands, lows to the woofers or bass drivers, mid-range frequencies to the mid-range speakers, and highs to the tweeters.

Speakers

The best sounding speakers feature a separate tweeter and woofer. This creates a "life-like sound stage" in your car for a more dynamic listening environment. Component speakers are somewhat more costly, but provide the absolute best car stereo sound.

Inexpensive speakers are ineffective at reproducing the frequencies your stereo can produce. Contrary to some belief, the size of your magnet does not necessarily indicate a better speaker.

Coaxial or Triaxial Speakers—A coaxial speaker has two distinct drivers layered on each other—a tweeter for highs and a woofer for lows.

A triaxial speaker has three drivers—one for highs, one for lows, and one for midrange. There is no real evidence that triaxial speakers are better than coaxial. The important thing to remember is speakers with real (i.e., separate) tweeters will produce the better sound.

Tweeters—These produce the high frequency sounds like cymbals, flute, upper piano register, etc., and should be mounted high up on your doors or in the dash.

Midrange Drivers—Midrange drivers and tweeters are responsible for producing all voice material and the mid to upper registers of most instruments. These should be mounted as close to the tweeters as possible to minimize phase disturbances.

Woofers—These produce the low frequencies and are mounted in the regular speaker holes, however the preferred location will be as low as possible.

Subwoofers—These are speakers that produce bass that is relatively non-directional. They can be mounted just about anywhere without sound

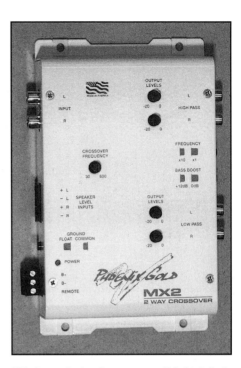

This is an electronic crossover. It is installed before the amplifier so it separates and filters the signal before it is amplified. It also allows you to select the frequencies that are sent to the speakers. You can also adjust the relative volume of each speaker.

quality or directionality problems, your trunk, behind the back seat, for example. In order to work effectively, subwoofers require installation in a box, but "infinite baffle" subwoofers do not.

Ideally, the music should sound as if it radiates from a single area, not from two distinct points. This type of problem is especially noticeable when you have tweeters mounted in the dashboard and midrange drivers mounted in the doors. Sometimes this is unavoidable, but most of the time there will be some small area towards the top of the door where the tweeter can be mounted.

Mounting Component Speakers

Choose the best locations for component speakers. This will differ with each model car but if you know the why behind selecting the location you will be able to get closer the first time around. The prime objectives of

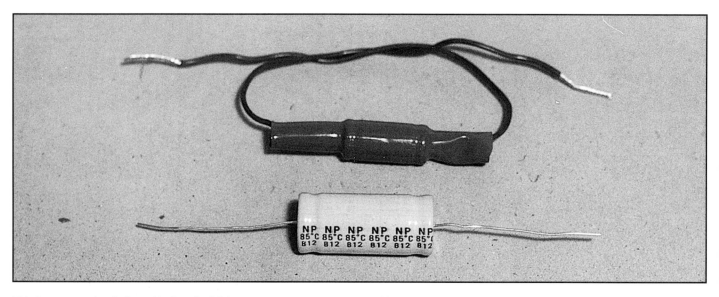

This is an example of a base blocker. Its job is to protect your tweeter and midrange speakers from being forced to reproduce low base that could cause the sound to be distorted, or worse, damage the speaker.

speaker mounting are:

• Position the speakers correctly in relation to the rest of the system
• Mounting them to a solid surface
• Making sure there are no air leaks between the front and back of the speaker cone
• Protecting the speakers from physical damage

The lower the frequencies a speaker reproduces, the more solid its mounting surface must be. This is necessary because a panel that vibrates acts like a second speaker and introduces its own sound into the listening area. The sound produced by the panel can create a low howling noise, degrading the quality of the music at certain volume levels.

If the speakers you are mounting are larger than 5" in diameter, you may have to reinforce the panel. The easiest way to do this is with a piece of plywood, or other hard board. Medium Density Fiberboard (MDF) is the preferred material because of its density, 3/4" for 5" diameter and 1" for sub woofers and boxes. MDF is available at most building supply stores. Many different methods are

used to secure these reinforcing baffle boards. The best method is to use a combination of adhesives and fasteners to secure them to the panel.

In most cases these baffle boards will be secured to the rear side of a panel, such as a door trim panel. In this case the front side of the door trim panel is cosmetic and it wouldn't be wise to have screw heads showing on the surface of the panel. Here we can use an epoxy to glue the baffle board to the rear side of the door's trim panel. Epoxies are available in formulations that cause them to dry in different lengths of time. The most useful for our applications is a 15 minute quick cure epoxy, available in most hardware stores. Be careful about getting a quicker cure epoxy; with some, the faster these materials cure the more brittle they are and can fracture if subjected to a sharp shock.

After the baffle board is cut to shape, cut for the speaker hole, and trial fitted a couple of times, it can be epoxied in place. Clamp the baffle board in place until the epoxy hardens. When dry, the speaker can be mounted and the door reassembled.

If you're securing a baffle board to the back side of a panel (the rear deck

in your car, for instance), the board can be pre-drilled so that it can be screwed into place as the epoxy is drying. Silicone adhesive can be used but you should be careful and keep it as thin as possible because the silicone remains flexible and if too thick will allow the board to vibrate slightly.

Preventing Air Leaks—This concern, more than any other in speaker mounting, will ultimately have the most effect on the performance of your sound system.

Speakers rely on the efficient transfer of their expanded energy to the air surrounding them. In order for the speaker to function properly, the air on the front side of the cone has to be separated from the air on the back side of the cone. Even very small leaks around the basket of a speaker can hurt a speaker's performance. Small leaks can whistle, and larger leaks can diminish a speaker's bass response. Prevent these leaks by being very accurate with your cutting procedures and by carefully inspecting the entire mounting of the speaker.

Often the manufacturers will mount a speaker to a steel bracket that is not sealed from the front to the rear. The

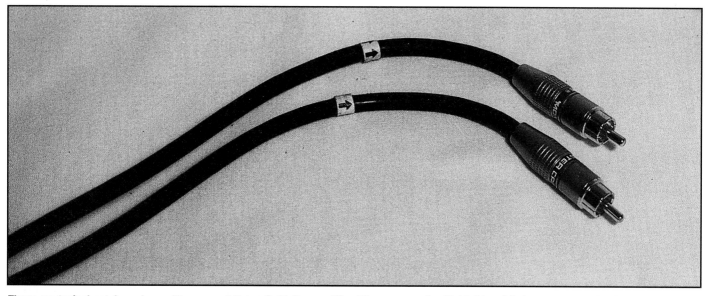
These are typical patch cords used to connect the radio to the amplifier. They are usually shielded to minimize any stray noise from being received.

sealing function on this type of speaker comes from a foam gasket fixed to the front of the speaker. The gasket presses against the backside of the car's trim panel thus sealing the cone.

Aftermarket speakers do not have this sealing gasket and the sealing function will be lost unless a new gasket is made. Paying attention to these types of small details will make the biggest sonic difference in your sound system installation.

Protecting Speakers—Protecting the speakers is necessary for the longevity of the system. The speakers must be protected from moisture, must be screwed tightly into place, and must be protected on the front side by grilles to prevent damage to the cones.

The only location where protection from moisture comes into play is in the doors. Doors have many holes in them, all of which perform different functions. Holes in the door along the front edge (hinge area) are a perfect place for water to enter. If you can seal these holes it is best, but if you can't then you have to somehow protect the speaker itself. This can easily be accomplished by using

speaker baffles. These are typically a water-proof closed-cell foam enclosure that seals the back side of the speaker cone. They can be loosely filled with poly fill stuffing (spun Dacron), which results in better sonic performance.

Stereo Troubleshooting

You will need a circuit tester, multimeter, buzz box and test light to troubleshoot a stereo installation

Testing for Speaker Shorts— Suppose you've installed a new stereo and speakers in your car. You turn it on for the first time, it sounds distorted, and the speaker cones move wildly in and out. It's possible that the speaker terminals are touching the metal of the car or that there's a break in the insulation surrounding the speaker wires allowing the bare wire to make contact with the car metal.

You can use a multimeter, a buzz box or a test light. A multimeter will give a reading in ohms and measure the amount of leakage to ground. A buzz box will make a noise, the strength of which will depend on how much current leaks to ground, and a test light will light up, dimly or brightly, depending on how much

current leaks to ground.

Unhook the speaker wires from the amplifier or radio. It is not necessary to disconnect the wires from the speakers. You will be reading from the wire to ground. Set the multimeter to the resistance or continuity setting. Adjust the needle to zero, touch the negative lead of the multimeter to a good bare metal component of the car. Touch the positive lead to each disconnected speaker wire. If everything is OK, the needle should not move.

If any lead produces a reading anywhere within the scale, the entire length of that wire (including at the speaker terminal) should be examined to see where it's making contact with bare metal. Once you've corrected that problem, your stereo should sound just fine.

If the stereo pops when it is turned on, this is generally due to the amplifier coming on first or too soon. If this is bothersome, a time delay relay can be installed to delay the turning on of the amp until after the radio is turned on for a few moments. ■

INTERIOR TIPS

11

A professional interior shop does interior work for a living. They have the proper tools and the expertise. When shopping for an upholsterer, don't even talk to someone that does furniture, because you will probably regret it. Automobile interiors are special and they have nothing in common. Look for someone that pays attention to detail, someone that plans the work rather than "winging it." Insist on seeing a sample of his work, talk to prior customers.

TRIM

No matter how much time and money you invest on your car and its interior, it will all be lost if your car doesn't have the necessary trim pieces or they are carelessly installed. There should be no reason to accept unbound carpeting, stitching that is crooked or one of my most hated, thread the does not blend with the fabrics but stands out and screams "here I am."

Adhesives and fasteners must be chosen carefully. Double-back tape and hot glue can soften and release, resulting in lost trim pieces. Clips salvaged from your donor car may be

This interior from an ERA GT40 Replica shows superb attention to detail. While not exactly plush, it is not intended to be. This interior is intended to have a period look for a classic sports car. Note the racing style harness, which should not be vintage.

the best method of all for attaching trim pieces.

One of the occasionally overlooked items are the headlight trim rings. If you are supplying your own headlight assemblies, make sure they come with trim rings. When you install the headlight assemblies, trial-fit the trim rings to ensure that the assemblies are lined up correctly.

Late-model MGB headlights have a trim ring that has a very small outside

diameter. These trim rings are a solution for a situation where trim rings were not provided. If need be, cut the ring and remove a small section from the rim, weld it back together and have it re-chromed.

CARPET

Consider the following points when choosing carpet:

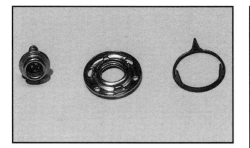

These clips are intended to hold your carpets in place without glue. The points from the fine ring (on top of the carpet) mate with the snap receiver on the underside of the carpet. The snap is attached to the floor and the carpet snaps in place making removal a snap while preventing it from creeping when you get in and out of your car.

• Jute padding, 40 oz. is preferred for insulation. 20 oz. is considered too thin. Maximum thickness, rug and insulation should not exceed about 1/2" thick.

• Foam rubber padding will do but is not preferred.

• Wool carpet, at over $55 per yard, is the most expensive but it is not good for a roadster because it will get wet and shrink.

• Velour carpet, at about $50 per yard, has nice texture and is easily cleaned and will not shrink.

• Nylon is the cheaper of your alternatives at about $15 per yard. Loop pile is rugged, resists soiling but can run if you try to drill through it. Cut pile carpet is the most difficult to keep clean.

Heel pads should be considered under the pedals. They are available in rubber or vinyl. Vinyl, unlike rubber, is available in numerous colors and will last a very long time.

SEATS

I will assume that the car has bucket seats. They should have approx-

Notice the detail in this interior. The carpets are all edge bound, and the seats all have piping on the edges. This is certainly a less plush interior, but this type of car requires just a basic interior.

imately 8 inches of travel adjustment and have an adjustable seat back. The capacity to tilt the seat bottom up and down is a nice feature but is not a necessity. The seats should be constructed to be firm enough so that the occupants will not sink into the seat.

Seat Cover Material

Vinyl, fabric or leather. Your choice of materials and color should be considered carefully. You may decide that it was not such a great idea to spend a fortune on black leather or vinyl for your seats the first time you burn your butt on them. A lighter fabric might be a wiser choice for a roadster. Dark leathers and vinyls might be a better choice for a sedan. The materials should be resistant to wear, and easy to clean.

If you purchase replacement covers and attempt to recover your seats yourself, you may find that they do not fit very well. While these covers

were made to the correct seat frame, the rubber or padding on those seats was probably brand new. Yours are old and somewhat compressed and as a result extra padding may be required to produce a good fitting and good looking job.

A smooth, flat seat will not prevent the occupants from sliding around as the car corners. Consider seats with side bolsters that are slightly raised to hold you in the seat.

Seats with headrests should be considered to reduce the possibility of whiplash injury during a rear-end collision.

SEAT BELTS

The seat belts in a street car should be comfortable. They should not make it difficult for the driver to lean forward (i.e., against the retractor forces of a self-adjusting belt system). The seat-belt should retract into a position that makes it easy for the

141

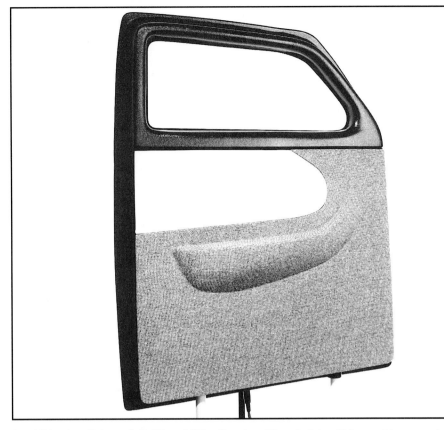

In addition to a flat panel, R. W. and Able offers ten different styles. This panel is covered with fabric that will give the interior a completely different feeling. The panels are large and can be located in any way, even on opposite sides of the car to reverse the patterns. The point is that because the panels are blank, you have greater flexibility.

These are one kind of the many door panel clips that are available for wood or masonite door panels. The retainer is driven (or pressed) into the door panel and the spring clip aligns with a hole in the door.

occupant to get in and out of the car, and it should not fall loosely so that it can be tangled or caught on anything.

Although a lap belt alone provides some protection for the vehicle passenger, a combination lap belt and shoulder harness is more effective because the shoulder harness minimizes the possibility that the occupant's head will be thrown against any part of the car's interior. An integrated shoulder harness and lap belt is considered an active three point system, meaning it is secured at three places.

Not only must safety belts be installed to restrain a vehicle occupant properly during a crash, but they should also be easy to put on and comfortable to wear; otherwise when given a choice, occupants (children especially) tend to avoid wearing them.

The most common seat belt complaints are associated with the shoulder belt part of three-point seat belt system. The proper location for the belt is across the chest, midway between the breasts at approximately the sternum. If the upper anchor is too high or inboard too much (toward the person's spine) the shoulder belt will rub or press against the wearer's neck. If the anchor is too low or too far outboard, the shoulder belt will press against the wearer's shoulder tip and possibly slip off.

Anchors

Be sure that any seat belt tabs are positioned so the load (or pull) is in a straight line (under tension) and not to the side as if you were trying to bend the tab over. If the belt anchors are bolted in, the bolts should be under a shear load.

The lap belt anchors should be positioned at a 45° fore angle to the floor or at an angle that is compatible with the direction of pull on the webbing under full load, and the width of the driver from each other. All of the mounting brackets should be attached directly to the frame or chassis of the car and limit the driver's body travel both upward and forward.

Ideally, the anchor for a shoulder harness should be anchored at a point even with or 4 inches below the top of the shoulder.

Bolts—According to the Government Regulation (49 CFR SEC 571.209), seat belt hardware should be at least 7/16-20 or preferably, 1/2-13. Most race sanctioning bodies such as the NHRA recommend grade 8 bolts.

DOOR TRIM

One of the worst things that can happen to your doors is if they open too far and the front edge strikes the fender. This will not only gouge the paint but could very well crack the fiberglass. Your doors need to be restrained. If your door hinges don't already have a limiting mechanism, you need to install stop straps. These

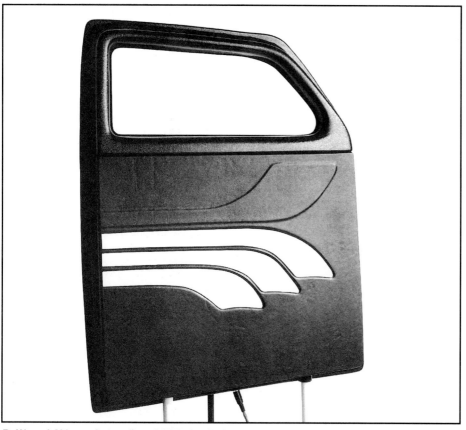

R. W. and Able markets a line of ABS plastic door panels that may just be the answer to your door panel problem. This panel is covered with vinyl and is held in place with a hook and loop fastening system. Armrests or door pulls can be added to finish the panels so they complement your interior.

are easily fabricated from leather or seat belt type webbing. One end attaches to the front of the door, near a hinge, and the other to the door jamb.

Door Panels

Inside door panels can be fabricated from heavy cardboard, pressboard, plywood (1/8") or vacu-formed polyethylene. Thin sheet foam can be used as padding under a wide variety of fabrics.

All too often, interior kits and backyard interior shops will use chrome screws to attach the door panels. If that isn't bad enough they make them even bigger by using cup washers to spread the load. When was the last time you saw screws and washers on your production auto? There is absolutely no reason to not use (production style) door panel clips to hold your door panels on. The

finished product will reward you every time you open the door to get in or out. Production door panels are held in place using metal panel clips around the perimeter, and with screws at subtle locations like through the armrest. If you need to make new door panels the process is the same regardless of the panel material you use.

You can make a template by holding paper or light cardboard against the inside of the door and tracing the outline of the door onto the template.

If the door is from a factory production model, it will likely have holes around the perimeter for panel clips. If you transfer the location of these holes to your template you will be able to use factory type panel clips. These clips can be purchased at most parts stores or they may be salvaged

from your donor car if they are still there. To use the panel clips you need to drill a hole in the door panel to hold the clips which then press into these holes. If your door is fiberglass, drill the holes every 6"–8" around the door, about 1" in from the edge. Position these holes carefully. The holes in the door panel need to be offset from the holes in the door. They are not directly in line with each other.

Cranks & Handles—Locating the holes for the window cranks and door handles is done by holding the template in place and pressing the template against the shaft. A small bit of grease on the end of the shaft will leave a mark on the template. From there on it is simply a matter of transferring the outline to the panel material, cutting and trimming the panel. Once fitted, the panel can be covered with matching upholstery.

Plastic Door Panels—Panels sculpted from ABS plastic can either be preformed or come in a flat sheet .125" thick. Kits are available consisting of enough material to cover both doors with a loop and hook fastening system, carpet clips and edge tape. The loop and lock system allows you to remove the door panel without having to pry the panel clips out of the door and chance breaking the edge of the panel. If you do happen to break the ABS you can glue it back together using ABS glue.

Hardboard only comes in flat sheets. It is cheap and easily obtainable at lumber yards and is worked the same way as the ABS.

VENTILATION

If your car doesn't have provisions for interior ventilation you only need to connect a piece of flexible duct from a clean high pressure area on the body and route it into the cockpit. Generally this duct will feed the

In order for a fresh air ventilation system to be effective, the inlet should be placed in a high pressure area. This car takes the fresh air from the front of the car near the grille opening.

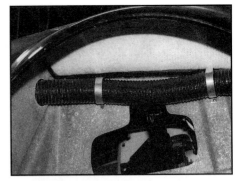

Notice how this flexible ducting is secured with metal straps that are screwed in place. The hole in the fender can be sealed with a bead of silicone or acrylic caulking.

If space is a problem, this style of fresh air inlet may be a solution for you. This inlet has a cable controlled damper to control the amount of fresh air.

This car has cable controlled dampers on each fresh air inlet.

This aluminum smoke pipe fitting measures approximately 3" in diameter and could be used to feed air into a foot box or heater box. After inserting the fitting into the panel, the tabs are bent over and caulking is applied to seal any air leaks. A damper can be constructed from sheet metal and a choke cable.

heater, which in turn directs all or part of the air through the heater core to the floor or to the windshield. Occasionally though, the fresh air inlet on the heater box can not be reached, so dampers are located somewhere in the foot box and do not tap into the heater box. If the fresh air is tapped into the heater box you will be able to temper the hot air as you drive, mixing exterior air with the heated air. You will also be able to get air movement through the cockpit as the car moves, without running the fan.

Intake Location

Locate the air intake in a high pressure area where you will get clean, fresh air. Remember, you will be breathing this air. If you take it from anywhere else you will most likely bring in fumes from the engine area that could contain carbon monoxide from leaking exhaust, smoke from any oil or coolant that could fall on hot exhaust or dust from your front brakes.

You have at least two points located in "clean" air. One is at the base of the windshield and the other is inside the grille opening. Since your body is most likely a reproduction of a body

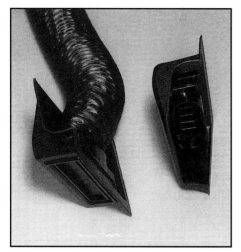

These kick panel louvers offer the advantage of directing the air flow to specific locations in the foot box or floor. They can be mounted on the kick panel, on the side of a console or under the dash. They measure about 6.5" wide by about 2" tall.

Heaters as small as one cubic foot are available for those crowded spaces. The flaps on this unit are opened to direct heated air to the foot box. If the flaps are closed, heated air is directed to the windshield. This heater is not set up to accept fresh outside air.

This is a vacuum-operated heater control valve. It is used to control the flow of hot water to the heater core. Cable operation heater control valves are also available.

Complete heat and air conditioning systems are available from Vintage Air and other manufacturers. Because of space requirements, some systems are designed to fit certain vehicles.

that doesn't have an opening at the base of the windshield, it will probably have to be the grille area. Mounting the intake as high as possible will minimize ingesting exhaust from other vehicles and shelter it from rain water or splashing from puddles. The best route for the duct will be high in the engine compartment or high inside the fender. Inside the fender is probably the better place, because it will be subjected to less engine and exhaust heat. If you must route the duct through the engine compartment consider insulating the ducting.

Because the air is taken from a high pressure area, you don't need to run the fan while the car is moving. Running the fan just to move the air around is unnecessary, and can also cause the occupants to become fatigued from the noise of the fan motor.

Most heater units have an opening for the fresh air to connect to. Your heater may have a round nipple about 4" in diameter or just an opening that seals to a hole in the donor car's firewall. If yours has a nipple, just slip the hose over it and clamp in place.

Making a Fresh Air Inlet—If your

heater box does not have a fresh air inlet, then you will need to fabricate one. A plate with a nipple of the proper size can be fastened with hardware or bonded with the appropriate adhesive to the heater box. Your fresh air inlet should have a flap of some sort that will allow you to close and seal this damper if the outside air temperature is too cool. The inlet flapper can be controlled with a push/pull cable. Most aftermarket heater systems should have all these parts included, so fabrication should be minimal.

Caution: Some dashboard A/C defusers will not withstand the elevated heat levels of your heater and may melt or get soft and deform. Make sure yours are rated for use with heat.

Heater Box

Your heater box should have an internal flap to divert the air through or around the heater core and flaps to divert the air from the floor to dash vents to defrost the windshield. Suppliers like Europa, Brooklands and Vintage Air should all have the pieces necessary to complete your heater/ventilation system.

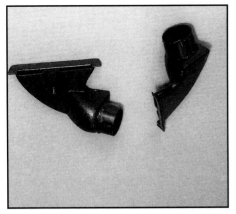

These defroster defusers are a compact 6" wide and about 4" tall, and they accept 2" diameter tubing. These may be the answer to your under dash clutter.

This 2" y connector is used to split the air flow. Sometimes you just don't have the room for two hoses.

Ducting Types

Flexible ducting is probably the easiest type of ducting to use. A length of ducting, a few clamps, inlet scoops, and discharges with dampers in the cockpit, and you're all done. Flexible ducting generally has a piece of spring wire wound through so it will hold its shape (round) and not collapse. Flexible ducting is available in a variety of materials including cloth, plastics, aluminum and stainless steel. You could use any of those but I don't recommend cloth because after a time it will rot and leak. Attaching the duct to the body is simply a matter of forming strips of aluminum around the duct and screwing or riveting it inside the fenderwell every foot or so. Keep the ducting as high as possible to keep it away from the tire as it is turned left and right.

Ridged Ducting—Ridged ducting is a little more time-consuming to create, but will make better use of the space you have. If you wanted to be more creative, you could fabricate a box on the inside of the fender where the fender meets the inner fender panel. A piece of ridged material could be bent and trimmed to fit up against the inside of the fender crown. You might need to use flexible duct to connect the ends to the heater box and the air intake. If you fiberglass the duct in, be prepared for "print through." That's when the adhesive softens the existing fiberglass and if conditions are correct you will see the bond line.

Ducting Outside the Car—If you want to be really creative, you can fabricate ducting by using Styrofoam® sheet (thin), planks or block as a mold and fiberglassing over it. The process is very simple—cut and glue the foam together, and sand it to fit the available space. Make this shape a little smaller than is needed, because you will be fiberglassing over it and it will end up slightly larger. With the shape on your bench, wrap it with plastic food wrap before you fiberglass over it so the fiberglass will not stick. After you apply a couple of coats of fiberglass, add a few tabs or anchors so it can be mechanically secured to the body.

If the shape is complex with a lot of bends, and the mold will not pop free, you can dissolve the foam by pouring a little acetone onto the Styrofoam. Be sure to let the fiberglass cure completely before you do this, and don't let the acetone stand very long on the new fiberglass or you could damage it. The plastic wrap will provide some protection to the fiberglass but not for long. The results will be a nice, hollow shape custom-fit to your body.

Note: Be careful what adhesive and resins you use. Some will dissolve certain types of foam.

WEATHERSTRIPPING

Once the body paint has cured for a while (ask the paint supplier or paint shop), the final installation of the weatherstrip, or gasket, can be done. If you are not sure where the weatherstrip goes, measure the thickness of the strip as it will be installed, take some modeling clay, and put on globs (thicker than the strip), where the gasket will go, and close the door. After the clay has been squeezed you can then measure the thickness and verify that the strip will be compressed enough to seal the door to the body. If the clay won't be compressed enough, then reroute the gasket to one side or the other.

Installation

Wipe the gasket channel clean of any paint overspray or residue from polishing or wet sanding. If you haven't already done so, pre-fit the gaskets in their respective channels and cut them to length. Do not stretch them. This will cause the rubber to get thinner, and if the adhesive allows the rubber to creep, then they will pull away from inside corners or gaps will appear at the ends. It is important to lay the gaskets on a clean, dry work surface to prevent them from attracting small objects and to keep them from becoming tangled. Apply adhesive along the entire length of the gasket and the channel where the gasket will sit. Of course you will follow the instructions on the container and allow ample time for the glue to "tack up." Locate the start point of the gasket down low (that way if the butt end of the gasket does come unglued, you'll be less likely to

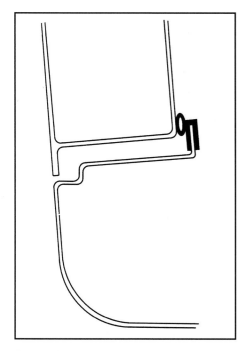

Door gaskets need to have some compression in order to seal and keep drafts and water out. Spending a little extra time here will minimize wind noise.

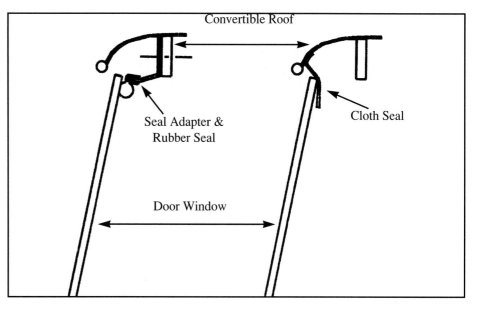

Some kits have poor window seals made from canvas. With care, a rubber seal could be fitted to seal against the glass.

have a leak) and work your way around the opening using a slight pressure on the gasket to make sure it is in full contact with the mating surface. Remember, do not stretch the gasket as you put it in. If the gasket should come loose and it has been stretched, then it could pop out of place and get caught between the door or trunk and the body.

If the gasket is the kind with a metal "U" channel with a rubber gasket attached to it, before you push it on for the final time you may want to consider applying a little silicone adhesive in the channel to prevent any water from coming in through that route. Don't assume anything. If it looks as if water may leak in, caulk it. There's nothing like the feeling of water running off the inside of the dashboard onto your legs and feet because water is leaking around the windshield or by the door gasket. The rugs get wet and begin to smell like your dog, and if it's your trunk then everything you put in will be wet. Take the time to do it correctly.

After the gasket placement is correct the proper door panels outline can be determined. Look for any possible areas that might leak water during your weekly washing or if you get caught in a rainstorm.

Windshield Gasket—If your kit is a convertible you will want to pay close attention to the weather seal around the windshield frame, the rear deck and around the window. Some donor cars and manufacturers don't have a seal around the side glass but instead have a flap. If your roof has a folding frame and you take your time you may be able to fabricate a seal for those windows. Before the cloth is installed on the frame, close and latch the frame. With the windows up, measure from the glass to a mounting point on the frame. Carefully sketch an adapter that will bolt to the frame and come close enough to the glass to hold a rubber weather seal. The weather seal can be the U-channel with a tube attached or a soft solid seal.

Gaskets are available in many different sizes and shapes so the hardest part will be deciding which profile or shape will do the best job for you. ∎

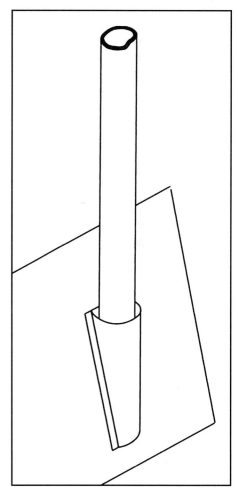

In order to seal out wind and water, a simple shield can be fabricated from light gauge tubing, fiberglass or plastic. The shield can be glued or screwed into place. A rubber seal should then be cut to slide down between the rollbar and the shield.

FINE-TUNING

W ell, there it is sitting in your driveway. The culmination of countless hours and enough money to pay for a college education. Now what? You drive it, and drive it, and drive, and drive, and drive.... That should be why you built it, but be prepared for some disappointments at first. As you drive your masterpiece, you will notice things that you don't like, or things that don't work as you expected or intended. But realize that there are adjustments to be made, each car is different and will require some massaging.

Items to look for include the exhaust note, rattles when you hit a bump, darting one way or the other as the front or rear hits a bump, excessive body roll as the car turns a corner, or a multitude of other minor problems. Don't worry, this part can be the most frustrating or rewarding part, depending on how you approach it. All I will remind you of is, you got this far by taking one step at time, and that is what you need to do when "fine tuning" your car.

Don't like the steering feel? Check to see that the steering is tight and the ratio (wheel movement to tire movement) is not excessive or sloppy. Is there movement of the steering shaft or u-joints? How about the

This car is cornering very flat through the turn, showing good roll resistance. The roll resistance can easily be improved by increasing the diameter of the anti-roll bar, using stiffer shocks or installing polyurethane bushings.

bearing mount? If you find that the steering is too slow (you turn the steering wheel too far to turn the wheels a little), a power steering rack has a faster ratio and might be the answer for you. A smaller steering wheel will allow you to turn it quicker but be careful. As the wheel gets smaller the effort required will increase.

Take the car up on the highway and check the self-tracking capabilities. The car should run straight on a flat surface (remember most highways are crowned to promote water run-off though). Does the wheel "self straighten" after you go around a corner or change lanes? If not, have

the caster rechecked. There should not be any darting back and forth after hitting a bump either. This could be a sign of "Bump Steer" or loose components and should be examined closer. If you used factory rubber suspension bushings, the suspension components may be moving under load. Aftermarket manufacturers offer just about every suspension component in polyurethane. They are effective and the improvement is immediate.

Make a list of any little problem, what happened and when or why it happened. Now all you need do is pick one at a time and deal with it.

SUSPENSION TUNING

The stiffness of the shock absorbers affects the rate that the body will roll and the resulting weight transfer. Stiffer shocks will slow the suspension movement down. Adding an anti-roll bar will slow the weight transfer down even more as the bar twists, without increasing any spring rates or making the ride too stiff.

Anti-Roll Bar

The anti-roll bar is a very important part of your car's suspension. It will share some of the roll resistance with the springs. In doing this, the anti-roll bar helps limit body roll and suspension travel during cornering. It only begins working when the car's body rolls from one side to other. When the car's body does try to roll, it resists the roll by taking weight off the inside wheel and transferring it to the outside wheel.

As a part of the "fine tuning" process you can experiment with larger front sway bars or by adding a rear anti-roll bar. You can design your bar linkage so that the leverage can be changed (effectively changing the stiffness). The shorter the lever arm, the less leverage and the stiffer the bar will act. By lengthening the lever arm the sway bar will act as if it is softer.

One of the most important uses of the anti-roll bar is to help balance the car for roll couple distribution. To illustrate how it works, let's suppose your car understeers going into a turn. Do you change to a softer front spring, or change to a softer anti-roll bar? A softer front spring means the car will dive more in the front when under hard braking. The front wheels are subjected to more camber change because the wheels are traveling more in the bump position. It is better to have the spring rates just stiff enough to resist the braking loads and let the

anti-roll bar resist body roll.

Mounting—As with the other suspension component, the softer the mounting materials the quieter the car will be, but at a sacrifice to handling crispness. The bar should be mounted as rigidly as possible so any loads applied to it will be applied to the twisting of the bar and not absorbed in compressing the bushings. In turn, more pressure is transferred (up or down) to the other tire. The best way to mount an anti-roll bar for a street application is in polyurethane blocks bolted to the chassis. If you plan on competing the car, an adjustable roll bar is recommended.

When you bolt the sway bar ends to the control arms, secure one side first then examine the other side. Both sides should be secured without twisting the bar.

Note: If you do have to push or twist the bar to get the bolts into the holes then you will have added a pre-load to the bar. Pre-load will result in more downforce on one side and less on the other. This could cause the car to respond differently when it turns from one side to the other. If for some reason the clearances are different, you can use washers to shim the mounts so there will be no pre-load.

And finally, a larger front anti-roll bar will tend to induce understeer, while the addition of a rear anti-roll bar will tend to induce oversteer.

Tires

Shorter, firmer tires have less side wall deflection. Tires with a shorter side wall tend to be less compliant with the road surface. The resulting ride will be harsher & noisier.

Miscellaneous Suspension Tips

• The softer the spring the freer the movement (more responsive to

changes) and softer the ride. Firmer springs will tend to produce a harsher ride. Springs that are too stiff prevent the suspension from following the irregularities of the road easily.

• Stiffer suspension bushings will induce crisper feel as the car reacts to cornering demands.

• The front end alignment is another area that will affect how your car drives and feels. Check it often, especially if the car isn't tracking straight, or there is a vibration through the steering wheel.

• To increase oversteer, try one of the following; to decrease oversteer try the reverse:

Increase front tire pressure.
Reduce rear tire pressure.
Add or move weight to the rear.
Increase front tire width.
Reduce rear tire width.
Add or increase rear roll stiffness with a stiffer sway bar.
Reduce front roll stiffness.

If none of these adjustments help, you should go back to your front end shop or to a race car chassis builder and discuss the problem. The technician should be able to suggest other adjustments. This process may take a few trips, but don't give up or get discouraged.

• Roll center is the point (centerline) that the body rolls around during cornering. The higher the roll center the more body roll the car will experience as the car goes through a turn. As the body rolls the suspension members move and affect weight transfer and wheel alignment. This in turn affects the stability of the car in a turn. If you lower the car, the roll center drops and the car will corner flatter and be more stable.

• Rear Axle Damper. If you discover under hard acceleration your rear axle tends to hop you can add an axle damper.

SPEEDOMETER

A question that never seems to be asked in public is, how do you dial in or set the gear ratio of your speedometer? Why do you want a calibrated speedometer in the first place? I can think of a number of reasons and most have to do with speeding tickets. I'm sure you can come up with a few of your own.

If you are using a mechanical speedometer you have a few options. You may be able to adjust the gear ratio using gears from the manufacturer of your drive train; if that doesn't work you can have a ratio converter constructed or you can have the speedometer re-calibrated. Chevrolet and Ford have replaceable speedometer gears in the transmission that are changed in order to set the ratio (see charts nearby).

Stewart Warner and VDO also offer Electric Programmable Speedometers that can be adjusted in the field by the owner to virtually any ratio. These offer the advantage of not requiring a speedometer cable or gear change as a mechanical speedometer does. A transmission sender unit is provided that is installed in place of the speedometer cable. Calibration is achieved by driving the car and setting switches on the back of the speedometer. The newer electronic speedometers have odometers that are LCD (Liquid Crystal Display). The older mechanical odometers had little wheels that would roll with an annoying click. The electronic units are a much improved system.

Calibrating Mechanical Speedos

For those that demand a cable-driven system, the process of setting the ratio consists of driving the car over a precisely measured distance and counting the number of revelations the cable makes, including parts of a revolution.

American cars are geared for the speedometer cable to turn 1000 revolutions per every mile driven. Changing tires or ring gears and pinion changes the revolutions by a percentage at all speeds. This percentage can be determined by one of the following methods:

1. Drive a measured 10-mile course after setting the trip odometer to "0." Note the reading at the end of the 10-mile course. A 9.4 reading indicates six percent slow. A 10.4 reading would indicate four percent fast.

2. Mark a 52-foot, 9 1/2" course on a driveway or parking lot with tape at the start and finish. Place a piece of tape on the rocker panel under the driver's door to match the start point on the pavement. Disconnect the speedometer cable from the speedometer head and place a paper clip on the speedometer cable core. You will need to count the revolutions. Move the car over the marked course, counting the cable revolutions as you go until you reach the tape marking the end of the course. The core will have turned ten times if the speedometer ratio is correct. However, if the core turned 9 1/2 times, you are five percent slow. If it turned 10 3/4 times, you are 7 1/2 percent fast.

Once you determine the percentage of difference, you may be able to correct it by changing the speedometer gears. If you have a Chevy or Ford tranny, see the charts

Chevy

Following is a listing of gears available for GM turbo 350 and 400 transmissions. By installing a driven gear with more teeth than the one on the Speedometer cable, the cable will turn slower and decreases the speed shown on the speedometer.

I. GM drive gears (gear on the end of the speedometer cable)

Part Number	No. of teeth
3987917	17
3987918	18
3987919	19
3987920	20
3987921	21
3987922	22
3987623	23

II. GM driven gears (the gear in the transmission that drives the Speedometer cable gear):

Turbo 350
Part Number	No. of teeth
6261783	8
6261782	9
8629547	15

Turbo 40
Part Number	No. of teeth
8629549	18
9629547	15
8440055	8

nearby for new gears.

Ford RWD Automatics

The speedometer drive gear is machined into the output shaft on Ford rear wheel drive automatic transmissions. Changing the "drive gear" is impractical, because it requires a new output shaft and

FORD

T-5 Manual Transmission Applications

Installation of the speedometer drive and driven gears shown in the following chart will provide approximately correct MPH readings. Ford Motorsport 7.5" and 8.8" axle ratios are installed in conjunction with the T-5 transmission, and P225/60VR15 Gatorback tires (815 revolutions per mile) when the indicated.

Motorsport Axle Ratio	Speedometer Drive Gear			Speedometer Driven Gear		
Axle Ratio	Part Number	Teeth	Color	Part Number	Teeth	Color
3.27:1	E3ZZ-17285-A	7	Yellow	CODZ-17271-B	19	Pink
3.45/3.55:1	E3ZZ-17285-A	7	Yellow	C1DZ-17271-A	20	Black
3.73:1	E3ZZ-17285-A	7	Yellow	C4DZ-17271-A	21	Red
4.10:1	E3ZZ-17285-B	6	Black	C1DZ-17271-A	20	Black

Automatic Transmission Applications

Axle Ratio	Drive teeth	Tire Size	Speedometer driven gear Part Number	Driven teeth	Color
3.27:1	7	225/60VR15	C7VY-17271-A	19	Tan
	7	225/60VR16	C7BZ-17271-B	18	Gray
	8	225/60VR16	D0OZ-17271-B	21	Purple
3.45/3.55:1	7	225/60VR15	C8SZ-17271-B	20	Orange
	7	225/60VR16	C7VY-17271-B	19	Orange
3.73:1	7	225/60VR15	D0OZ-17271-B	21	Purple
	7	225/60VR16	C8SZ-17271-B	20	Orange

complete transmission tear down. To determine the number of drive gear teeth, simply remove the extension housing and count them. Most have 7 or 8 teeth. Listed below are some of the more popular performance axle ratios and tire combinations.

Special applications, driven gear calculation example:

Step 1—If your axle/tire combination is not in the above charts, you can calculate the number of teeth required on the driven gear by using this formula:

Driven Gear Teeth = Drive Gear Teeth x Axle Ratio X Tire rpm/1000.

As an example, plug in the following numbers for a T-5 transmission.

T-5 Trans

Drive Gear Teeth =7
Axle Ratio = 3.73:1
Tire rev. per mile =815 (225/60VR15).

You would select a driven gear with the closest whole number of teeth, that would be the 21 tooth C40Z-17271-A part.

Summary—If the drive gear is changed to one with more teeth, the Speedometer will show a decrease in speed. Fewer teeth will show an increase in speed. The percentage of change depends on how many more or fewer teeth are on the gears compared to the gears that you are replacing.

If after all of that you still can not "set" your speedometer, Stewart Warner or most speedometer repair shops can make a ratio adapter that will make the necessary correction. These are occasionally referred to as "Drive Joints" or "ratio converters." These gear reduction boxes compensate for tire or gear changes that cause your speedometer to read wrong. ■

CONTRIBUTORS LIST

ERA Cars
608-612 Main Street
New Britain, CT 06051
860 224 0253

Carrera Shocks
5412 New Peach Tree Rd.
Atlanta Ga. 30341
770 451 8811

ADDCO
715 13th St.
Lake Park, Fla. 33403
800 338 7015

COOL IT, Thermo Tec Products
PO. Box 96
Greenwich. Oh. 44837
419 962 4556
419 962 4013 fax
800 274 8437

Rockford Fosgate
546 South Rockford Drive
Tempe, AZ. 85281
602 967 3565

Wilwood Engineering (Brakes)
461 Calle San Pablo
Camarillo, California 93012
805 388 1188

ECI (Engineered Components Inc.)
(Brakes)
PO. Box 841
Vernon, CT. 06066
203 872 7046

Stabalus Gas Springs
92 County Line Rd.
Colmar Pa, 18915 9607
215 822 1982.

Emhart Fastners, Inc.
510 River Road
Shelton, CT. 06484
203 924 9341
800 225 5614 fax

Specialty Power Windows
2087 Collier Rd.
Forsyth, Ga. 31029
800 634 9801

**TCI Transmissions &
Torque Converters**
601 224 8972

Energy Suspension
960 Calle Amanexer
San Clemente, Ca. 92672
714 361 3935

VDO /Yazaki
188 Brooke Rd.
Winchester, VA. 22603
703 665 0100,

Stewart Warner Instruments
580 Slawin CT.
Mount Prospect, IL. 60056
800 927 0278

Accel
8700 Brookpark Road
Cleveland, OH. 44129
216 398 8300 213

Sanderson Headers
202 Ryan Way
South San Francisco, CA. 94080
415 583 4590
800 669 2430

Doug Thorly Headers
1561 Commerce St.
Corona, CA. 91720
909 735 7280

MAC Products
43214 Black Dear Loop, Unit 113
Temecula, CA 92590-3473
(909) 699 9440
(800) 367 4486

Flow Master
707 544 4761
800 544 4761

Imperial Eastman, Inc.
6300 West Howard St.
Niles, Il, 60714-3492
888 467 8665

Neutronmics Ent.
11421 W. Bernardo Court
San Diago, CA. 92127-1639
619 674 2250
EMAIL: NEUTRONICS.COM

Walbro Automotive Fuel Systems
810 377 1800
Michigan

Tanks Inc.
PO. Box 400
Clearwater, MN 55320
612 558 6882 phone & fax

First Enertia (Fuel shut off switch)
P.O. Box 704
Grand Blanc, MI 48439
810 695 8333

Vintage Air.
10305 I.H. 35 North
San Antonio, TX. 78233
800 862 6658

Badger Interior Coachworks
259 Great Western Road
South Dennis, Ma. 02660
508 394 2680

R. W. and Able, Inc.
P.O. Box 2110
636 Nord Avenue, #D
Chino, CA. 95927
(919) 896-1513

Steele Rubber Products
Highway 150 East
Denver, NC 28037-9735
704 483 9343
http://www.steelerubber.com

Flow Kooler
289 Prado Rd.
San Luis Obispo, CA. 93401
805 544 8841

Walker Radiator
694 Marshall Ts.
Memphis TN. 38103
901 527 4605

Modine Radiators
1500 DeKoven Ave.
Racine MI 53403
800 276 5095

Ron Francis Wire Works.
167 Keystone Road
Cheaster, PA 19013
610 485 1981

Painless Wiring
9505 South Paula Dr.
Fortworth, TX 76116-5929
800 423 9696
http://www.painlesswiring.com

Rhode Island Wiring Services
PO. Box 434
W. Kingston, RI. 02892
410 789 1955

Centech Wiring
7 Colonial Drive
Perkimenville, Pa 18074
610 287 6730

Cole Hersee
20 Old Colony Ave.
S. Boston MA. 02127-2467
617 268 2100

Snap Action
1260 Rte 22 West
Mountianside, N.J. 07092

Total Performance
400 South Orchard St.
Wallingford, CT. 06492
203 265 5667

Tweeter etc.
508 771 2400
508 778 6746

**Ford Motor Sport Performance
Equipment.**
44050 N. Groesbeck Highway
Clinton Township, MI. 48036-1108
810 468 1356

Callaway Cars
2 High St.
Old Lyme, CT. 06371
203 434 9002

Chevrolet Motor Sport Tech.
810 492 6871
810 492 9084 fax
Warren Michigan.

Alan L. Colvin
PO 3533
Dayton Iohio 45401
Chevrlotte by the Numbers.
937 277 9320

The Car Channel
www.carchannel.com

Howell Engine Development Industries
6201 Industrial way
Marine City MI 48039
810 765 5100

Holley Carburetors
1801 Russellville Road
PO. Box 10360
Bowling Green, KY 42102-7360
502 745 9530

Digital Fuel Injection
29387 Lorie Lane
Wixom, MI 48393
810 380 1322

K&N Engineering
P.O.Box 1329
Riverside, CA 92502
909 684 9762
800 858 3333

S & W Race Cars. (Roll Bar)
11 Mennonite Circle
Spring City, PA. 19475
800 523 3533
610 948 7303

Perfection Automotive Products.
Catalic Converters
800 468 4970

Competition Cams
3406 Democrat Rd.
Memphis, TN
910 366 1897

Edelbrock
2700 Calf. St.
Torrance, CA. 90503
800 739 3737

Crane Cams
530 Fentress Blvd.
Daytona, FL 32114
904 252 1151 x 4203

B.F. Goodrich/Michelin
South Carolina
803 458 6957

Fibre Glast Developments Corp.
1944 Neva Dr.
Dayton, Ohio 45414
800 838 8924

P.P.G.
189 East View Ave
Cranston, RI. 02920
617 729 7580

Prism Powder Coatings
12 Kendrick Rd. Unit #9
Wareham, MA.
508 295 5601
Research Source list

Factory Five
18 Kendrick Rd.
Wareham, MA 02571

TABLES

Table #1

Recommended Torque Values
SAE Grade 2, 5, 8, Cap screws, bolts and studs.

Torques listed are suggested values on parts with a coating of light oil as would be received from the manufacturer. These values do not apply to plated or otherwise lubricated parts.

Size & Thread	Grade 2 Load lbs.	Grade 2 Torque lbs.	Grade5 Load lbs.	Grade5 Torque lbs	Grade 8 Load lbs.	Grade 8 Torque lbs.
1/4-20	1300	6	2000	11	2850	12
1/4-28	1500	7	2300	13	3250	15
5/16-18	2155	13	3350	21	4700	25
5/16-24	2400	14	3700	23	5200	30
3/8-16	3200	23	4850	38	6950	50
3/8-24	3600	26	5600	40	7900	60
7/16-14	4400	37	6800	55	9600	85
7/16-20	4900	41	7850	60	10700	95
1/2-13	5850	57	9050	85	12800	125
1/2-20	6550	64	10200	95	14400	140
9/16-12	7550	80	11600	125	16400	175
9/16-18	8350	91	13000	140	18000	195
5/8-11	9300	111	14500	175	20300	245
5/8-18	10500	128	16300	210	23000	270

Table #2

General Conversion Table for Torque Units

to Obtain	Multiply by	Inch oz.	Inch lbs.	Ft-lbs.	Meter Kilograms	Newton Meters
Inch ounces	1	16	192	13.89	1389	141.6
Inch pounds	.06251	1	12	.8680	86.80	8.851
Foot pounds	.005208	.083332	1	.07233	7.233	.7376
Centimeter kilograms	.07201	1.152	13.83	1	100	10.20
Meter Kilograms[3]	.0007201	.01152	.1383	.01	1	.1020
Newton-Meters	.007061	.1130	1.356	.09806	9.806	1

1 or divide by 16
2 or divide by 12
[3] Meter Kilogram (mkg) is also known as Meter Kilopond (mkp)

Table #3

Inch-Metric Conversion Table.

Inches Frac.	Dec.	mm	Inches Frac.	Dec.	mm
1/64	0.015 625	0.3969	33/64	0.515 625	13.0969
1/32	0.031 250	0.7938	17/32	0.531 250	13.4938
3/64	0.046 875	1.1906	35/64	0.546 875	13.8906
1/16	0.062 500	1.5875	9/16	0.562 500	14.2875
5/64	0.078 125	1.9844	37/64	0.578 125	14.6844
3/32	0.093 750	2.3812	19/32	0.593 750	15.0812
7/64	0.109 375	2.7781	39/64	0.609 375	15.4781
1/8	0.125 000	3.1750	5/8	0.625 000	15.8750
9/64	0.140 625	3.5719	41/64	0.640 625	16.2719
5/32	0.156 250	3.9688	21/32	0.656 250	16.6688
11/64	0.171 875	4.3656	43/64	0.671 875	17.0656
3/16	0.187 500	4.7625	11/16	0.687 500	17.4625
13/64	0.203 125	5.1594	45/64	0.703 125	17.8594
7/32	0.218 750	5.5562	23/32	0.718 750	18.2562
15/64	0.234 375	5.9531	47/64	0.734 375	18.6531
1/4	0.250 000	6.3500	3/4	0.750 000	19.0500
17/64	0.265 625	6.7469	49/64	0.765 625	19.4469
9/32	0.281 250	7.1438	25/32	0.781 250	19.8437
19/64	0.296 875	7.5406	51/64	0.796 875	20.2406
5/16	0.312 500	7.9375	13/16	0.812 500	20.6375
21/64	0.328 125	8.3344	53/64	0.828 125	21.0344
11/32	0.343 750	8.7312	27/32	0.843 750	21.4312
23/64	0.359 375	9.1281	55/64	0.859 375	21.8281
3/8	0.375 000	9.5250	7/8	0.875 000	22.2250
25/64	0.390 625	9.9219	57/64	0.890 625	22.6219
13/32	0.406 250	10.3188	29/32	0.906 250	23.0188
27/64	0.421 875	10.7156	59/64	0.921 875	23.4156
7/16	0.437 500	11.1125	15/16	0.937 500	23.8125
29/64	0.453 125	11.5094	61/64	0.953 125	24.2094
15/32	0.468 750	11.9062	31/32	0.968 750	24.6062
31/64	0.484 375	12.3031	63/64	0.984 375	25.0031
1/2	0.500 000	12.7000	1	1.000 000	25.4000

Table #4

Sheet Metal Gauges in decimals of an inch and millimeters U.S.S. Mfg. Standard Gauge

Sheet metal gauge	Inches (approx.)	mm (approx.)
3	.2391	6.073
4	.2242	5.695
5	.2092	5.314
6	.1943	4.935
7	.1793	4.554
8	.1644	4.176
9	.1495	3.797
10	.1345	3.416
11	.1196	3.038
12	.1046	2.657
13	.0897	2.278
14	.0747	1.897
15	.0673	1.709
16	.0598	1.519
17	.0538	1.367
18	.0478	1.214
19	.0418	1.062
20	.0359	0.912
21	.0329	0.836
22	.0299	0.759
23	.0269	0.683
24	.0239	0.607
25	.0209	0.531
26	.0179	0.455
27	.0164	0.417
28	.0149	0.378
29	.0135	0.343
30	.0120	0.305

Table #5

Wire Size (Gauge) vs Current Carrying Capacity.

Wire size AWG	OHMS (resistance) per 1000 ft	Current Carrying Capacity @ 700 CM/AMP
00	0.0779	190
0	0.0983	151
2	0.1563	95
4	0.2485	60
6	0.3951	38
8	0.6282	24
10	0.9989	15
12	1.588	9
14	2.525	6
16	4.016	4
18	6.385	2
20	10.15	1

Table #6
Drill-Tap Chart

Screw Size	Dec. equiv.	Threads per inch	Tap Drill size	Dec. Equiv.	Clearance Holes Close fit		Free fit	
					Size	Dec.	Size	Dec.
0	.060	80	3/64	.0469	52	.0635	50	.7000
1	.073	72	53	.0595	48	.0760	46	.0810
2	.086	56	50	.0700	43	.0890	41	.0960
		64	50	.0700				
3	.099	48	47	.0785	37	.1040	35	.1100
		56	45	.0820				
4	.112	36	44	.0860	32	.1160	30	.1285
		40	43	.0890				
		48	42	.0935				
5	.125	40	38	.1015	30	.1285	29	.1360
		44	37	.01040				
6	.138	32	36	.1065	27	.1440	25	.1495
		40	33	.1130				
8	.164	32	29	.1360	18	.1695	16	.1770
		36	29	.1360				
10	.190	24	25	.1495	9	.1960	7	.2010
		32	21	.1590				
12	.216	24	16	.1770	2	.2210	1	.2280
		28	14	.1820				
14	.242	20	10	.1935	D	.2464	F	.2570
		24	7	.2010				
1/4	.250	20	7	.2010	F	.2570	H	.2660
		28	3	.2130				
5/16	.3125	18	F	.2570	P	.3230	O	.3320
		24	I	.2720				
3/8	.375	16	5/16	.3125	W	.3860	X	.3970
		24	Q	.3320				
7/16	.4375`	14	U	.3680	29/64	.4531	15/32	.4687
		20	25/64	.3906				
1/2	.500	13	27/64	.4219	33/64	.5156	17/32	.5312\
		20	29/64	.4531				

TABLE 7
Springs & Shocks.

1. Overall weight of your car:
2. Axle weight, Front:_____Rear:_____

2a Leverage Ratio.
The amount of travel that the shock has for each inch of travel at the wheel.
Front:_____Rear:_____

3. Static ride height & the angle that the shock will be installed at.
Installed (static) Angle, Front:_____Rear:_____

4. Determine the fully extended and fully compressed lengths, and the amount of travel or stroke.
Extended_____Compressed_____Stroke_____

TABLE 8
Driveline, Universal Joint Alignment

Note: All angles are in the horizontal plane.

1. Transmission (crankshaft center line angle).

2. Rear axle(pinion center line angle).

3. Driveshaft angle
Single _____ Dual _____

Do angles 1 & 2 intersect £, (not good) or are they parallel £ (good)? Re-align the drive line if the angles intersect

4. Universal joint angle
Front _____ Rear _____

5. Maximum recommended Drive shaft speed = Drive shaft length divided by 5.
Length _____ divided by 5 = Max _____ RPM

Table #9
Drill Sizes
Number vs. Decimal

80 - .0135	54 - .055	28 - .1405	2 - .221
79 - .0145	53 - .0595	27 - .144	1 - .228
78 - .016	52 - .0635	26 - .147	A - .234
77 - .018	51 - .067	25 - .1495	B - .238
76 - .020	50 - .070	24 - .152	C - .242
75 - .021	49 - .073	23 - .154	D - .246
74 - .0225	8 - .076	22 - .157	E - .250
73 - .024	47 - .0785	21 - .159	F - .257
72 - .025	46 - .081	20 - .161	G - .261
71 - .026	45 - .082	19 - .166	H - .266
70 - .028	44 - .086	18 - .1695	I - .272
69 - .0292	43 - .089	17 - .173	J - .277
68 - .031	42 - .0935	16 - .177	K - .281
67 - .032	41 - .096	15 - .180	L - .290
66 - .033	40 - .098	14 - .182	M - .295
65 - .035	39 - .0995	13 - .185	N - .302
64 - .036	38 - .1015	12 - .189	O - .316
63 - .037	37 - .104	11 - .191	P - .323
62 - .038	36 - .1065	10 - .1935	Q - .332
61 - .039	35 - .110	9 - .196	R - .339
60 - .040	34 - .111	8 - .199	S - .348
59 - .041	33 - .113	7 - .201	T - .358
58 - .042	32 - .116	6 - .204	U - .368
57 - .043	31 - .120	5 - .2055	V - .377
56 - .0465	30 - .1285	4 - .209	W - .386
55 - .052	29 - .136	3 - .213	X - .397
			Y - .404

General Conversion table, just in case I missed something in the other tables.

To Convert From:	To:	Multiply By:	To Convert From:	To:	Multiply By:
Length					
Inch	Millimeter	25.4	Millimeter	Inch	.03937
Foot	Meter	.3048	Meter	Foot	3.28084
Yard	Meter	.9144	Meter	yard	1.093613
Mile	Kilometer	1.609347	Kilometer	Mile	.62137
Area					
Sq. inch	Sq. millimeter	645.16	Sq. Millimeter	Sq. inch	.00155
Sq. Foot	Sq. Meter	.092903	Sq. Meter	Sq. foot	10.763915
Sq. Yard	Sq. Meter	.836127	Sq. Meter	Sq. Yard	1.195991
Volume					
Cubic inch	Cubic Millimeter	16387.06	Cubic Millimeter	Cubic inch	.000061
Cubic feet	Cubic Meter	.028317	Cubic Meter	Cubic feet	35.314662
Cubic yard	Cubic meter	.764555	Cubic meter	Cubic yard	1.307950
Gallons	Liter	3.785412	Liter	Gallon	.264172
Quart	Liter	.946353	Liter	Quart	1.056688
Mass					
Ounce	Gram	28.349520	Gram	Ounce	.035274
Pound	Kilogram	.453592	Kilogram	Pound	2.204624
Short Ton	Kilogram	907.185	Kilogram	Short Ton	.00110
Force					
Ounce-Force	Newton	.278014	Newton	Ounce-Force	3.596941
Pound-Force	Newton	4.48222	Newton	Pound-Force	.224809
Bending Moment					
Pound-Force Inch	Newton Meter	.112985	Newton-Meter	Pound-Force Inch	8.850732
Pound-Force Foot	Newton-Meter	1.355818	Newton-Meter	Pound-Force Foot	.737562

(continued)

To Convert From:	To:	Multiply By:	To Convert From:	To:	Multiply By:
Pressure, Stress					
Pound-Force, psi	Kilo Pascal	6.894757	Kilo Pascal	Pound-Force, psi	145038
Foot of Water	Kilo Pascal	2.988980	Kilo Pascal	Foot of Water	334562
Inch of Mercury	Kilo Pascal	3.386380	Kilo Pascal	Inch of Mercury	.295301
Energy, Work, Heat					
Foot-Pound-Force	Joule	1.355818	Joule	Foot-Pound-Force	.737562
British Thermal unit	Joule	1055.056	Joule	British Thermal Unit	.000948
Calorie (cal)	Joule (J)	4.1868	Joule (J)	Calorie (cal)	.238846
Kilowatt Hour (kW-h)	Joule (J)	3600000	Joule (J)	Kilowatt Hour (kW-h)	2.78-7
Power					
Foot-Pound Force/Second	Watt	1.355818	Watt	Foot-Pound Force/Second	.737562
British Thermal Unit/Hr	Watt	.293071	Watt	British Thermal Unit/Hr	3.412142
Horsepower	Kilowatt	.745700	Kilowatt	Horsepower	1.34102
Angle					
Degree	Radian	.017453	Radian	Degree	57.295788
Temperature					
Degree Fahrenheit	Degree Celsius	(F - 32)/1.8	Degree Celsius	Degree Fahrenheit	1.8xC +32

COST ESTIMATING TABLE

		Wheels and Tires	
Kit Cost	$_____	Wheels	$_____
Paint Frame	$_____	Tires	$_____
		Total Wheels and Tires	$_____
Rear Suspension		Fasteners	
Ford 8.8" Rear End, new	$_____	Chrome or stainless	$_____
Ford 8", 8.8" or 9", rebuilt	$_____	Body	
Disc Brake Conversion	$_____	Task	
Coilover Shocks	$_____	Material cost	
Four Link	$_____	Body mount	$_____
Subcontract Installation	$_____	Installation labor, 8 hours	$_____
Total Rear Suspension	$_____	Prep and Paint	$_____
		Windshield	$_____
Front Suspension		Installation labor, 3 hours	$_____
Rebuild Kit	$_____	Windshield Wiper Assembly:	$_____
Steering Rack	$_____	Door latches	$_____
Steering Column, Tilt	$_____	Installation labor, 2 hours	$_____
Steering Shaft Parts	$_____	Tail lights	$_____
Aftermarket Sway Bar, front	$_____	Installation labor, 1 hour	$_____
Aftermarket Sway Bar, rear	$_____	Headlights	$_____
Total Front Suspension	$_____	Installation labor, 1 hour	$_____
		Fuel tank	$_____
Brake System		Installation labor, 2 hours	$_____
Master Cylinder & Booster	$_____	Wiring harness	$_____
Rear Disc Brake Option	$_____	Installation labor, 12 hours	$_____
Front Disk Upgrade, 11"	$_____		
Proportioning Valve	$_____	**Interior**	
Residual Pressure Valve/2	$_____	Drop in	$_____
Metering Valve	$_____	Installation labor, 7 hours	$_____
Brake Tubing	$_____	Carpeting	$_____
Flex Lines	$_____	Installation labor, 4 hours	$_____
Total Brake Cost	$_____	Gauges	$_____
		Installation labor, 5 hours	$_____
Engine / Transmission		Steering wheel	$_____
5.0 or 5.7-L Engine, New	$_____	Installation labor, 1 hour	$_____
Exhaust System	$_____	Stereo/Speakers	$_____
Custom Headers	$_____	Installation labor, 2 hours	$_____
Radiator	$_____	Antenna, power	$_____
Electric Fan	$_____	Installation labor, 2 hours	$_____
Engine chrome kit	$_____	Shifter	$_____
Transmission	$_____	Installation labor, 2 hours	$_____
Shifter	$_____	Seats	$_____
Kick Down &Throttle cables	$_____	Installation labor, 2 hours	$_____
Fuel Lines	$_____	Seat Belts, 3 point	$_____
Driveshaft, shortened	$_____	Heater/AC	$_____
Total Engine /Transmission	$_____		

COST ESTIMATING TABLE
(continued)

Total Parts cost $_____

Total Labor cost $_____

Miscellaneous Costs
Under coat $_____

Misc. paint , adhesives and caulking

   Total Misc. cost $_____

Registration costs, plates, etc. $_____
Insurance cost $_____
Sales tax $_____
Excise tax $_____

TOTAL ESTIMATED COST TO BUILD YOUR CAR
         $_____

TOOLS CHECKLIST

Basic Hand Tools
Roll-away and Tool Chest
Hammers, Ball Peen, large and small, Nylon (1).
Chisel and Center Punch set.
Screwdrivers (non chrome tips)
Adjustable Wrenches
Vise Grips, assortment, large and small
Pliers and Cutters
Offset, reversible screwdrivers, flat and Phillips Head
Socket sets, Deep/Shallow sockets, Metric and SAE. 3/8" and 1/2" drive with assorted length extensions and universal joints
Nut Drivers, (with hollow shank) 3/16" - 1/2"
Torx tips set
Hex Bit head tips, 5/32" - 3/8"
Hex Key Set, SAE 5/64" - 3/8"
Hex Key Set, Metric, 1.5mm - 8mm
Wrenches, Combination, SAE 1/4" - 1"
Wrenches, Combination, Metric6mm - 19mm
Wrenches, Flare Nut, SAE 3/8" - 7/8"
Wrenches, Flare Nut, Metric 9mm - 17mm
Torque Wrench, 1/2" drive

Scissors, 2 pieces
Tin Snips, right hand
Tin snips, left hand
Clamp set, C Clamp and Pony
Scribe
Tape Measure, 25'
Machinist scale or metal ruler
Combination Square
Vise, 6"
Hack saw
File set
Soldering Iron
Pop Riveter
Wire Strippers
Volt Ohm Meter
Clamp Light
Jack stands
Hydraulic Jack
Creeper
Drop Light, Fluorescent
Fire Extinguisher
Dust pan and Broom

Power Tools
Shop Vacuum
Saber saw, electric
Electric Drill, 1/2"
Reciprocating saw
Tap and Drill set
Drill bits
Hole Saw Kit
Bench Grinder
Disc grinder

Optional tools
Electric Drill, variable speed, reversible
Bench Sander
Small Drill Press
Angle vise
Heat Gun
Impact Wrench
Small Compressor
Air (mini) Saw
Air ratchet
Blowing gun
Oxygen and Acetylene Torches
Arc Welder
Brake Line Flaring tools
Tubing bender
Tubing Cutter

Owner's Manual

Make copies of these two pages, then fill in all information and keep this in a safe place.

MODEL & ID NUMBERS

Make & Year:_____

MSO:_____

VIN:_____

Body #:_____

Engine Casting #:_____

Transmission/Casting #:_____

Frame Serial #:_____

DIMENSIONAL DATA

Length:_____

Width:_____

Height:_____

Ground Clearance:_____

Wheelbase:_____

Track Fr.:_____Rr.:_____

Curb Weight:_____

Weight Distribution:_____

CAPACITIES & FILTERS

Engine Oil :_____

Engine Oil Filter:_____

Air Filter:_____

Fuel Filter:_____

Fuel Capacity :_____

Transmission Fluid Capacity:_____

Coolant capacity:_____

Power Steering fluid Capacity:_____

Rear End capacity:_____

Brake Fluid:_____

TUNE UP INFORMATION

Ignition Timing:_____

Ignition Module/Point #:_____

Spark Plug #:_____

Spark Plug Gap:_____

Spark Plug Wire #:_____

Firing Order:_____

Idle Speed:_____

FRAME & SUSPENSION

Make & Year:_____

Front

Suspension Type:_____

Springs:_____

Steering Box:_____

Shock Absorbers:_____

Wheels:_____

Tire:_____

Toe:_____

Caster Left:_____Right:_____

Camber:_____

Bushings:_____

Sway bar:_____

Rear

Type:_____

Make & Year:_____

Rear Axle:_____

Shocks:_____

Spring Rate:_____

Wheels:_____

Tires:_____

Sway Bar:_____

Bushing:_____

Brakes

Master Cylinder:_____

Piston Diameter:_____

Pedal Ratio:_____

Weight Bias:_____

Power Booster:_____

Caliper Piston Diameter:_____

Rotor Diameter:_____

Wheel Cylinder (or caliper):_____

Piston Diameter:_____

Drum (or rotor) Diameter:_____

ENGINE

Make & Year:_____

Number of Cylinders:_____

Machining by:_____

Bore :_____

Stroke :_____

Stock Displacement :_____

Current displacement :_____

Crank type:_____

Connecting Rods:_____

Pistons :_____

Compression Ratio:_____

Rings:_____

End Gap :_____

Main Bearings:_____

Rod Bearings:_____

Cylinder Heads:_____

Chamber Volume:_____

Valve Springs Specs:_____

Installed Specs:_____

Flywheel/Flex Plate:_____

Camshaft :_____

Lifters:_____

HP:_____

Torque:_____

Engine Electrical

Starter :_____

Alternator :_____

Voltage Regulator :_____

Distributor:_____

Ignition Modifications:_____

Carburetor / Injection:_____

Exhaust Manifolds :_____

Mufflers:_____

TRANSMISSION

Make & Year :_____

Model :_____

Clutch/Torque Converter:_____

Gearing:_____

Shifter

Driveshaft Length :_____

Universal Joints:_____

BODY

Radiator :_____

Hoses:_____

Fan:_____

Thermostat:_____

Coolant Type:_____

ACCESSORIES

Donor Vehicle:_____

Front Bumper:_____

Rear Bumper :_____

Door Handles/Latches:_____

Trunk handle / Latch :_____

Hood release / Latch:_____

Windshield:_____

Roof:_____

Fuel Tank:_____

Lighting:_____

Steering Column:_____

Side Windows:_____

GAUGES, LIGHTS & WIRING

Gauges:_____

Wiring:_____

Fuse Box:_____

Head Lamps:_____

Parking Lamps:_____

Driving / Fog Lamps:_____

Tail Lamps:_____

Stop Lamps:_____

Plate Lamp:_____

Dash Lamps:_____

Misc Lamps:_____

Seats :_____

Air Conditioner:_____

Misc:_____

MAINTENANCE

Mileage:_____

Engine Oil:_____

Transmission Lube:_____

Rear End Lube:_____

Filters:_____

Air:_____

Oil:_____

Transmission:_____

Fuel:_____

INDEX

A

ABS systems, 4546
Acceleration defined, 28
Adhesives, 12
  hot metal, 12
  solventbased, 12
Aftermarkets, 6164
  Accel, 6263
  Edelbrock, 63
  Holley, 62
  Howell Engine Development, 6364
Air intakes, engine, 9495
Alternators, 121
Ammeters, 133
Amp hour ratings, 121
Amplifiers
  power, 136137
  and speakers, 136139
Antiroll bars, 149
Axles
  dampers, 2223
  weights, 35

B

Bars, antiroll, 149
Batteries, 120
Body
  assembly, 8388
    attaching body, 8687
    attaching fiberglass panels, 85
    correcting poor fitting parts, 8788
    trial fittings, 8485
  doors, 8890
    bracing, 89
    nonfitting, 88
    reassembling, 8990
    shaky, 8889
    warped, 89
  fiberglass and other composites, 7983
  fibers, 8081
  front end, 9099
    inspection, 9192
    reducing cowl shake and flex, 9091
    vibration prone areas, 91
  hood/trunk gas springs, 99103
  insulation, 103107
  mounting, 8586
  post curing, 8182
  powder coating, 83
  prep, 8283
  resins, 80
  storage, 84
  tips, 79108
  tire and wheel clearance, 107108
Bolts, 11, 142
Bonding pieces, 12
Brakes
  ABS systems, 4546
    electronic, 46
    mechanical, 4546
  building it on paper, 3639
    donor car system, 3839
    increasing performance, 3638
  installation tips, 4245

bleeding, 44
brake lines, 4244
documentation, 45
lines, 4142
  flare types, 4142
  mild steel, 41
  rubber vs. braided stainless steel, 42
  tubing requirements, 42
pedal feel, 45
system components, 3942
tips, 3646
troubleshooting, 4445
Budgeting, 46
  parts lists, 5
  payment, 6
  shopping, 56
Bump steer, 2021
Bushings, 2527
  leaf spring, 2627
  polyurethane, 26
  rear control arm, 27
  rubber, 26
  strut rods and control arm, 26
  sway bar, 27

C

CAGS (computer aided gear selection), 72
Camshafts, 4950
  duration, 50
  lift, 50
  overlap, 50
Carburetors, 5357
  recommendations, 5657
  selection, 5456
    air capacity, 5455
    vacuum vs. mechanical secondaries, 56
    volumetric efficiency (V.E.), 5556
Carpets, 140141
Caster, 21
Catalytic converters, 6869
CCA (cold cranking amps), 120
Center of gravity, locating, 101102
Chassis
  front end, 2122
  inspection, 1516
    square, 1718
    twist, 17
    welds, 1617
  painting, 24
  rear end, 2224
    axle dampers, 2223
    fuel tanks, 23
    leaf spring wrap up, 2223
    radiators, 24
    tank vents, 2324
  steering racks, 1820
  suspension geometry, 2021
  tips, 1524
Circuit breakers, 122123
Clubs, 2
Coil springs, 3435
Connectors
  installing, 127
  solderless or crimp, 124127

D

Documentation, 89
  donor car information, 9
  owner's manual, 9
Doors, 8890
  bracing, 89
  nonfitting, 88
  panels, 143
  reassembling, 8990
  shaky, 8889
  trim, 142143
  warped, 89
Drive ratios, 78
Driver controls and aids, 114119
  gauge layouts, 117118
  gear shifts, 117
  GM steering columns, 116117
  pedal assemblies, 114115
  rear view mirrors, 118
  seats, 116
  steering columns, 116117
  switches, 117
  windshield wipers and washers, 118119
Driveshafts, 7376
  angles, 7476
  lengths, 7374
  vibration, 74, 76
Drivetrains
  gear selection, 7678
    aspect ratios, 7778
    effective drive ratios, 78
    equivalent drive ratios, 78
    oversize tires, 77
    section height and width, 77
  tips, 7178
  transmissions, 7173
    Chevy, 7172
    Ford, 7273
    GM automatics, 7172
    tips, 73
Dual plane manifolds, 5759

E

EGO (Exhaust Gas Oxygen) sensors, 60
Electrical systems, 120139
  components, 120124
    alternators, 121
    amp hour ratings, 121
    batteries, 120
    circuit breakers, 122123
    circuit protection, 122123
    cranking power, 120121
    fuse box locations, 123
    fuse panels, 122
    fusible links, 122
    relays, 123124
    voltage regulators, 121122
  flashers, 134
  reserve capacity, 121
  stereo systems, 135136
  troubleshooting, 133135
    light, 134
    start up, 134135
Electrical wiring concepts, 124128

Electronic systems; See Electrical systems
Engines
  air intakes, 9495
  cooling, 5153
      carburetors, 5357
      radiators, 5153
  EPA laws, 48
  exhaust systems, 6670
      catalytic converters, 6869
      factory manifolds, 6667
      mufflers, 70
      tips, 6970
      tubular headers, 6768
  fuel cutoff switches, 65
  fuel injection, 5964
      aftermarkets, 6164
      Ford, 6061
      port injection, 60
      throttle body injection (TBI), 59
      tuned port injection (TPI), 60
  grounding, 131
  intake manifolds, 5759
  modifications, 4951
      camshafts, 4950
      roller rockers, 5051
  new vs. used, 48
  newer, 4849
  selection, 4749
      fourbangers, 48
      V6 considerations, 48
      V8 considerations, 4748
  throttle opening rate, 6466
  tips, 4770
  TPI primary components, 58
EPA laws, 48
Exhaust systems, 6670
  catalytic converters, 6869
  factory manifolds, 6667
  tips, 6970
      crossover pipes, 69
      pipe and muffler locations, 69
      pipe size, 6970
      scavenging, 70
  tubular headers, 6768

F

Fasteners, 1013
  adhesives, 12
      hot metal, 12
      solventbased, 12
  bolts, 11
  bonding pieces, 12
  gaskets, 13
  nuts, 11
  recommendations, 11
  sealants, 1213
  washers, 1112
      liquid thread lockers, 12
      lock, 1112
Fiberglass
  attaching panels, 85
  and other composites, 7983
  tips, 82
Fibers, 8081
Firewalls, sealing, 129130
Flashers, 134
FRP's (fiber reinforced plastics), 79
Front end, 2122, 9099
  engine air intakes, 9495
  firewalls, 9293
  grille openings, 95
  hood and hood scoops, 9599

fiberglass options, 98
  making plenums, 96
  making templates, 9798
  measurements, 9697
  modifying air cleaner housing, 99
  securing scoop floors, 9899
inspection
  adding strength panels, 9192
  strengthening ribs or channels, 92
steering braces, 9394
Fuel
  cutoff switches, 65
  gauge needle jump, 133
  injection, 5964
      Accel, 6263
      aftermarkets, 6164
      Edelbrock, 63
      Holley, 62
      Howell Engine Development, 6364
  tanks, 23
Fuses
  box locations, 123
  panels, 122

G

Garages, 1314
  safety, 1314
Gas springs
  hood/trunk, 99103
  worksheet, 102
Gaskets
  using, 13
  windshield, 147
Gauges
  ammeters, 133
  fuel gauge needle jump, 133
  layouts, 117118
  oil pressure senders, 132133
  sender installation, 133
  Stewart Warner electric, 132
  VDO electric, 131132
Gears
  selection, 7678
      aspect ratios, 7778
      effective drive ratios, 78
      equivalent drive ratios, 78
      oversize tires, 77
      section height and width, 77
  shifts, 117
GM steering columns, 116117
Grille openings, 95

H

Headers, tubular, 6768
Heat
  insulation, 105
  metal shields, 105106
Heater boxes, 145146
Hinges, 8788
Holley Carburetors, 5455
Hood and hood scoops, 9599
Hood/trunk gas springs, 99103
  gas spring worksheet, 102
  installation, 102103
  locating center of gravity, 101102
      hoods, 101
      trunk lids, 101102
Hot metal adhesives, 12

I

Insulation, body, 103107
  heat insulation, 105

metal heat shields, 105106
noise and vibration, 106107
proper insulation location, 105
thermal insulating materials, 105106
Intake manifolds, 5759
Interiors
  carpets, 140141
  door trim, 142143
  seat anchors, 142
  seat belts, 141142
  seat cover material, 141
  seats, 141
  tips, 140147
  trim, 140
  ventilation, 143146
  weatherstripping, 146147

K

Kit Car, 2
Kit Car Illustrated, 2
Kit owners, 6

L

Leaf spring wrap up, 2223
Liquid thread lockers, 12

M

Manifolds
  dual plane, 5759
  factory, 6667
  intake, 5759
  recommendations, 59
  singleplane, 59
Manuals, owners', 9, 164165
Manufacturers, 6
Mechanics, common sense law of, 13
MIG (metal insert gas), 10
Mirrors, rear view, 118
Mufflers, 70

N

NAPA (National Auto Parts Association), 65
Noise and vibration, 106107
  identifying sources, 106107
  insulating paths, 107
Noise Killer, 107
Nuts, 11

O

Oil pressure senders, 132133
Owens Corning, 79
Owners' manuals, 9, 164165

P

Painting chassis, 24
Parts
  assembly, hinges, 8788
  correcting poor fitting, 8788
  lists, 5
  management, 78
Payment of parts, 6
Pedals
  assemblies, 114115
  gas and brake, 115
Planning and organization, 610
  documentation, 89
      donor car information, 9
      owner's manual, 9
  parts management, 78
  tools, 910
      recommendations, 910
      warnings, 10

Plenums, making, 96
Port injection, 60
Post curing, 8182
Powder coating, 83
Power amplifiers, 136137
Pumps, water, 52

R

Radiators, 24, 5153
  fans, 51
  shrouding, 5152
  thermostats, 5253
  troubleshooting, 53
  water pumps, 52
Ratio converters, 151
Rear end, 2224
  axle dampers, 2223
  fuel tanks, 23
  leaf spring wrap up, 2223
  radiators, 24
  tank vents, 2324
Rear view mirrors, 118
Relays, 123124
Repanels, 14
  examining, 3
  getting it in writing, 4
  maintenance, 4
  referrals, 3
  research, 2
  test drive, 23
  usage of, 12
Resins, 80
Ride height, 3234
Rochester Carburetors, 54
Rods, strut, 26
Roll bars, 109113
  installation tips, 111113
  measuring custom, 110111
    floor plates, 111
    main hoops, 111
    rear braces, 111
    seat crossmembers, 111
    templates, 110111
  single hoop, 110111
Roller rockers, 5051

S

Safety, 1314
ScotchLok connectors, 127128
Sealants, 1213
Seat anchors, 142
Seat belts, 141142
Seat cover material, 141
Seats, 116, 141
Senders
  installation, 133
  oil pressure, 132133
Service loops, 45
Shocks
  losses, 30
  mounting, 2830
  relocating, 3032
    front, 3132
    rear, 32
  selection, 28
  and springs, 2732
  theory, 28
Single plane manifolds, 59
Solventbased adhesives, 12
Speakers, 137
  and amplifiers, 136139

components, 137139
  mounting, 137139
  preventing air leaks, 138139
  protecting, 139
Speedometers, 150151
  calibrating mechanical, 150
  Chevy, 150
  Ford RWD automatics, 150151
  Ford T5 Trans, 151
  GM, 150
Splicing wires, 127128
Spring weight and length, calculating, 35
Springs, coil, 3435
Sprung weight, 35
Steering
  columns, 116117
  cooling braces, 9394
  racks, 1820
  wheel clearances, 116
Stereo systems, 135136
  selection, 135136
  troubleshooting, 139
  unit, 136
Stewart Warner electric gauges, 132
Strut rods, 26
Suspension
  bushings, 2527
    leaf spring, 2627
    polyurethane, 26
    rear control arm bushings, 27
    rubber, 26
    strut rods and control arm bushings, 26
    sway bar, 27
  coil springs, 3435
    calculating spring weight and length, 35
  geometry, 2021
  ride height, 3234
  shocks and springs, 2732
  stops, 3334
  tips, 2535
  tuning, 149150
    antiroll bars, 149
    tips, 149150
    tires, 149
Switches
  fuel cutoff, 65
  using, 117

T

Tables, 153163
  cost estimating table, 162163
  drill sizes, 159
  drilltap chart, 157
  driveline, universal joint alignment, 158
  general conversion table, 160161
  inchmetric conversation table, 155
  sheet metal gauges, 156
  springs and sockets, 158
  tools checklist, 163
  torque unit conversion table, 154
  torque values, 154
  universal joint alignment, 158
  wire size (gauges) vs. current carrying capacity, 156
Tanks
  fuel, 23
  vents, 2324
TBI (throttle body injection), 59
Templates, making, 9798
Thermal insulating materials, 105106
Thermostats, 5253
Throttle opening rate, 6466

TIG (tungsten insert gas), 10
Tires, 107108, 149
  oversize, 77
  and wheel clearances, 107108
Tools, 910
  recommendations, 910
  warnings, 10
TPI (tuned port injection), 58, 60
Transmissions, 7173
  Chevy, 7172
  Ford, 7273
  GM automatics, 7172
  tips, 73
Trim, 140
Trunk gas springs, 99103
Tuning
  fine, 148151
  suspension, 149150
Twist, 17

U

Unsprung weight, 35

V

V.E. (volumetric efficiency), 55
VDO electric gauges, 131132
Ventilation, 143146
  ducting types, 146
  heater boxes, 145146
  intake locations, 144145
Vibration, 91, 106107
Voltage regulators, 121122

W

Washers, 1112, 118119
  liquid thread lockers, 12
  lock, 1112
Water pumps, 52
Weatherstripping, 146147
  installation, 146147
  windshield gaskets, 147
Weber Carburetors, 54
Welds, 1617
Wheel clearances, 107108
Wheels, 108
Windshields
  gaskets, 147
  wipers
    arms, 118119
    motors, 119
    and washers, 118119
Wires, splicing, 127128
Wiring
  concepts, 124128
    gauges, 131133
    installing connectors, 127
    solderless or crimp connectors, 124127
    splicing wires, 127128
    wire sizes, 124
    wiring tools, 126
  harnesses, 128131
    grounding, 130131
    installation, 129
    sealing firewalls, 129130
  tools, 126
Worm screw mechanisms, 100

ABOUT THE AUTHOR

Doug McCleary has been an automobile enthusiast longer than he has held a driver's license. He started building his first Hot Rod before he was sixteen. He has owned and built many different cars over the years, from classics to reproductions, and has always worked within the Mechanical Engineering field.

Doug and his wife have competed in numerous rallies and autocrosses throughout the New England region. In 1987, Doug founded the New England Specialty Car Association and administered it for seven years. During that period, he organized most of the club events and produced as well as participated in many automotive charity events to benefit children.

Doug's introduction to writing started with producing training programs, the club newsletter and articles recounting the club's many events during the late 80's and mid 90's. As a freelance writer, Doug is a regular contributor to the McMullen-Argus publication, *Kit Car Illustrated*.

Doug and his wife Mary, currently reside, with their children, in Cape Cod, Massachusetts. ■

HANDBOOKS

Auto Electrical Handbook: 0-89586-238-7
Auto Upholstery & Interiors: 1-55788-265-7
Brake Handbook: 0-89586-232-8
Car Builder's Handbook: 1-55788-278-9
Street Rodder's Handbook: 0-89586-369-3
Turbo Hydra-matic 350 Handbook: 0-89586-051-1
Welder's Handbook: 1-55788-264-9

BODYWORK & PAINTING

Automotive Detailing: 1-55788-288-6
Automotive Paint Handbook: 1-55788-291-6
Fiberglass & Composite Materials: 1-55788-239-8
Metal Fabricator's Handbook: 0-89586-870-9
Paint & Body Handbook: 1-55788-082-4
Sheet Metal Handbook: 0-89586-757-5

INDUCTION

Holley 4150: 0-89586-047-3
Holley Carburetors, Manifolds & Fuel Injection: 1-55788-052-2
Rochester Carburetors: 0-89586-301-4
Turbochargers: 0-89586-135-6
Weber Carburetors: 0-89586-377-4

PERFORMANCE

Aerodynamics For Racing & Performance Cars: 1-55788-267-3
Baja Bugs & Buggies: 0-89586-186-0
Big-Block Chevy Performance: 1-55788-216-9
Big Block Mopar Performance: 1-55788-302-5
Bracket Racing: 1-55788-266-5
Brake Systems: 1-55788-281-9
Camaro Performance: 1-55788-057-3
Chassis Engineering: 1-55788-055-7
Chevrolet Power: 1-55788-087-5
Ford Windsor Small-Block Performance: 1-55788-323-8
Honda/Acura Performance: 1-55788-324-6
High Performance Hardware: 1-55788-304-1
How to Build Tri-Five Chevy Trucks ('55-'57): 1-55788-285-1
How to Hot Rod Big-Block Chevys:0-912656-04-2
How to Hot Rod Small-Block Chevys:0-912656-06-9
How to Hot Rod Small-Block Mopar Engines: 0-89586-479-7
How to Hot Rod VW Engines:0-912656-03-4
How to Make Your Car Handle:0-912656-46-8
John Lingenfelter: Modifying Small-Block Chevy: 1-55788-238-X
Mustang 5.0 Projects: 1-55788-275-4

Mustang Performance ('79–'93): 1-55788-193-6
Mustang Performance 2 ('79–'93): 1-55788-202-9
1001 High Performance Tech Tips: 1-55788-199-5
Performance Ignition Systems: 1-55788-306-8
Performance Wheels & Tires: 1-55788-286-X
Race Car Engineering & Mechanics: 1-55788-064-6
Small-Block Chevy Performance: 1-55788-253-3

ENGINE REBUILDING

Engine Builder's Handbook: 1-55788-245-2
Rebuild Air-Cooled VW Engines: 0-89586-225-5
Rebuild Big-Block Chevy Engines: 0-89586-175-5
Rebuild Big-Block Ford Engines: 0-89586-070-8
Rebuild Big-Block Mopar Engines: 1-55788-190-1
Rebuild Ford V-8 Engines: 0-89586-036-8
Rebuild Small-Block Chevy Engines: 1-55788-029-8
Rebuild Small-Block Ford Engines:0-912656-89-1
Rebuild Small-Block Mopar Engines: 0-89586-128-3

RESTORATION, MAINTENANCE, REPAIR

Camaro Owner's Handbook ('67–'81): 1-55788-301-7
Camaro Restoration Handbook ('67–'81): 0-89586-375-8
Classic Car Restorer's Handbook: 1-55788-194-4
Corvette Weekend Projects ('68–'82): 1-55788-218-5
Mustang Restoration Handbook('64 1/2–'70): 0-89586-402-9
Mustang Weekend Projects ('64–'67): 1-55788-230-4
Mustang Weekend Projects 2 ('68–'70): 1-55788-256-8
Tri-Five Chevy Owner's ('55–'57): 1-55788-285-1

GENERAL REFERENCE

Auto Math:1-55788-020-4
Fabulous Funny Cars: 1-55788-069-7
Guide to GM Muscle Cars: 1-55788-003-4
Stock Cars!: 1-55788-308-4

MARINE

Big-Block Chevy Marine Performance: 1-55788-297-5

**HPBOOKS ARE AVAILABLE AT BOOK AND SPECIALTY RETAILERS OR TO
ORDER CALL: 1-800-788-6262, ext. 1**

HPBooks
A division of Penguin Putnam Inc.
375 Hudson Street
New York, NY 10014